**VALUE AND VISION** *in American Literature*

# VALUE AND VISION

## *in American Literature*

LITERARY ESSAYS IN HONOR

OF RAY LEWIS WHITE

EDITED BY Joseph Candido

OHIO UNIVERSITY PRESS ▪ *Athens*

Ohio University Press, Athens, Ohio 45701
© 1999 by Joseph Candido
Printed in the United States of America
All rights reserved

Ohio University Press books are printed on acid-free paper ∞ ™

03 02 01 00 99    5 4 3 2 1

*Library of Congress Cataloging-in-Publication Data*
Value and vision in American literature : literary essays in
    honor of Ray Lewis White / edited by Joseph Candido.
        p. cm.
    Includes bibliographical references and index.
    ISBN 0-8214-1291-4 (alk. paper)
        1. American literature—History and criticism.  I. Candido, Joseph,
    1945–    . II. White, Ray Lewis.
    PS58.V35 1999
    810.9—dc21
        99-30999

# Contents

# CONTENTS

# Foreword
## *Ray Lewis White: A Tribute*

As Ray White likes to tell his story, it all began with Sputnik. If not for the national crisis of confidence about American higher education sparked by the Russians' 1957 triumph, Congress would not have passed the National Defense Education Act, and without the NDEA, Ray White might never have left the family dairy farm. Without Sputnik, a young Ray White might not have escaped from a future of milking and shoveling manure in the impoverished Appalachians of southwestern Virginia, a world that he now tersely describes as "primitive." Without the NDEA, Ray White would not have been able to enter Emory and Henry College, only a few miles from the farm but in a sense another planet, a place where the young man already in love with books and ideas could imagine another life for himself, a literary life. The government was eager to loan the nation's youth low-interest money to ensure the future of freedom through education, and Ray, having decided that this poor farm boy would have a Ph.D. in English, did his part by dreaming himself free of manure-shoveling and into the world of scholarship and the storyteller's art.

He chose to do his graduate work at the University of Arkansas in Fayetteville, a college town in the heart of Ozark highlands similar to his native Appalachians, if even poorer and in those days perhaps even more "primitive." But the town then was and still is a remarkably literary place, attractive to a rich variety of writers and other intellectuals by virtue both of its natural beauty and of its freedom from the problems of less isolated cultural centers, if also free of their amenities. At the center of this literary world, when Ray White arrived in the fall of 1962, was the university's English Department, an engaging blend of eccentricity and distinction that Ray seems instinctively to have recognized as just the diverse group of mentors he needed to help forge his own identity as a scholar. Some among them must have helped prepare him to understand Sherwood Anderson's notion of the "grotesque," like the romantic poetry professor who began each class by unburdening his otherwise empty briefcase of numerous bottles and envelopes containing his medications for the day, medications prescribed to treat an ailment that he confessed to his pupils to be varicose veins of the scrotum, and lining them up on the front edge of his desk.

Others, though, provided valuable models for the habits of mind and work that would mark his own career. Duncan Eaves, for instance, a Restoration scholar whose enormous learning and extraordinary eloquence made his classroom a stage on which the passions and intrigues of literary London in the long eighteenth century came to life three times a week, produced in Ray White and his peers an enthusiasm for catching the spirit of the flesh-and-blood people behind the printed words. Ray would carry this enthusiasm into his own work, especially on Sherwood Anderson. But Ray also learned from Eaves the necessity of tempering enthusiasm with scholarly precision. Eaves's edition of the letters of William Gilmore Simms, which he had published just before Ray's arrival in Fayetteville, exhibits the same respect for facts and judicious sifting of evidence that distinguish Ray's later editions of Anderson's correspondence.

Perhaps even more influential was Eaves's work with his friend and colleague Ben Kimpel on what would become the definitive biography of Samuel Richardson, published a few years after Ray left Arkansas. Those of us who never knew Ben Kimpel sometimes find it difficult to believe the universal assertion of those who did: that he knew simply *everything* that is worth knowing about the Western tradition and a good deal else too. But Ray and many others insist that every conversation with Ben Kimpel, every classroom lecture, was a guided tour through the very best that has been thought or said in every part of the world and that knowing him was a deeply inspiring experience. If the Kimpel and Eaves book on Richardson established a standard of biographical criticism for its time, one that has guided Ray's own superb literary sleuthing, surely the influence of Ben Kimpel's encyclopedic mind can be seen in the breadth of subjects that mark Ray White's bibliography: books and articles on Anderson and many other American writers, of course, but also on Charles Dickens, Guy de Maupassant, Mikhail Sholokhov, Raja Rao, Kawabata Yasunari, R. K. Narayan, Par Lagerkvist, and others.

Others influenced him at Arkansas, most notably his dissertation director, H. Blair Rouse, who first inspired in Ray a passion for bibliography when he employed the first-year graduate student and fellow Virginian as a research assistant. But Ray was eager to do his own research and to write his own books. He left Fayetteville in the summer of 1965, six years before finishing his degree, to take up his first full-time academic appointment at North Carolina State and continue work on a project that he began in Arkansas, his first book, a critical collection of essays on Sherwood Anderson. This volume and the others pertaining to Anderson that Ray White produced through the late 1960s and early 1970s helped inaugurate a new and broad appreciation of this great storyteller who spent his last years in the same Virginia highlands where Ray spent his youth. Critical interest in Anderson has continued largely undiminished to this day, and Anderson's place in American literary history is now firmly established. After surveying Ray's fifteen books and dozens of articles on Anderson (including the Rouse-directed dissertation, a critical edition of *Marching Men* published in 1972), any fair judge of the development of Anderson studies must conclude that no one has done more than Ray White toward fulfilling the "hope" that he offers in his introduction to Anderson's memoirs, that Anderson would someday "be loved and understood" so that "others may learn how to write and how to live" from him.

A broader survey of Ray White's scholarship leaves many strong impressions: a deep and sympathetic curiosity about the creative process and the people who make art, a commitment to the intrinsic benefits of literary knowledge and insight for improving the quality of the individual life, and a genuine delight in the storyteller's art of making the world a more interesting and, sometimes, a better place to live. Most conspicuous, though, is his passion for detail, resting on a faith (shared with Anderson, of course) that the deepest truths often lie in the barest and humblest facts, whether of a life or of a text. Setting the record straight—establishing a text and its history, uncovering the truth behind the writer's version of his life, or charting the fluctuations in a writer's stock on her way to critical acceptance—has always been for Ray White the precondition of intelligent interpretation.

Ray's students certainly understood the point. As a key member of the graduate faculty at Illinois State University for thirty years, Ray White taught classes in research methods and American literature in which, by all accounts, respect for the facts was enforced as a special obligation in the face of the profession's increasingly evident fascination with ideologies of all kinds. But enforced without rancor, since he is spoken of as an elegant and generous teacher with a gift for making literary scholarship, in the words of one of his former doctoral students, "an adventure, a treasure hunt, just a lot of fun." As a colleague, he is similarly regarded as one generous with his time and his ideas when his department or university might benefit. Many of his contributions to Illinois State might illustrate the point, but one stands out. The Ph.D. in English Studies at ISU, still one of the more innovative doctoral programs in the country almost thirty years after Ray White designed it, is a tribute not merely to his genius for navigating the treacherous waters of academic bureaucracy but, more important, to his genius for making the values that have inspired his scholarship—breadth of learning, meticulous preparation, and a vision of literary study as a complex approach to understanding human affairs—come alive in the classroom and in the academic curriculum generally.

Ray White retired as Distinguished Professor of English at Illinois State at the end of the 1998 spring semester. To commemorate this event and to express their appreciation for Ray's generous support for his graduate alma mater, his friends in the Arkansas English Department offer this collection of essays. The essays are written by current Arkansas faculty, alumni of the Arkansas English Department and the Illinois State program, and a handful of leading Americanists invited by the Arkansas faculty to participate. Various both in their subjects and in their approaches to literature, these pieces constitute an apt tribute to Ray White's own broad literary interests while concentrating on the area of study in which his legacy will be most conspicuous, American literature. My colleagues and I hope that this gift of the fruits of so much literary labor will be received in the spirit in which it is offered, as the most sincere gesture that members of our profession can make to honor (in the words that Ray applied to Anderson in his dissertation) "a life devoted to literature."

# Preface

This gathering of essays is a tribute from the English Department at the University of Arkansas to Ray Lewis White in appreciation of his generosity and in honor of his achievement. The department's aim in shaping the volume and soliciting its contributors was threefold. We wanted, first, for the book to have a distinctly "Arkansas" flavor (hence the inclusion of five members of our graduate faculty) so that we could honor Ray personally and in so doing reflect our pride in the fact that it was in Fayetteville that Ray undertook the literary apprenticeship that would lead to a lifetime of scholarly accomplishment. Second, we wanted the book to reflect Ray's influence and reputation in the field of American literature; therefore, we sought contributions from some of his close friends and colleagues, people on whose personal and professional lives Ray had and continues to have a lasting influence, as well as other respected scholars widely acquainted with his work who knew him first and foremost through his scholarship. Third, and most important, we wanted the book to make a genuine contribution to the field of American literature. We felt all along that the fittest tribute to Ray would be a book whose contents both he and the profession at large could respect, and we offer it to him, and to all other interested readers, in that hope and spirit.

At first blush it may appear that a volume containing not a single reference to the life and work of Sherwood Anderson is an odd one indeed to honor Ray's life and work, particularly since Anderson is the writer with whom Ray is most closely identified. A word of explanation is perhaps in order. In soliciting the essays for this volume, we deliberately placed no restriction on contributors regarding content or approach. Our aim throughout was to allow authors the freest rein to pursue any topic or interest of their own, with the sole restriction that their essays be previously unpublished and on a topic relating to American litera- ture. Yet the result, oddly Andersonless as it proved to be, nevertheless in its own way reflects both the scholarly accomplishment of Ray White and, indeed, even to some extent, the literary accomplishment of the author to whom he was so deeply devoted. What strikes one about the essays that appear below is how resolute they are as a group in recover- ing the neglected, reassessing the familiar, or challenging the orthodox. Taken either individually or as parts of a loosely unified whole, they vir- tually without exception seek to find in the subtle or overlooked details relating to an author or a text some defining characteristic or set of char- acteristics that bring a sudden clarity. In other words, they exhibit a stance toward the study of literature that Anderson himself famously exhibited toward the study of character and which Ray consistently upheld throughout his academic career. In their ideological eclecticism, too, they gesture, modestly perhaps yet surely, toward the kind of schol- arly life Ray led—a life of uncommon breadth and intellectual charity. No single collection of essays can adequately reflect the enormous criti- cal diversity of an intellectual career like Ray's, embracing as it does such disparate figures as Anderson, Vidal, Stein, Böll, Lagerkvist, Grass, Narayan, Zweig, West, Hecht, Hemingway, Yasunari, Cleaver, Rao, Steinbeck, Stevens, Sholokhov, Mencken, Holman, Dos Passos, Barth, Lockridge, and others—but we hope that our collection, in spirit at least, gives some intimation of the adventuresomeness and inclusiveness that marked Ray's intellectual life.

Michael Reynolds's "A View from the Dig at Century's End" opens the volume and, to some degree, stands as an implicit challenge to all that follows. Approaching the enterprise of literary investigation from the vantage point of a biographer whose task is to weigh evidence and evaluate facts (in his case a five-volume life of Ernest Hemingway), Reynolds invites us to imagine the interpretive enterprise as if it were an archaeological dig: every scrap we find is important, and one scrap is never enough. In so doing, he issues a clarion call for more scholars and fewer critics, and asks us to consider five "obvious" questions relating to the genesis, background, and cultural context of literary art as we form our critical judgments. In one way or another each essay that follows engages, in its own way and on its own terms, the questions Reynolds so forcefully poses and, even more important, the theoretical implications they raise.

Keneth Kinnamon's "The Politics of 'The Snows of Kilimanjaro'" is related to Reynolds's piece both by its interest in Hemingway and by its investigative method. Kinnamon sifts through various aspects of Hemingway's ambivalent attitude toward wealth and those who possess it, and in so doing seeks to shed fresh light on the political aspects of Hemingway's fiction. Noting particularly the author's financial dependency on the good offices of Gus A. Pfeiffer, the rich uncle of his second wife, Pauline, and contrasting this acquiescence to wealth with Hemingway's openly radical politics of the early 1930s, Kinnamon asks us to see Harry's "betrayals of himself and what he believed in" in "The Snows of Kilimanjaro" as a statement that can apply not only to Hemingway's art of fiction but also to his betrayal of his political belief in the oppressive and corrupting power of wealth. Jackson J. Benson also turns his attention to biographical facts in "Wallace Stegner: Artist as Environmentalist." Benson is concerned with the formation of Stegner's keen "environmental conscience," which he associates with Stegner's childhood growing up on the prairie, where he had few diversions except for animals and nature and where he experienced the harshness of an abusive father and the tenderness of a loving mother. Seeing Stegner's response to this explosive triumvirate of Nature, Father, and Mother as forming the basis of his literary imagination, Benson both examines the development of Stegner's "environmental conscience" and emphasizes his friendship with Bernard DeVoto as a crucial element of its full expression.

In Linda Wagner-Martin's "'The VaNe Sisters' and Nabokov's 'subtle and loving' Readers," we have the first of a series of critical essays on novels that rely heavily on close readings of selected episodes. In Wagner-Martin's essay, however, the twin interests in biography and cultural context that figure so prominently in the three preceding essays are forcefully employed to serve the ends of feminist criticism. Basing her analysis of the text on the fact that Nabokov saw in his own marginalized status in an American university an analogue to a woman's status in a heterosexual love relationship, Wagner-Martin uncovers subtle nuances in the text of "The Vane Sisters" that reshape our perception of the story almost entirely and in the process also help to reshape our understanding of Nabokov both as a man and a writer. Brian Wilkie is also interested in reshaping our attitudes toward an author and a text, in this case Harold Frederic's *The Damnation of Theron Ware*. In a richly textured and highly allusive essay, Wilkie urges a reevaluation of the work beyond the status of mere local color realism by calling our attention to a narrative technique through which Frederic creates polarities only to have them dissolve into unities or fragment kaleidoscopically. The result of this "confounding of affects" is a narrative that presents us with an irresolvable conflict in which two separate and perfectly valid senses of "good," one based on traditional morality and the other on antinomian spiritual energizing, become equally valid. Polarities are also the subject of Robert Cochran's "Lessons of the Bear," a concise analysis of Saul Bellow's *Henderson the Rain King* that focuses on the bipolar means by which the protagonist, Eugene Henderson, acquires knowledge. From Atti the lion Henderson acquires a style of action—a "mode of becoming"; but from Smolak, the bear with whom he experiences a twice-a-day roller-coaster ride in an Ontario amusement park, he discovers "a way to be."

David Kesterson's examination of the Roman Carnival as apocalypse in *The Marble Faun* and Ann Fisher-Wirth's "*El Otro Sud:* Willa Cather and Cormac McCarthy" both seek to contextualize their respective authors' works. Kesterson's highly detailed analysis is concerned with Hawthorne's knowledge of the Roman Carnival—particularly how our understanding of Hawthorne's use of the carnivalesque in the novel can subtly yet clearly direct our attitudes toward Kenyon, its protagonist. Fisher-Wirth posits a new way of looking at Cather and McCarthy based on their shared imaginative longing for the old Southwest and their joint preoccupation with "the American 1848"—the period just after the U.S. victory in the Mexican War which prompted heightened feelings of nationalism and Manifest Destiny. Her discussion of this connection focuses on *Death Comes for the Archbishop, Blood Meridian,* and *The Crossing,* seeing in the connection between the latter and *Death Comes for the Archbishop* the two seemingly different authors' shared affinities for "God, the desert, and the telling of stories."

Reassessing the relationship—and indeed the relative status—of two authors who are often forced (unfairly) by critics to inhabit the same critical space is also Noel Polk's intention in "Welty and Faulkner and the Southern Literary Tradition." Polk's thoughtful assessment of each writer on his or her own terms rather than on some ex post facto Platonic ideal of what constitutes "great," "tragic," or "heroic" writing, spurs his impassioned defense of Welty's ability to evoke a more intensely "local" understanding of traditionally cosmic concerns that is no less cosmic for being un-Faulknerian. Faulkner's relationship to another of his great contemporaries is also the concern of John Caldwell Guilds, who examines Faulkner and Henry James through the lens of the "pragmatic humanism" of James's equally famous brother, William. Guilds's reading of *Absalom, Absalom!* in light of *The Ambassadors* allows us to see that for each author the achievement of fairness and equity in human affairs sometimes requires the abandonment of principle. Susan Swartwout's "Revolution Has Not Yet Entered Their Souls: The Jilting of Katherine Anne Porter," the last essay on prose fiction in our collection, revealingly examines Porter's changing attitudes toward Mexico by looking closely at the textual changes in the two versions of her short story "Hacienda." Here we may say, at the "dig" of the text itself, one finds just the sort of scraps Reynolds asks us to consider when he insists that in literary investigation "we've got to know the place."

Our collection concludes with four highly original essays on poetry. Stephen Cushman's "Poems of the Civil War: Past and Present" amounts to a full reassessment of the contours of Civil War poetry from the 1860s to the present day. Although Cushman finds that much Civil War verse deserves the blanket dismissal it so often receives, his detailed analysis of poems both familiar and unfamiliar nevertheless forces us to rethink our stereotypical picture of nineteenth- and twentieth-century poetry on the war. Perhaps the most formidable act of literary recovery in our collection is Jim Elledge's meticulously argued essay on the gay World War II love poetry of the now largely neglected

Dunstan Thompson. Elledge's study of the texture of Thompson's verse makes an eloquent case both for its literary and psychological complexity and for its explicit and unapologetic homoeroticism. Similarly eloquent is Dave Smith's "Warren's Ventriloquist: J. J. Audubon," a revealing study of the autobiographical dimension of Robert Penn Warren's narrative poem *Audubon: A Vision*. In an argument that elucidates the many technical subtleties of Warren's text, Smith demonstrates that for Warren the search for language is always an act of self-definition and further that the poet gambles with a poetic form in *Audubon* that creates a living character with whom he identifies.

Sidney Burris's "Stephen Dedalus and the New Formalism" both draws the volume to a close and, in a manner of speaking, opens it up again by echoing in another key the sort of cautionary advice to the critic with which Michael Reynolds began the volume. Wary (and weary) of the New Formalist nostalgia for past poetic achievement, Burris shows how resistant the *actual* poetic tradition is to such overgeneralizing. He draws on the experiences of Stephen Dedalus in *A Portrait of the Artist as a Young Man* to demonstrate that Joyce was skeptical of precisely such "monolothic appropriation" of the past and concludes that the literary past is "a radically varied congregation of voices" that requires "discrimination, bias, and judgment" for its just evaluation. In its urging of a highly individualized and informed sensibility that shuns any "indiscriminate reading of literary history," Burris's essay may not *precisely* situate us in the intellectual space occupied by Reynolds's scholar, but it does nonetheless echo Reynolds's enjoinder that to write well "we've got to know the place." How we know it, and indeed how well we know it, the essays in this collection attempt to demonstrate. It would be no small accomplishment, however, to know it as surely as Ray Lewis White knew it and to write about it nearly as well.

**VALUE AND VISION** *in American Literature*

# A View from the Dig at Century's End

**H**aving spent the last twenty-five years reconstructing the life of Ernest Hemingway in what is now closing out as five volumes, I sometimes feel blessed to have had this opportunity; at other times I feel that I was, in a Faulknerian sense, doomed to complete the project. For example, had I not met Ray Lewis White at the beginning of my career, someone else would have written these books. The seeds for the biography were planted when Ray and I shared an office as lowly instructors at North Carolina State University. He was fresh out of the University of Arkansas Ph.D. program; I, armed only with an M.A., was back from four years in the U.S. Navy. During office discussions of our classroom teaching, I told Ray about the historical accuracy of *A Farewell to Arms*. Ray realized that I had the groundwork for a casebook on the novel. Together we divided the research tasks, produced a proposal, sent it to Scribner's, and received a rejection letter. Ray went on to write and edit his important Sherwood Anderson books and articles. I went back to graduate school for my Ph.D., using the work we had done as the first step toward a dissertation, which became *Hemingway's First War* (1976). That book raised the question about Hemingway's reading, the answer to which raised the question of a new biog-

1

raphy. Thus was Ray godfather to the work I have done in Hemingway studies, making it altogether appropriate that I should be thanking him these many years later.

My last volume, *Hemingway: The Final Years,* appears in 1999, the Hemingway centennial, which will be a media celebration. The National Portrait Gallery will open an exhibit of Hemingway portraits. In Key West, Ketchum, and Oak Park there will be celebrations. In Boston, Nobel and Pulitzer prize winners in fiction will gather at the Kennedy Library to discuss Hemingway's impact on this century's writers. At the same time, scholars will be working in more detailed fashion on what needs to be redone, rethought, and in many cases done for the first time. Born in the last year of the last century, Ernest Hemingway imprinted himself deeply into the literature, culture, and social psyche of an America changing from an upstart nation into a world power. That generation of the 1890s—F. Scott Fitzgerald, William Faulkner, and Hemingway—changed forever how Americans wrote about themselves and how others saw us. Perhaps, as this century and this millennium end, those of us who are neither theorists nor critics might take on the difficult and frequently tedious task of completing the literary history of Ernest Hemingway and his fellow Modernists, completing the literary history of this century's first half. When finished, we will have a far more complex, more interdisciplinary, more detailed, and, God help us, more interesting history than those we were handed in graduate school a generation back.

Hasn't it all been done? Of course it has, but not yet well enough. Using an analogy from mapping, we have a literary history written mostly at the 1:500,000 scale when we need it done at 1:100,000. The standard one-volume Hemingway biography is 564 pages for a life of sixty-one years, which translates out to forty days of his life per every page. By the time I am finished with my Hemingway work, I will have written about 2,000 pages or one page per every eleven days. I still remember when my first application to the National Endowment for the Humanities came back with the reader's report: "We have one Hemingway biography. We don't need another one." Maybe cursory readers do not need more information, but they at least deserve accurate information, and early biographies lay out the map, leaving plenty of blank spaces that are easy to paper over if each page covers a month or more. Early biographies rely heavily on personal interviews, of which there is nothing more misleading, for there are no objective witnesses. The only way for a writer to get a fair shake is to outlive his or her enemies, then outlive the friends, who are frequently worse. We should remember T. S. Eliot's advice that each generation needs to write its own books. The unspoken corollary must also be kept in mind: those books may tell us more about the generation that wrote them than their nominal subject matter.

That generation of scholars and critics who came out of World War II created and immortalized the Hemingway Code, which operated the same way in all of his fiction. They also created a Hemingway Hero, who was simply Hemingway in disguise, a doppelganger who aged as Ernest aged, forming a seamless continuum. This neat paradigm explained **3** everything we needed to know about the texts: the character was actually Ernest, and his code of behavior did not change. The unspoken corollary led many a reader and scholar to believe that the fiction was Hemingway's biography, a biographic trap large enough to hold an elephant. For example, because the young man in "Out of Season" is fishing before the season has opened, more than one writer has told us that this was the case at Cortina in 1923 when the Hemingways were there. Wrong. The fishing season had already opened when Ernest returned from his journalism assignment in the Rhur. What difference does it make? What takes place between husband and wife is largely beneath the surface of that story. Without the surface tension produced by the illegal fishing, there would be no iceberg. The entire story would be under water. So it was not the "found" story as Hemingway told Scott Fitzgerald but a carefully crafted fiction.

As long as one keeps to the anointed Hemingway texts, ignoring many of the short stories, *Death in the Afternoon,* and *To Have and Have Not,* the inherited paradigms are plausible, even comforting. But as soon as one returns to the texts without the tinted glasses provided by the postwar generation, the paradigms begin to crater. I remember so clearly the 1976 Alabama Hemingway Conference when an older scholar was telling us that every story Hemingway wrote contained the journey as its central motif. Example followed example, forcing all the texts into this neat explanation. Then, Alfred Kazin rose up in the audience, interrupting the speaker, saying, "Oh, Leo, come off it. You know that's not right." It was an exhilarating moment when the continuum was thrown into doubt.

From the vantage point of century's end, that first wave of Hemingway criticism reflects the needs and values of the generation that fought World War II. They wanted order in their lives, rules to live by, and a unified field theory that explained the text, early or lately written. While they were formulating, Hemingway was writing *Garden of Eden,* which, had it been published, would have sent the Code and the Hero theories into a tailspin. That same generation told us that Hemingway was not very well educated and did not understand the complexity of his own work, which required a college professor to explain it to him. (Never, never imagine that you know better than the author about his own text.) They told us that Hemingway's best work was in the 1920s and that after *A Farewell to Arms* the quality fell off. Which tells us about their taste and very little about Hemingway's texts.

On her deathbed Gertrude Stein is reported to have been asked by Alice B. Toklas, "Lovie, what is the answer?" To which Gertrude replied, "In that case, what is the question?" True or apocryphal, the anecdote is appropriate to the issue of reevaluating our literary inheritance: so much depends on the question one asks. It is the question that is difficult to formulate; the answer can be found if the question can be first imagined. Ask the wrong question, or the self-serving question, and the answer will be in kind. Ask which is Hemingway's best work, and someone will tell you the answer, but it won't be me. That question does not interest me. When asked, I tend to give an existential answer: whichever book or story I happen to be reading or working with at the moment. Or when the fit is upon me, I quote Walt Whitman:

> Showing the best and dividing it from the worst, age vexes
> age,

Knowing the perfect fitness and equanimity of things, while
      they discuss, I am silent.

The questions that I do ask are fairly obvious:

What triggers the text? Given the stories he might have written, why
was this text produced at this time by this writer?

What is the background for the text in the writer's life?

What is happening in his immediate surroundings that contributes to
the text?

What is happening in the wider cultural context that contributes to
the text?

What does the text tell us about the time and place in which it was
written?

Consider for a moment Hemingway's breakthrough novel—*The Sun
Also Rises* (1926).

This book could not have been written in 1915 because there was not
yet a war-weary generation to populate it or a reading audience coming
of age during Prohibition. The novel could not have been published in
1935 because in the middle of the Great Depression, few readers would
have been interested in the sexual problems of a bunch of drunks in Paris
and Pamplona. *The Sun Also Rises,* which is now treated by historians as
a period artifact, is not trapped in time, but it is certainly anchored there.
One can ignore the novel's historical context, for *The Sun* outshines its
own time, but to know its context is to read a richer novel.

As well as the scholar can manage, I suggest he or she must gather
data before formulating explanations. All too frequently, thesis-driven
research selects data that prove the answer that was known before the research began. As a geologist's son and a would-be engineer, I find it difficult to know the answer before I have done the research. I start with
questions. For example, how can you explain an author who would write
"Hills Like White Elephants" while on his honeymoon with his second
wife, an ardent Catholic who refused to practice birth control? If I have
a model, it comes from archaeology. I view Hemingway's life as if it were
an archaeological dig located in time and space. Chronology of events is
crucial to my methodology. Like the archaeologist, first and always I am

looking for ways to date artifacts. To fudge or distort the time line would be as dishonest for me as it would be for an archaeologist to fudge on the dating of a pot shard.

Consider, for example, what Hemingway did when his wife, Hadley, lost his early manuscripts. Carlos Baker tells us that after Hemingway returned to the Paris apartment to verify the loss, he went the next day to see Gertrude Stein. She gave him a "very fine lunch." He stayed there until train time, talking and reading "a lot of Gertrude's new stuff."[1] The source for this information is Hemingway's letter to Edmund Wilson written November 25, 1923—a year after the event. Unfortunately, when Ernest was in Paris visiting Gertrude, Miss Stein and Miss Toklas were vacationing in Provence at St. Remy. I know this from the dates on Stein letters from 1922.

**6**  What difference does it make? If the ladies had been in Paris, Hemingway would have visited them. No one is hurt by his invention. But why did he invent the visit, the meal, the discussion, and reading Gertrude's new stuff? Because he wanted to impress Edmund Wilson that he, Ernest Hemingway, as yet unknown in America, was an insider among the literary avant-garde of Paris, a writer to be taken seriously by Wilson. This analysis shows us a much shrewder Hemingway than the one he portrayed later in *A Moveable Feast*. The incident also underscores the mistake of letting anyone, much less a writer, construct his or her own biography—something that Hemingway was doing from 1918 to the end of his life.

Once, when he knew me fairly well from my several visits, Carlos Baker told me, "Hemingway lied to me! Why would a grown man tell lies?" I don't think that Carlos had seen the unpublished fragment in which Hemingway said:

> It is not unnatural that the best writers are liars. A major part of their trade is to lie or invent and they will lie when they are drunk, or to themselves, or to strangers. They often lie unconsciously and then remember their lies with deep remorse. If they knew all other writers were liars it would cheer them up.[2]

I would urge all literary biographers and cultural historians to hold that caveat in mind when approaching their subject matter. With Hemingway, one must always find corroborating evidence. For example, it was my good fortune to find his second wife's diary of their 1933 African safari, which gives us a benchmark from which to measure Hemingway's version in *Green Hills of Africa*. Here is an overly long portion of my take on Hemingway in Africa based on Pauline's journal, and not on *Green Hills* as almost every other biography has done.

Getting laden trucks up the slippery, wet, dirt road to the crater rim took most of the morning before Christmas, leaving Pauline alone staring out into the mist of the huge, flat, green caldera beneath her, where famous lions were said to roam. When the men came up after pushing and cursing the trucks, Ernest asked her to go somewhere else, for he was having an attack of diarrhea. He didn't want to go into the three foot grass because there might be snakes. That afternoon they took one car down into the crater where she and Ernest saw their first lioness, driving to within fifty feet of her. After killing two zebra for bait and driving back toward the lioness, Percival, Pauline, and Ernest were stunned by an explosion going off beside Ernest's head. His rifle, strapped to the car top and supposedly unloaded and uncocked, fell to the ground beside his door and unexplainably fired. Visibly shaken, Pauline's first thought was that Ernest had been killed. . . .

The last day of the year went out to a chorus of missed shots and curses. The morning began with Ernest missing a Roan antelope followed by three missed shots at a leopard. Later he wounded a cheetah which everyone tracked up and over the hill for more than a sweaty hour without finding him. That afternoon Charles fired six or seven shots at an Impala, finally bringing him down. Next morning, the first of the new year, Pauline, worn out from hiking in the brush, stayed in camp while Ernest was out redeeming his sorry shooting of the previous day. Before noon he had killed a warthog, and a cheetah, and then he and Charles killed three buffalo which Pauline had to see. So they sent Ben Fourie, the mechanic and driver, an hour back to camp to haul her to the killing ground where she admired the dead buffs with ticks still crawling on them. Too much heat, too much dust, too much male talk, Poor Old Mama, as they were now calling Pauline, had reached her limits. Making strenuous demands upon her in the field, the men, who apparently did not understand either her disappointments or her fears, frequently added to Pauline's melancholy. A long way from St. Louis, she was trying, almost desperately at times, to be the outdoors wife Ernest so wanted her to be.

8

Three days later, approaching by car a mated pair of lions on a slight hill, the group was surprised when the two predators came toward the vehicle, the lion to one side, his mate to the other. To Pauline's rising anxiety, the men agreed that she should shoot the male lion which had grown huge in her eyes by the time they got her out of the car. As she took aim, Percival said, "For Christ sake don't shoot the lioness!" She looked up, wondering could she be shooting the lioness, which, of course, was on the opposite side of car. As she resighted down the rifle barrel, she could hear Charles struggling to get out of the car. Afraid the lions would spook, she hurried her shot, apparently missing. The lions quickly disappeared into a dry stream bed thick with brush. No amount of beating about the edges of the donga could bring them back in sight. Pauline returned to camp in silent despair. Ernest, she noted later, had remained inside the car unable to save her should the lion have charged.[3]

If you read my entire chapter on the safari, *Green Hills* will become a slightly different book. You will also have a better understanding of Hemingway's artistry that transformed the thing itself into art, and you will appreciate Pauline a lot more.

Pauline Pfeiffer Hemingway—the mother of two Hemingway sons—was the daughter of a wealthy St. Louis father who moved the family to Piggott, Arkansas, where he became a gentleman farmer and the village patron. Between 1927 and 1936, while their marriage was sound, Pauline was wife, mother, bookkeeper, travel arranger, tax accountant, and banker for Hemingway's most productive ten years: five books, his *Esquire* "Letters," and several classic stories including "Hills Like White Elephants," "A Clean Well Lighted Place," and "The Snows of Kilimanjaro." These ten years were his most productive literary period, made possible largely by his wife's devotion to his talent. Ernest Hemingway became Pauline's art form. Without her resources, both financial and intestinal, Hemingway might have become another of the truly lost generation—the writer of one or two books who could not have supported himself through writing.

It was Pauline's trust fund producing $6,000 a year during the Great Depression that allowed Hemingway to remain a self-employed writer—he did not make enough money from his writing to support his lifestyle until *For Whom the Bell Tolls*. It was Pauline's doting, wealthy, and childless uncle Gus Pfeiffer who bought them automobiles, paid for their Key West house, and gave them $25,000 worth of stock to pay for the African safari. For ten years, Pauline never wavered in her support of Ernest's obsessions: deep sea fishing, Spanish bullfights, African safaris, Wyoming hunting, his beloved fishing boat, the *Pilar*. That she was not a very good rifle shot, that she was often seasick, that she preferred big city life to the limited pleasures of Key West never came between her and her husband's passions or his career. When he needed seclusion to write, she was protective; when he needed a change of scene, to be with her husband she would consign her sons to the nanny, for she knew how badly he fared when alone.

Knowing more about Pauline enriches several of the Hemingway texts produced during her tenure, just as knowing where Hemingway was at any given date can be crucial in understanding one of his letters or dating one of his manuscripts. If you bring together all of his incoming and outgoing correspondence, know where he was and what he was reading, then you have the local context to frame the text. "Big Two Hearted

**9**

River" tells us very little about Ernest Hemingway in 1919 just back from the war. (The experience upon which he based the story was on the Fox River. The first draft has three young men. Hemingway never fished the Big Two-Hearted. On the actual fishing trip there was no burned-over country.) To use the story as if it were biography is to miss its only verifiable biographic importance: the state of Hemingway's mind that early summer of 1924 when he wrote the story.

The interests of audience and artist, as William Butler Yeats understood, do not always coincide. Fortunate and favored is the artist born into that conjunction of antinomies where his art and audience are one. If ever an American writer appears so blessed, it would seem to be Ernest Hemingway. In his public life and prose, he became a national icon, his photograph needing no identifying caption. He lived by his trade for almost forty years, never consciously sacrificing his art for book sales. Thirty-eight years after his death, all his work remains in print, translated into languages too numerous to count; at least ten biographies repeat the incidents we all now know by heart; and several shelves of books, not to mention hundreds of articles, explain exactly what his stories were about and how he wrote them. And yet he escapes us still: complex, contradictory, irritating, unpredictable, a modernist raised on the virtues of the previous century. We want him to be our contemporary, but he is not and maybe never was. He was raised on self-reliance and the myth of the American West; we, his living readers, were raised on political confusion and the myth of social security. Nowhere are these differences more apparent than in our inability to appreciate Hemingway's interest in revolutionaries and blood sport—interests that surface in various ways in his fiction.

Which leads, round aboutly as John Barth might say, to a few words about *To Have and Have Not*—a strange novel told in different voices, which generally is said to be one of the worst books Hemingway wrote and certainly not worth reading. That sort of judgment—about Hemingway or any writer—always perplexes me. Can you imagine an archaeologist throwing out an imperfect pot as not worth studying, discarding a flawed Clovis spear point as unimportant? If we are trying to reconstruct our literary history, there are no unimportant artifacts. Nor are there any shortcuts. *To Have and Have Not* is a significant artifact in the study of Ernest Hemingway. To put it into perspective, I first examined every page of the Key West newspaper for the 1930s, every page of the *Havana Post* for periods he was in Cuba. I read every available letter to and from Hemingway in public and private collections. I studied the holograph manuscript and its several revisions. I read memoirs, biographies, and collections of letters. I pored through the historical records of Key West and collected a pile of period photographs. Interviews with two of Hemingway's contemporaries resulted in two hundred pages of typed transcription. All of this sifting in the dig gave me the evidence to restore the several contexts that produced *To Have and Have Not.* Even a broken pot, imperfectly restored, can tell us something about that time and place. As Hemingway explained to his editor, Max Perkins, the **11** themes of this newly conceived novel were "the decline of the individual" and his "re-emergence as Key West goes down around him" and "a hell of a lot more."[4] His private notes were rough, hurried and contradictory, not an outline but a working through of ideas. There were three themes running sometimes in parallel, sometimes in counterpoint, reinforcing each other. The first was local: the rise and fall of Harry Morgan in tandem with the decline of Key West into penury and its resultant destruction by government bureaucracy. The second theme would contrast the two islands—Cuba and Key West—both tropical, both aquatic, both Hispanic and Anglo but with their power structures reversed. The third theme was the overview pulling the two stories together: the dream of what might have been in the new world, the promise of Eden so quickly destroyed by greed and politics. He would include the lost dream, the death of the Cuban revolution that began so idealistically, and the rise of oppressing army control. Inside this plan, there were to be other parallels and contrasts of characters and events, enrichments and further complications. He would give his readers the Matecumbe vets in their darkest night going under as the hurricane's surge swept across the island, give them the revolutionists in the same storm running dynamite out of Key West and into Cuba, and give them finally the betrayal that brought everything together: the bridge that had to be blown, the Key West and Cuban revolutionists betrayed but not defeated, and it all going down to failure. [You recognize that bridge for it reappears at the heart of *For Whom the Bell Tolls*.] A *War and Peace* in miniature, *To Have and Have Not* was conceived as a far more ambitious and complicated book than the one we now read.[5]

If we don't understand what happened to Key West and the country in the 1930s, we deprive Hemingway of the audience for whom he wrote, Americans mired in the Great Depression. We also miss a crucial step in the development of Hemingway's social commitment. In 1929, Frederic Henry is reduced to a society of one, having deserted the Italian army and the Great War, standing alone in the neutral rain of Switzerland. In *Green Hills of Africa* (1934), the narrator tells himself that if things become unbearable in the United States, a man can always leave and go elsewhere, writing off the American experiment as a failure. But in *To Have and Have Not* (1937), Hemingway takes the first step away from ego-centered characters when Harry Morgan learns the hard way that man alone is no fucking good. Two years later in *The Fifth Column*, the American counterintelligence man, Philip Rawlings, is ready to sacrifice himself for the good of the cause. When the self-centered Dorothy wants to go with him at the final curtain, he tells her: "Where I go now I go alone, or with others who go there for the same reason I go."[6]

It is but a short step from Philip's position to that of Robert Jordan (*For Whom the Bell Tolls*, 1940) a year later. Having done his duty in a battle that was doomed to failure, Jordan lies dying on the Spanish pine needles, committed not to an ideology but to the Spanish land and its people. He tells Maria to leave him where he has fallen, adding, "What I do now I do alone. . . . Each one must do it alone. But if thou goest then I go with thee. It is in that way that I go too."[7]

My point is simple: the route from point A to point F is not necessarily a straight line. If you bypass B, C, D, and E, you have been dishonest. As Edward Albee told us in *The Zoo Story*, sometimes it is necessary to go a long way out of your way in order to come back a short distance correctly. To read most current views of Hemingway's 1930s is to

12

be told that between *A Farewell to Arms* in 1929 and *For Whom the Bell Tolls* in 1940 there is no need to read anything but some of the short stories. To accept this view is to subscribe to a literary history too dilettantish and too precious for me to bear. It also fails to realize how necessary *Death in the Afternoon, Green Hills,* and *To Have and Have Not* were to Hemingway's development. Without his 1930s experiments, he could never have written *For Whom the Bell Tolls,* his epic novel, just as "The Snows of Kilimanjaro" was his epic short story: in both, he gave the reader a story within which was embedded an entire collection of short stories. The critics who said he repeated himself were missing the obvious. Always experimenting, always reaching beyond his last effort, Hemingway never repeated the form.

What I say of Hemingway studies, I say as well for this century's literary history. The Modernist period is littered with paper trails enough to complicate an entire collection of Borges stories. Literary history is the Garden of Forking Paths. In the archaeological dig, we must sift with a fine screen, measuring and correlating every artifact because one piece of evidence is never enough to support a circumstantial case. We need more scholars and fewer critics. Better training in research methods is vital. We need better tools and more cooperation among scholars. We need on-line databases. We need a comprehensive means of locating archived manuscripts and letters. We need authoritative texts, but first we must train the next generation to edit those texts properly. The reevaluation of where we have been in this century's literature will not be accomplished by the dispassionate or by the unobsessed. But we must find and train those willing to make the effort, and in the end, as Mr. Eliot once suggested, we may come to know the place for the first time.

# Notes

1. Carlos Baker, *Ernest Hemingway* (New York: Scribner's, 1969), 103.
2. Item 845, Hemingway Collection, John F. Kennedy Library, Boston.
3. Michael Reynolds, *Hemingway: The 1930s* (New York: Norton, 1997), 160–62.

4. EH-Perkins, July 11, 1936 (Cat Cay); Ernest Hemingway, *Selected Letters* (New York: Scribner's, 1981), 447–48.

5. Item 211, Hemingway Collection, John F. Kennedy Library, Boston.

6. Ernest Hemingway, *"The Fifth Column" and Four Stories* (New York: Scribner's, 1969), 83.

7. Ernest Hemingway, *For Whom the Bell Tolls* (New York: Scribner's, 1940), 463.

# The Politics of "The Snows of Kilimanjaro"

"The Snows of Kilimanjaro" is the story of the last afternoon and evening of a writer on safari in East Africa who is facing death after a thorn scratch has become infected and gangrene has set in. This man, Harry, is attended by his wife, Helen, whom he reviles as a "rich bitch" whose money has corrupted him, preventing him from realizing his genuine literary talent. More justly he subjects himself to a merciless examination, silently admitting that he has changed his old style of life—"traded it for security, for comfort too." As he waits for the end he recalls to himself episodes from the past, printed in italics and rendered vividly to the reader, all of which could have been the subject of literature if he had husbanded his talent more carefully. As his wife clings to the hope that a rescue plane from Nairobi will arrive to save him, Harry, alert to the numbness of his gangrenous leg and to the vultures and a hyena loitering near the camp, knows better. Death comes that evening as his wife instructs the servants to carry his cot into their tent. As or just before he dies Harry has a dream-vision of the rescue plane arriving and taking him not to Arusha and then Nairobi but instead to the "great, high, and unbelievably white"[1] summit of Mt. Kilimanjaro, called, in the Masai language, "the House of God." The conclusion brings the reader down from this height to the wife in their tent awakened by the hyena closing in to feed on Harry's corpse.

Widely regarded as one of Hemingway's half-dozen finest short stories, if not as he himself thought perhaps his very finest,[2] "The Snows of Kilimanjaro" has generated a large body of critical and scholarly commentary. No fewer than 120 separate items appear in checklists by Jackson J. Benson and Paul Smith,[3] which do not include book reviews or anything appearing in the last decade. Scholarly treatments have included the close study of the final typescript by Robert Lewis and Max Westbrook,[4] amplified by details retrieved by Paul Smith from earlier typescripts; search for sources of the intriguing epigraph about the mountain and its frozen leopard carcass; analysis of imagery and symbolism; discussion of point of view and narrative method, especially the use of italicized flashbacks; identification of such themes as death, life as pain and loss, "life-in-death and death-in-life," artistic integrity and the lack thereof, spiritual rebirth, the failure of love, marital disorder, misogyny; and comparison of Hemingway's story to works by Milton, Bunyan, Thoreau, Tolstoy, Conrad, Ambrose Bierce, and William Golding.

A recurrent critical concern—and the focus of this essay—is the relation of "The Snows of Kilimanjaro" to its author's life. To what extent is Harry a fictional version of Hemingway himself? Is the woman his second wife, Pauline Pfeiffer? In what ways does the story derive from their safari with Philip Percival in late 1933 and early 1934, already treated in the nonfiction novel *Green Hills of Africa* (1935)? With the exception of one episode from the American West, probably in northern Wyoming, Harry's italicized memories refer to scenes and events from the first three decades of the century, but do Hemingway's experiences in the early Depression years have any effect on "The Snows of Kilimanjaro"? Before turning to such issues, though, it might be well to examine the author's own account of the genesis of his story.

In "The Art of the Short Story" Hemingway relates that he gave an interview to reporters on his way back from Africa in early April 1934 in which he spoke of returning to Africa as soon as he could make enough money to do so: "Well it was in the papers and a really nice and really fine and really rich woman invited me to tea and we had a few drinks as well and she had read in the papers about this project, and why should I have to wait to go back for any lack of money? She and my wife and I could go to Africa any time and money was only something to be used intelligently for the best enjoyment of good people and so forth. It was a sincere and fine and good offer and I liked her very much and I turned down the offer. . . . [In Key West] I start to think what would happen to a character like me whose defects I know, if I had accepted that offer. So I start to invent and I make myself a guy who would do what I invent."[5]

Since this account of the origin of the story has never been corroborated, the identity or even the existence of such a woman is not known. Hemingway's penchant for "invention" made him a sometimes unreliable source for his own activities or those of others. On the other hand, given his fame and sexual magnetism, we cannot discount entirely this putative offer from "a really nice and really fine and really rich woman."[6] If true, **17** Hemingway, however tempted, would be painfully aware of the similarity of such a ménage à trois to the actual threesome that developed after Pauline Pfeiffer joined Hadley and Ernest in Schruns in late December 1925. If the episode did not happen, the invented woman may have some relation to the actual Jane Mason, with whom Hemingway had an affair in Havana and who has long been considered the prototype of Margot Macomber in the other great story deriving from that first safari. Harry's "rich bitch" epithet would be more applicable to Jane than to Pauline, who was devoted to her husband and patient with his shortcomings, as *Green Hills of Africa* attests. The common denominator of the three women is their money. Other details do not fit the invented wife of the story. Although a good shot like Harry's wife, Pauline had not been previously married, did not have a series of lovers or grown children or a stable of horses, had not been a heavy drinker, and after her second cesarean could no longer risk pregnancy by exercising "a great talent . . . for the bed." As for Jane Mason, she was still in her middle twenties when Hemingway was writing.[7]

Hemingway's account of the origin of the story states that the protagonist is a projection of himself if he had yielded to the temptation of an unearned second safari financed by "a really nice" woman who would bring out the considerably less than nice "defects" of "a character like me." The diction is ambiguous: character meaning dramatis persona or character in the Damon Runyon sense? The syntax describing the beginning of composition is also slippery: "So I start to invent and I make myself a guy who would do what I invent." Is Hemingway saying that he is transforming himself into an autobiographical persona who would behave as his creative invention dictates, or is he saying that he will make *for* himself a character who will do as his author directs? In any event, he is describing the story as a revealing hypothetical fictional autobiography about what did not happen but could have. Moreover, as all readers of "The Snows of Kilimanjaro" who are familiar with Hemingway biography immediately recognize, most of Harry's italicized recollections correspond to actual events in the author's life: riding the Orient Express on his way back to Paris in October 1922, skiing in western Austria in 1924–25 and 1925–26,[8] whoring in Constantinople, observing the Greco-Turkish conflict, picking blueberries in northern Michigan, living in the Place Contrescarpe in Paris, holding a horse's tail to descend a mountain at night in the American West, hearing war stories from the Western Front. And, of course, Harry's immobilized condition on the Serengeti Plain and his dream-vision of escape by air to the purity of the heights of Kilimanjaro correspond roughly to Hemingway's attack of amoebic dysentery with severe diarrhea requiring air transportation from the bush back to Nairobi on January 16, 1934.

But various critics have pushed the similarities much farther, emphasizing Harry's failure to write about such good material as his memory has stored, indulging instead in the slothful self-indulgence made possible by the wealth of his wife: "each day of not writing, of comfort . . . dulled his ability and softened his will to work so that, finally, he did no work at all."[9] This condition, the argument goes, mirrors the author's own situation at the time. Between 1925 and 1929, Hemingway published *In Our Time, The Torrents of Spring, The Sun Also Rises, Men Without Women,* and *A Farewell to Arms.* In the following six years only a guide to bullfighting, a collection of short stories, and a book on hunting in Africa appeared. Such a view drastically oversimplifies the operation of a writer's imagination, which seldom moves with metronomic regularity.

It also overlooks some relevant biographical data. Dr. Clarence E.

Hemingway committed suicide in November 1928, leaving Ernest as the head of the family with corresponding financial responsibilities and expenditures of time. *Death in the Afternoon* is a book that required substantial scholarly research in the vast literature of *tauromaquia* as well as close observation of scores of corridas. Late in 1930 an automobile accident in Montana resulted in the most painful of the many injuries he sustained over his lifetime. His right arm, severely fractured with extensive nerve damage and paralyzed wrist, required seven weeks of immobilization in a Billings hospital, followed by three more months of convalescence in Piggott and Key West before he could write again. Despite such contretemps, Hemingway the writer could hardly be called idle. From 1930 to the appearance of "The Snows of Kilimanjaro" in August 1936, he published a long article on the economics of bullfighting; *Death in the Afternoon; Winner Take Nothing*, consisting of fourteen short stories, including such major ones as "After the Storm," "A Clean, Well-Lighted Place," "The Gambler, the Nun, and the Radio," and "Father and Sons"; letters to the editors of *Hound and Horn* and the *New Yorker;* "One Trip Across," which became the first part of *To Have and Have Not;* nine introductions, statements, or essays in books and pamphlets by other hands; a couple of poems; *Green Hills of Africa;* a report on the hurricane of 1935 as it affected the war veterans on Lower Matecumbe Key;[10] an article for *Outdoor Life;* and twenty-nine articles for *Esquire.* Admittedly much of this production was topical or occasional rather than permanent, but its quality has generally been underestimated. Edmund Wilson paints with far too broad a brush when he characterizes the *Esquire* pieces as "rubbishy."[11] One of the best was "The Horns of the Bull" (later titled "The Capital of the World," an excellent short story), and "Notes on the Next War: A Serious Topical Letter" and "Wings Always Over Africa: An Ornithological Letter" are prescient and powerful commentaries on Mussolini's invasion of Ethiopia, ranking among the very best of Hemingway's political writings.

Unlike Harry, then, Hemingway had certainly not "softened his will to work." Also unlike Harry, it could not be said of the author of *In Our Time, The Sun Also Rises,* and *A Farewell to Arms* that "it was never what he had done, but always what he could do."[12] Hemingway, however, was genuinely concerned about his relation to the rich, especially wives with more money than he possessed. Toward the rich in general he was deeply ambivalent. Although they are attacked bitterly in "The Snows of Kilimanjaro" and even more bitterly in *To Have and Have Not,* Hemingway had long associated with friends more affluent than himself. Much has been made of his upper-middle-class origins in Oak Park, but the Hemingways hardly qualified economically for such status. Physicians today almost always have an annual income in six figures, but medicine was much less lucrative early in the century, especially for doctors who were reluctant to press for payment of overdue bills, as was Dr. Clarence E. Hemingway. Since the family was a large one, Dr. Hemingway tried his best to limit expenses, but his wife and daughters did not always cooperate. Like Scott Fitzgerald, though to a lesser degree, Hemingway grew up in a community where many families were better off than his.

20

In "The Snows of Kilimanjaro" Harry muses that "it was strange . . . that when he fell in love with another woman, that woman should always have more money than the last one."[13] This was certainly true of Hemingway in his procession from Agnes von Kurowsky to Hadley Richardson to Pauline Pfeiffer. It is also true that he did not avoid friendships with wealthy people, though such was his personal vitality and charm that the rich usually sought him out. While still a boy of nineteen convalescing from his war wounds, he was taken under the wing of the distinguished Italian diplomat Count Giuseppe Maria Greppi, and Bellia Pier Vicenzo of Turin, a wealthy contractor, virtually adopted him into his family, styling himself Hemingway's "papa Italiano."[14] Hemingway's commanding Red Cross officer in the war was Captain James Gamble, a Yale graduate and a wealthy member of the soap manufacturing family. Twice Hemingway's age, Gamble cultivated his friendship, taking him to the picturesque Sicilian village of Taormina for a week of rest and relaxation with all expenses paid in late December 1918. As Michael Reynolds comments dryly, "Hemingway did not see Gamble's money as an impediment to friendship."[15] Additional invitations were for an entire cost-free year in Italy and, on a later occasion, five months in Rome, but Hemingway declined because of his involvements with Agnes and then Hadley.

It was to Paris, not Italy, that Ernest and Hadley went three months after their marriage on September 3, 1921. There they were not "very poor and very happy," as Hemingway states in the memorable last sentence of *A Moveable Feast*, but quite comfortable and very happy, thanks primarily to Hadley's trust fund and only secondarily to her husband's income from the *Toronto Star*. The final chapter of the Paris memoir also describes the insidious entry into the happy life of the Hemingways of the charming and wealthy Gerald and Sara Murphy, introduced by John Dos Passos, the "pilot fish." "Then you have the rich and nothing is ever as it was again." Indeed, in wildly extravagant hyperbole Hemingway states that when such people as the Murphys have "taken their nourishment from the happy and talented," they depart and "leave everything deader than the roots of any grass Attila's horses have ever scoured."[16] Thus near the end of his life Hemingway's animus against the rich, including his second wife, Pauline, is at least as intense as the similar feelings expressed by Harry in "The Snows of Kilimanjaro." Like Hadley, Pauline brought a trust fund to her marriage with Ernest, only larger.

She also came with a family, and Ernest became much more involved with—and indebted to—its members than was the case with his other in-laws. Though born in Iowa, her father, Paul Pfeiffer, had become rich in St. Louis before moving in 1913 to Piggott, a small town in the extreme northeast corner of Arkansas, where he bought cheap land and built an agricultural empire of more than sixty thousand acres.[17] His brothers were also rich, especially Gustavus A. Pfeiffer, who lived in New York and ran his pharmaceutical, patent medicine, and perfume enterprises. Throughout his second marriage, Ernest benefited from generous gifts from the Pfeiffer family, beginning with a thousand dollar wedding check to Pauline from her parents. For his part, Uncle Gus had advanced money for the newlyweds' stylish Paris apartment. In contrast, ten days after the wedding Ernest received a check for one hundred dollars from the *New Republic* for his article "Italy 1927" (later called "Che Te Dici La Patria"). With royalties from his previous books going to Hadley and *A Farewell to Arms* not yet out, it is clear where the money was as Hemingway's second marriage got under way.

It continued to flow in throughout their life together, especially from

Uncle Gus. The problem was that Ernest felt obliged to read his numerous letters, such as one dated September 17, 1927, from Homestead, his Connecticut estate, praising the pioneering spirit of the United States as superior to European culture and urging his nephew-in-law to come home again: "You have been away how many years—isn't it time to reacquaint yourself with your native land which in spite of its faults is the greatest although the richest country in the world." Banal, smug, sententious, Uncle Gus was as generous with his avuncular advice as he was with his money. His prose style, too, must have made Ernest wince with its prolixity and its poetic diction (e.g., "finny tribe"). Characteristically the letters are long, whether written in small cursive or typed, but Ernest or Pauline had to plow through them, for they often compensated for the boredom they induced with news of another gift, such as the new Ford announced in an eight-page letter of January 22, 1928. When Patrick Hemingway was born on June 28 of the same year, Uncle Gus dispatched a letter with three checks, one for Ernest, one for Pauline, and one for the infant to start him "on the road to Thrift and Wealth." As a gesture of appreciation for his bounty, Ernest dedicated *A Farewell to Arms* to Uncle Gus. In the following year, as Ernest was researching taurine literature for *Death in the Afternoon*, Gus wrote his corporate representative in Barcelona to search for and purchase a large number of relevant books and magazines unobtainable in America and difficult to find even in Spain, instructing him to "send me the bill for all expenses which you may incur by reason of this request." A more substantial bill was paid by Uncle Gus less than a year later—$8,000 for the big house on Whitehead Street in Key West, deeded to Ernest. Then in late 1933 he furnished it for Ernest and Pauline with Spanish antiques shipped from the peninsula. His business interests continuing to prosper even as the Depression deepened, Gus wrote to Ernest on February 5, 1932, enclosing a letter from a yacht broker in New York concerning a 135-foot pleasure craft for sale at the bargain price of $35,000. The letter concludes: "Between now and the time I come to Florida you might be thinking it over, and at that time we can discuss it." The implication seems to be that he is offering to buy it for Ernest. By the time that the *Pilar*—a 38-foot fishing craft, not a luxury yacht—was purchased, Hemingway was able to

**22**

borrow enough from Max Perkins and Arnold Gingrich to pay the purchase price of $7,500. But in the meantime Uncle Gus had provided the $25,000 needed for the African safari, and he even promised to pay the taxidermy bills not only for Ernest and Pauline but for their Key West friend Charles Thompson as well.[18] Paul and Mary Pfeiffer also gave money to their daughter and son-in-law during the years preceding "The Snows of Kilimanjaro," but on a much smaller scale.

Against this biographical background it is easier to understand Harry's vitriolic comments about the rich and his self-loathing for living off his wife's fortune, consisting of "all the money there was."[19] Hemingway himself was a working writer, not one whose reliance on his wife's family was so extreme that it "dulled his ability and softened his will to work so that, finally, he did no work at all." Hemingway salvaged his pride, but he could not dispel the malaise out of which the story grew.    **23**

Whether one emphasizes the role of the putative wealthy New York woman or the Pfeiffer family as crucial in the genesis of the story, more seems involved than either personal pride or prostitution of one's talent, literary or sexual. As shadows darken that late afternoon on the Serengeti Plain, Harry ruminates: "You said that you would write about these people, about the very rich; that you were really not of them but a spy in their country; that you would leave it and write of it and for once it would be written by someone who knew what he was writing of."[20] The metaphor of espionage is striking, as is the designation of the very rich as "the enemy." This was the language of the left, the language of William Z. Foster and Norman Thomas and even FDR, who was denouncing the "malefactors of great wealth." Hemingway's story does not indict its protagonist for espionage but for going over to the enemy, for succumbing to the debilitating life of the leisure class instead of exposing it. "The Snows of Kilimanjaro" may, at least to this extent, be said to have its politics. But there is more.

Harry's italicized flashbacks have been scrutinized closely by many critics, especially the long one on the Place Contrescarpe in Paris. Here the recollection is indisputably Hemingway's as well as Harry's; indeed, he later uses it in *A Moveable Feast*. But one part of it has been utterly ignored, precisely the part that is explicitly political. The Place

Contrescarpe is working-class Paris, a neighborhood rife with alco-
holism and prostitution. Its inhabitants *"were the descendants of the Com-
munards and it was no struggle for them to know their politics. They knew
who had shot their fathers, their relatives, their brothers, and their friends
when the Versailles troops came in and took the town after the Commune and
executed anyone they could catch with calloused hands, or who wore a cap, or
carried any other sign he was a working man. And in that poverty, and in
that quarter across the street from a Boucherie Chevaline and a wine cooperative he had written the start of all he was to do."*[21]

Unlike his neighbors, whose left politics were hereditary and class-
determined, Hemingway had to struggle to determine his. Raised in a
progressive Republican family in which both grandfathers were Union
veterans, he encountered a very different politics among his Italian comrades in World War I: socialism, anarchism, bolshevism. Back in Oak
Park he cast his first and only vote in an American presidential election
for Eugene V. Debs, then incarcerated in the Atlanta Federal Peniten-
tiary as a self-described "flaming revolutionist."[22] The following month
Hemingway was writing and editing for the *Cooperative Commonwealth*,
whose motto was "All for Each, and Each for All."[23] Returning to Europe
in December 1921 as a correspondent for the *Toronto Star*, he covered the
International Economic Conference in Genoa, the rise of Mussolini,
communist violence in Paris, runaway inflation in Germany, the Greco-
Turkish conflict in Thrace, growing Soviet influence in the Balkans,
French political parties, and similar topics, gaining an extensive knowledge of European politics. Even after he left the *Star* in September 1924,
he retained his interest in political matters, often saving clippings or
entire newspaper pages with relevant articles. His correspondence, too, is
sprinkled with political comments, mostly on leftist topics. Moreover, in
1927 and 1928 he was working on a picaresque novel about an American
revolutionist and his son. He wrote to Max Perkins on March 17, 1928,
that he had completed twenty-two chapters and forty-five thousand
words but that he was putting it aside to work on a story that was to become *A Farewell to Arms*.[24]

Hemingway was, however, highly critical of American communists
and their "shitty house organ," *New Masses*, which had turned down "An

Alpine Idyll." On April 12, 1931, he wrote to Scott Fitzgerald: "Have you become a Communist like Bunny Wilson? In 1919–20–21 when we were all paid up Communists Bunny and all those guys thot it was all tripe— as indeed it proved to be—but suppose everybody has to go through some political or religious faith sooner or later. Personally would rather go through things sooner and get your disillusions behind you instead of ahead of you."[25]

But Hemingway's disillusions were shaken just two days later. Revolutionary ferment in his beloved Spain forced the abdication of King Alfonso XIII on April 14, 1931, and continued throughout the spring and summer. These events were observed closely by Hemingway, who had arrived in Madrid on May 15 for the San Isidro bullfights. Reporting to Dos Passos on the chaotic situation, he said that "we could have a fine time here now. Communists have *no money at all*—or could make a pretty good show." The radical painter Luis Quintanilla explained to Hemingway the necessity of the revolution in Spain. His judgment seemed vindicated by subsequent events, for the Republican-Socialist coalition won a resounding victory in the June elections. Hemingway wrote to Waldo Pierce in early November: "Spain was very nice with the revolution. Had a fine time all spring and summer—." At the end of the year the Cortes unanimously (368–0) adopted the Constitution of the Second Republic. It declared Spain to be "a democratic republic of workers of every class, organized in a regime of liberty and justice."[26] It was to this democratic republic of workers that Hemingway made the most intense political commitment of his life.

Back in the United States and working on *Death in the Afternoon*, Hemingway was disturbed by the deepening Depression and disgusted by Hoover's machinations. "W're in the S house now," he wrote to Mike Strater. "Well to hell with it." Doctrinaire communism certainly did not seem a way out, though, and he continued to reject didacticism in fiction. Writing to Dos Passos he qualified his praise of *1919* with this caveat: "If you get a noble communist remember the bastard probably masturbates and is jallous as a cat. Keep them people, people, people, and don't let them get to be symbols. . . . don't let them suck you into any economic Y.M.C.A." Two months later he added: "I can't be a Communist because

**25**

I hate tyranny, and, I suppose, government. But if you're ever one it's swell with me." Other recent converts or potential converts aroused his ire, however. In a subsequent letter to Dos Passos he contrasted his early radicalism with the socially irresponsible aesthetes who were now demanding political engagement: "It's damn funny when I used to get the horrors about the ways things were going those guys never took the slightest interest or even followed it. They were all in Europe and got worked up over Tristan Tzara when the god damnedest things were happening." Now they are saying, "'Dont you see the injustice, the Big Things that are happening. Why don't you write about them etc.'"[27]

He also must have been annoyed by the gratuitous attacks on him in the pages of *New Masses*. In a review of Archibald MacLeish's epic poem *Conquistador*, Sol Funaroff called such a focus on the past "the yearning of decadent bourgeois sophisticates for a simpler life . . . similar to the delights Ernest Hemingway takes in bullfighting." The following month Philip Rahv in "The Literary Class War" called the characters in *The Sun Also Rises* "effete hypochondriacs [Was Jake merely imagining that his member was missing?], cataleptic individualists—the human dust of finance capitalism."[28]

But Hemingway, who more than once in his correspondence expressed approval of "intelligent assassination" as a political act, did not consider himself less radical than Malcolm Cowley or Max Eastman or even Mike Gold. When a limited edition publisher from Kansas City expressed his hope that Hemingway would swing to the left, the response was invective worthy of Thomas Nashe. If a revolution ever came, Hemingway promised, he would "see that all limited edition publishers were shot and all their stinking little souls distributed to relieve sanitex shortage." A month later he explained: "I will not outline my political beliefs to you since I have no need to and since I could be jailed for their publication but if they are not much further left than yours which sound like a sentimental socialism I will move them further over."[29]

In addition to Spanish and American politics, there was Cuba. During three years preceding the composition of "The Snows of Kilimanjaro" Hemingway spent much time fishing the Gulf Stream out of Havana—almost thirty weeks in all. He took shorter trips as well, such as the one with John Dos Passos in 1934 to celebrate May Day. All the while he was a close observer of the turbulent political situation on the island. Depression had hit Cuba at least as hard as its neighbor to the north. As the price of sugar plunged and unemployment spread, unrest was inevitable. President Gerardo Machado met it with brutal repression, followed by increased opposition, which prompted further repression. The crisis came in August 1933, when a general strike spread across the country and the U.S. ambassador, Sumner Welles, joined the effort to oust Machado. Losing the support of the military as well, the dictator fled to Nassau. After three more weeks the provisional government collapsed and a revolutionary junta took its place. Early in 1934 it was replaced by a conservative regime installed by Fulgencio Batista, who controlled the army, and a new U.S. ambassador, who declared that the revolutionary junta led by Ramón Grau San Martin and Antonio Guiteras drew its support from "the ignorant masses who have been misled by utopian promises."[30] The presence of the battleship *Wyoming* in Havana Harbor underscored the point.

Hemingway's sentiments were clearly on the side of the Cuban Revolution of 1933, however much he scorned stateside parlor radicals. Before going to the island in early April, Hemingway had Alfred Dashiell of Scribner's ask a college classmate at the State Department to issue what was in effect a safe-conduct pass, which would be "useful when he has been held up by some ambitious fascist." Writing from Havana to his mother-in-law on August 14, 1934, Hemingway seemed hopeful that a Cuban postal strike indicated that the conservative "govt. is very wobbly and may fall before the projected November revolution." In the memorable opening scene of "One Trip Across," Harry Morgan tells the three young Cuban revolutionaries that he cannot transport them to Key West even though, he says, "I'm all for you." Moments later they are shot down by government gunmen. In 1935 Richard Armstrong of the *Havana Post* sent Hemingway a graphic account of a similar incident and included a photograph of corpses with the caption "Being gentlemen obnoxious to the government." About this time Hemingway was helping leftist Cuban painter Antonio Gattorno, just as he had helped a Spanish counterpart, Luis Quintanilla. To Arnold Gingrich he explained: "He is on his ass in Havana having won a gigantic competition which the last revolution [i.e., the counterrevolution of 1934] buggared up (we lost) so never paid."[31] "*We* lost." Hemingway was expressing his solidarity with the Cuban revolutionary left and implying his opposition to the wealthy Cuban right and its American overlords.

Placed in the context of Hemingway's politics of the early 1930s—his scorn of the nouveau American left and his support of Cuban and Spanish radicals—two key passages in "The Snows of Kilimanjaro" can be seen in a new light. Although it was "no struggle" for the hereditarily oppressed proletariat of the Place Contrescarpe "to know *their* [emphasis added] politics," it had been a struggle for Harry—and Hemingway—to arrive at such knowledge, a central element of which was hatred of the rich. When Harry analyzes the destruction of his talent, he recognizes his own responsibility, especially "betrayals of himself and what he believed in."[32] Readers of the story customarily relate this statement to his failure to maintain his commitment to the art of fiction, a valid interpretation, but surely it can also be understood as a betrayal of his political belief that wealth both corrupts and oppresses.

Placed in the context of Hemingway's literary career in the 1930s, "The Snows of Kilimanjaro" is not only his greatest artistic achievement since *A Farewell to Arms* but a key transitional point between the disengagement of *Death in the Afternoon* ("Let those who want to save the world if you can get to see it clear and as a whole") and *Green Hills of Africa* on the one hand and the commitment of *To Have and Have Not* ("a man alone ain't got no bloody fucking chance"), *The Spanish Earth*, *The Fifth Column*, and *For Whom the Bell Tolls* on the other.[33]

Recognizing the politics of "The Snows of Kilimanjaro," a submerged portion of the iceberg, does not negate the validity of the other dimensions of meaning identified over the last six decades, nor does it compromise the superb artistry with which this masterful story is executed. It does help us to enhance our understanding of what Susan Beegel calls Hemingway's "craft of omission." It also demonstrates, as *For Whom the Bell Tolls* does more amply, that as long as didacticism can be avoided, art and politics are not necessarily incompatible in Hemingway's fiction.

28

# Notes

1. Ernest Hemingway, *The Fifth Column and the First Forty-nine Stories* [hereafter SK] (New York: Charles Scribner's Sons, 1938), 156, 160, 174.

2. Roger B. Linscott in his "On the Books" column states that "looking backward from the vantage point of 1946, Hemingway considers '"The Snows of Kilimanjaro' . . . about as good as any of my stories" (*New York Herald Tribune Book Review* [December 29, 1946], 13). In "The Art of the Short Story," Hemingway says that it and "The Short Happy Life of Francis Macomber" "are as good short stories as I can write" (Jackson J. Benson, ed., *New Critical Approaches to the Short Stories of Ernest Hemingway* [Durham: Duke University Press, 1990], 8). And A. E. Hotchner quotes Hemingway at the Whitehead Street house in Key West: "This is where I wrote 'The Snows of Kilimanjaro' . . . and that's as good as I've any right to be" (*Papa Hemingway* [New York: Random House, 1966], 161). Hemingway would have been grimly aware of the irony of writing a story railing against the rich in a house bought for him by his wealthiest benefactor.

3. Jackson J. Benson, *The Short Stories of Ernest Hemingway: Critical Essays* (Durham: Duke University Press, 1975), 311–75; Benson, ed., *New Critical Approaches to the Short Stories of Ernest Hemingway*, 393–458; and Paul Smith, *A Reader's Guide to the Short Stories of Ernest Hemingway* (Boston: G. K. Hall, 1989), 349–61.

4. Robert Lewis and Max Westbrook, "'The Snows of Kilimanjaro,' Collated and Annotated," *Texas Quarterly* 13 (Summer 1970): 64–143.

5. Benson, ed., *New Critical Approaches*, 8.

6. Whether or not the woman existed, shipboard reporters did indeed interview Hemingway, who said he intended "to work like hell and make enough money so that I can go back to Africa and really learn something about lions" (*New York Herald Tribune*, April 4, 1934, 4. See also *New York Times*, April 4, 1934, 18).

7. SK, 159. For more information on the "sexual coolness" between Pauline and Ernest, see Bernice Kert, *The Hemingway Women* (New York: Norton, 1983), 248. In a 1998 television documentary Gregory Hemingway linked his father's affair with Jane Mason to his parents' sexual problem. Disregarding the age issue, A. E. Hotchner states flatly that Hemingway portrays Jane as Helen as well as Mrs. Macomber. See *Hemingway and His World* (New York: Vendome Press, 1989), 130.

8. Harry remembers four winters there, but there were only two for Hemingway, who is perhaps thinking of Chamby and Cortina in 1922–23 and Gstaad in 1926–27.

9. SK, 157.

10. "Who Murdered the Vets?" *New Masses* 16 (September 17, 1935): 9–10.

11. "Letter to the Russians About Hemingway," *New Republic* 85 (December 11, 1935): 135.

12. SK, 157, 158.

13. SK, 158.

14. Vicenzo to Hemingway, February 9, 1920, Hemingway Collection of the John F. Kennedy Library, Boston (hereafter cited as JFK-HC).

15. Michael Reynolds, *The Young Hemingway* (Oxford: Basil Blackwell, 1986), 126.

16. Ernest Hemingway, *A Moveable Feast* (New York: Charles Scribner's Sons, 1964), 211, 207, 208. See also Linda Patterson Miller, ed., *Letters from the Lost Generation: Gerald and Sara Murphy and Friends* (New Brunswick: Rutgers University Press, 1991).

17. The Pfeiffer letterhead proclaimed that Paul and Mary Pfeiffer, president and secretary-treasurer of Piggot Land Co., Inc., were "owners of over fifty thousand acres of highly improved and cut over lands in rich St. Francis, Cache, and Black River valleys. Well drained. . . . These lands grow fine Clover, Corn, Cotton, Wheat and Truck Crops. Mild winters and fine pastures make this an ideal Hog, Cattle and Poultry Section. Served by both the Cotton Belt and Frisco Railroads." The Pfeiffer holdings eventually reached the astonishing total of 63,000 acres.

18. All letters cited from Gustavus A. Pfeiffer are in the JFK-HC.

19. SK, 158.

20. SK, 157.

21. SK, 167–68.

22. Ray Ginger, *The Bending Cross: A Biography of Eugene Victor Debs* (New Brunswick: Rutgers University Press, 1949), 387.

23. This motto appears on the masthead of the first page of volume 1, no. 4 (May 1920) in the Carlos Baker Collection of the Princeton University Library (hereafter PUL).

24. Matthew J. Bruccoli, ed., *The Only Thing That Counts: The Ernest Hemingway/Maxwell Perkins Correspondence* (New York: Scribner, 1996), 69.

25. Carlos Baker, ed., *Ernest Hemingway: Selected Letters, 1917–1961* (hereafter *SL*) (New York: Scribner, 1981), 261, 339. Hemingway's low opinion of *New Masses* in 1926 did not prevent him from contributing to it in 1935.

26. *SL*, 341, 344. Carlos Baker, *Ernest Hemingway: A Life Story* (New York: Scribner's, 1969), 222, on Quintanilla. For the historical events in Spain, see Rhea Marsh Smith, *Spain: A Modern History* (Ann Arbor: University of Michigan Press, 1965), 430–35.

27. Hemingway to Strater, January 28, 1932, PUL. Hemingway to Dos Passos, March 26, 1932, *SL*, 354; May 30, 1932, *SL*, 360; October 14, 1932, *SL*, 374. Compare the last letter here to the flashback in the story mentioning Tristan Tzara and the American poet (Malcolm Cowley), SK, 164. See also Kenneth G. Johnston, "The Silly Wasters: Tzara and the Poet in 'The Snows of Kilimanjaro,'" *Hemingway Review* 8 (Fall 1988): 50–57.

28. *New Masses* 8 (July 1932): 26; 8 (August 1932): 7–10.

29. On "intelligent assassination," see letter to Dos Passos, October 14, 1932, *SL*, 374. Hemingway to Paul Romaine, July 6, 1932, *SL*, 363; August 9, 1932, *SL*, 365.

30. Luis E. Aguilar, *Cuba 1933, Prologue to Revolution* (Ithaca: Cornell University Press, 1972), 224. For Hemingway and Cuban politics in the 1930s, see Mary Cruz, *Cuba y Hemingway en el gran rio azul* (Havana: Union de Escritores y Artistas de Cuba, 1981).

30

31. Alfred Dashiell to Stuart Grumman, March 31, 1933, JFK-HC; Hemingway to Mary A. Pfeiffer, August 14, 1934, JFK-HC; Ernest Hemingway, *To Have and Have Not* (New York: Charles Scribner's Sons, 1937), 4; Richard Armstrong to Hemingway, June 1, 1935, JFK-HC; Hemingway to Gingrich, June 4, 1935, *SL*, 413.

32. SK, 158.

33. Ernest Hemingway, *Death in the Afternoon* (New York: Charles Scribner's Sons, 1932), 278; *To Have and Have Not*, 225.

# Wallace Stegner

*Artist as Environmentalist*

Wallace Stegner would seem to have been born with a feeling in his bones for the land around him—alert even in early childhood to its smells, sounds, and sights. By contrast to most of us who motor on through life, he established relationships with places, sometimes the most God-awful barren places. Always he yearned to know more about any place he might find himself, but particularly in the West, the region he considered home. When he came across a place that was unfamiliar to him, he wanted to know its physical history and geological composition, as well as the record of man from the earliest natives, to the white explorers, to waves of settlers who stayed or just passed through. The land stimulated his senses, called forth his imagination, and led him to wonder or contemplation. He was a storyteller and seemed to know instinctively that the land had many stories to tell and that any story about people worth telling tied them somehow to their natural environments.

What are the circumstances that might lead someone to become so attached to the land and eventually become an environmental activist? In Wallace Stegner's case we know that the ground was prepared for him by an intimate relationship with nature during childhood. Spending his summers while growing up on the last homestead frontier in Saskatchewan (from 1914 to

1920), he was without playmates, alone with his parents, who through the long days were preoccupied with trying to make the farm function. But rather than suffering from loneliness as one might expect, he found joy in being solitary in nature. He has said in looking back, "The bond with the earth that all the footed and winged creatures felt in that country was quite as valid for me."[1] Perhaps this reaction is characteristic of all those who eventually become concerned with preserving the natural environment.

From the ages of five to eleven, Wallace found himself on a desolate prairie three to four months a year, a place with "searing wind, scorching sky, tormented and heat-warped light, and not a tree,"[2] a place where livestock could roam for days without encountering the fence of a neighbor. Yet, amazingly enough considering such a barren and hostile environment, Stegner could still look back on a childhood not of suffering and boredom but of "wild freedom, a closeness to earth and weather, a familiarity with both tame and wild animals."[3] His years on the homestead marked him as a Westerner for life. As he has said, "Expose a child to a particular environment at his susceptible time and he will perceive in the shapes of that environment until he dies."[4]

Aside from the empty flatness of the 320 acres of the homestead, its most salient feature was its dryness. There was a source of water—just barely. A short ways off the property near the Montana line, there was a coulee which in most seasons didn't really run with water but seeped to the surface and in the spring formed small pools. Wallace and his father would fetch water for the family and livestock from those pools and carry kegs back on their wagon. Wheat was their crop, but it required summer rainfall, and in four years out of five, they were dusted out. During a sixth summer there was so much rain that the wheat was ruined by rust. The family's hopes were dashed, and Wallace's father, who, despite his many flaws, was a hard worker, gave up in disgust and turned to bootlegging to make a living and after a few months moved the family to Montana. In looking back, the author has said that but for a few inches of rain, his family would have become naturalized citizens and he would have been a Canadian.

That bitter defeat and the missing few inches of rain was a hard, early lesson that was ingrained in his consciousness and later became a major theme in his environmental writing. Lack of rain or aridity, he repeatedly would observe, was the factor that above all defined the West. And lack of water, as well as poor land and water laws, became a defining problem for the success or, more often, lack of success for the settlers in the West.[5] Wallace's father's failure to make it as a farmer was a harsh experience for the entire family—even more difficult to accept as time went on because this time in Saskatchewan was the only period that they were together as a family in a home of their own. But it was not until much later, after Wallace had done the research for his biography of John Wesley Powell, that he really understood the basis for that failure and its meaning.

As a child on the prairie, he was more than just painfully aware of the bareness of his surroundings and the weather. He became aware, too, of **34** the animals around him, as he would put it in the title of a novel in his later years, *All the Little Live Things*.[6] He looked upon them with an attitude much like that of the Native American. "The earth was full of animals," he has said about his childhood, "—field mice, ground squirrels, weasels, ferrets, badgers, coyotes, burrowing owls, snakes. I knew them as my little brothers, as fellow creatures, and I have never been able to look upon animals in any other way since."[7] With time on his hands, no playmates, and parents deeply engaged in the backbreaking work of carving out a farm in the wilderness, he became far more observant of his surroundings than most children of that age. His senses, which made continuous connection with his surroundings, formed his "internet," his window to the natural world and its drama, as opposed to the virtual worlds that so entrance our contemporary children.

An important influence leading Wallace to such an early appreciation of nature was a mother who taught him the beauty both of books and of his surroundings, so that the two, literature and the environment, were joined together for him in a positive way in his mother's example early in life. In addition to the positive influences of his mother was the negative influence of a father who came to stand in Wallace's mind for all the careless, selfish exploiters of nature in the West. Just as bulbs and fruit trees need both the cold of winter and the returning warmth of spring to blossom, so did Wallace need both the hatred for an opportunistic and abusive father and the love for a beauty-seeking and generous mother for his environmental conscience to develop.

An early autobiographical story based on Stegner's childhood on the homestead brings together all three of these elements—the land, mother, and father. "Bugle Song" is a quiet story, one that creates an atmosphere of solitude through its very quietness.[8] What drama there is is carried almost subliminally in a subtext of conflict in gender roles involving the boy, but a conflict he is too young to recognize. With only his mother nearby—his father is presumably out working on the homestead—the boy is left to his own devices on the hot and monotonous prairie. We see him first as hard and insensitive to the suffering of animals. He seems to perform his grisly task of trapping gophers and killing them (and on occasion feeding them to his pet weasel) with grim satisfaction as part of the masculine frontier role.

**35**

Although absent during the course of the story, it is obviously the father, or his spirit, that dominates this family, and he is the model that the boy feels he should emulate. The mother protests the boy's cruelty and he ignores her, yet he does follow her wishes in preparing for school in the fall by reading his poetry book, and in this and the romantic daydreams generated by the poems he reflects her softer, more civilized approach to life. Thus, a second conflict in the story, connected to the first but different in kind, is developed between the active, instinctive, and physical on the one hand, and the life of the mind—the imagination and the stimulation of the imagination by literature and by nature—on the other.

Both conflicts would persist in Stegner's consciousness throughout his life, and similar contrasts as we see them in "Bugle Song" between male and female roles, between insensitive and sensitive, caring and uncaring are carried as themes throughout his fiction. We can recognize in these contrasts the conflict at the heart of the Western archetype, and the adult Stegner, who plumps down squarely on the side of the mother, becomes a writer who spends much of his career refuting the mythic West and our rationale for exploitation in the doctrine of Rugged Individualism. This in turn would lead him to such environmental activities as refuting the arguments of the Sagebrush Rebellion—Western landowners and developers, and the politicians they controlled, who wanted the federal government to "return" federal land to the states. That land, Stegner pointed out repeatedly in several essays, was never owned by the states.[9]

In his childhood, often alone on the prairie or isolated in his house in town during the harsh winters, Wallace Stegner became an omnivorous reader, and as a small and weak boy, he found his only successes came by achievement in school. Out of such a background, one could predict that he might become a writer, but he never thought of it as even a possibility. Nevertheless, following a long, circuitous route, as described in his essay, "Literary by Accident," he eventually became by his late twenties both writer and teacher of writing.[10] His first major success came with *The Big Rock Candy Mountain* (1943), the story of his own growing up and the conflict between the values of his father and mother.[11] In depicting his father as exploiter and mother as conserver, the novel is an early reflection of the author's evolving environmental conscience.

But the work that really established him as a writer of environmental literature was his biography of John Wesley Powell.[12] It brought Powell to the public mind as an early hero in the conservation struggle and brought to the fore the history of the mistakes and controversies of Western land and water policy. In reminding us of Powell's assertion, which so infuriated his politician-booster contemporaries, that most of the West beyond the one-hundredth meridian was either desert or near desert and that settlement and development must take this into account, Stegner's book can take its place alongside such seminal conservation works as Rachel Carson's *Silent Spring*. In the West water meant survival, not only for people but for the land itself and all its creatures.

Although embracing Powell's values, Stegner did not write the book out of a passion for environmentalism, but as a tribute to a man he admired. Powell came to his attention because his doctoral adviser at the University of Iowa suggested he write his dissertation on a colleague of Powell's, Clarence Edward Dutton, a nineteenth-century scientist, civil engineer, and literary naturalist. Just by chance the Stegner family had a cabin on the Fishlake Plateau, right in the middle of the high plateaus that were Dutton's territory. Wallace realized that "all of a sudden history crossed my trail. I found that when I went up Seven Mile I found I knew

36

what had happened there sixty, seventy years before."[13] The literary and the natural environments once again came together in his life.

Although the groundwork had been laid from childhood to maturity, Wallace Stegner as environmental activist did not emerge until midlife in the early 1950s, after he had written many short stories and novels and had nearly finished the research for the Powell biography. Just researching and writing the Powell book taught him a great deal, not only giving him detailed knowledge of the fight for conservation in the West but also providing a different mind-set, a realization of how important and ongoing the battle had been and still was. In addition to his work on Powell, as an inveterate traveler and camper throughout the West, Wallace remained connected to the land, aware of its natural and historical values, but it took a moment, a moment of transformation, that would take him from sympathizer to activist.

**37**

To trace the history of that moment, we need to look briefly at Stegner's teaching career, which began at a small Lutheran college in Illinois while he was a doctoral student, to the University of Utah after his degree, and then to the University of Wisconsin. He found he had no chance, during the depths of the Depression, to get promoted and gain tenure at either of those universities, so from Wisconsin he went on to Harvard University as a Briggs-Copeland Fellow. There he met famous literary figures, two of whom were particularly important to him—Robert Frost and Bernard DeVoto. They became mentors to him—Frost in literature and DeVoto in conservation and both in regard to humankind's relations with nature.

Readers have noticed how often Stegner in his fiction quotes Frost, and it could be said that Frost provided a background of metaphor which Stegner adopted and brought into his own talent for figurative language to deal with nature in literary terms. Both Frost and Stegner were basically realists: in the poetry of the one and the fiction of the other, life can be hard and nature, while it can be beautiful, can also be unforgiving. While nature and a consciousness of nature dominate the work of both men, neither writer ever treats it sentimentally.

But it was DeVoto who would provide the moment of transition for

Stegner. They became close friends in Cambridge and had a lot in common, since both had come out of the West to the East and both were non-Mormons from Utah.[14] Both were involved in writing both fiction and history. During the 1940s and 1950s, DeVoto's was one of the few voices in the mainstream media as an advocate of the preservation of public lands and supporter of the National Park Service (he had a bully pulpit in his "The Easy Chair" column for *Harper's*). The two men played tennis and badminton together, and Stegner and his wife, Mary, were regulars at DeVoto's Sunday evening martini get-togethers of Harvard luminaries. DeVoto was vociferous and argumentative in support of his convictions, and over the years that Stegner was at Harvard (1939–45) he got an earful of DeVoto's passion for conservation.

Stegner left Harvard after World War II to go to Stanford to found its creative writing program. In 1952 he took a trip around the Colorado Plateau and Grand Canyon areas of the West to do research for the Powell biography and came back fuming over the complaining he had heard throughout the region about the Bureau of Land Management and the Park Service. Many of the complaints were unjustified and founded on false information, such as the supposition, once again, that the federal government had taken public lands away from the states. He and DeVoto had been corresponding regularly about his research for the Powell book, and in a phone conversation on his return from his trip, he revealed his anger about the attacks on federal land management, which in his view were motivated by greed. If public lands were handed over to the states, then the lumber, mining, and cattle industries would have a much easier time influencing local officials to adopt the lands for their own uses and an easier time ignoring the larger public interest.

DeVoto listened impatiently and then told him, "For God's sake, man, don't tell me. I know all about it. You need to sit down and write about it, get the article published, and spread the word."[15] And Stegner did. That was the moment an activist was born. That first article was "One Fourth of a Nation: Public Lands and Itching Fingers," and he had a very difficult time finding a magazine that would publish it. Finally, his agents got it placed with *Reporter* magazine for the May 1953 issue.[16]

Wallace Stegner went on to write some sixty articles entirely or par-

tially devoted to conservation, preservation, and environmental problems
and with various subjects and venues. Following his initial *Reporter* article in 1953, he published a piece in the *New Republic* in 1954 called "Battle for the Wilderness" and another in 1955 for *Sports Illustrated* called
"We Are Destroying Our National Parks."[17] Probably his most common
topic was the aridity of most of the West, which was misunderstood or
simply denied, and the multitude of problems that resulted. But he also
wrote several articles about the need to preserve our chronically under-
funded national parks, the need to set aside wilderness areas as defined by
law, and the need to keep public lands in the hands of the federal government. Other subjects included overpopulation, pollution, rugged individualism, the history of the environmental movement, the history of
public lands, and land law. He also wrote essays about various key figures
of the movement, including Ansel Adams, Aldo Leopold, Henry David
Thoreau, and Bernard DeVoto.

**39**

He published these works in diverse magazines, ranging from *Satur-
day Review, Holiday, American Heritage, Esquire, Westways,* and *Atlantic,*
to *Smithsonian, Living Wilderness, Wilderness,* and *Sierra Club Bulletin.*
These last few he tended to avoid as preaching to the already converted,
although one of his best essays, a history of the environmental movement
in America called "It All Began with Conservation," appeared in *Smithsonian.*[18] Mainstream publications tended to avoid such articles, which
they may have considered too specialized in interest, too editorializing,
or too doctrinaire. Stegner, however, had the advantage of being a well-
known author of fiction and nonfiction whose work, regardless of subject, required editorial attention, if not always acceptance, and his agents
worked hard to place his environmental essays in magazines where they
would likely do the most good. Furthermore, one of Stegner's favorite
genres was the travel article (which he used to finance his and his wife's
travel), and in many of these articles he was able to slip in bits of advocacy or information that implied conservation. For example, he did an
article on Lake Powell for *Holiday,* which, although doing justice to the
beauties and advantages of the lake, clearly mourns the loss of Glen
Canyon because of the Glen Canyon Dam at Page, Arizona.[19]

Probably Stegner's best-known and most often reprinted piece of environmental writing is his "Wilderness Letter" (1961). He was asked by David Pesonen to help strengthen his argument for the preservation of wilderness areas in a report he was preparing for the Outdoor Recreation Resources Review Commission. Stegner's son Page has said that his father in reply wrote what is now known by every environmentally conscious soul on the planet as the "Wilderness Letter," an argument for the restorative value of wilderness that like Aldo Leopold's "The Land Ethic" and Henry David Thoreau's "Walking" has become one of the central documents of the conservation movement.[20] The letter is beautifully written, yet it was never intended to be published. Stegner brought every tool of his trade as artist to his task, and nearly every sentence of its six printed pages is memorable. The arguments against preserving land as wilderness depended on the idea that in such areas resources would be "locked up" (a potent argument against wilderness during World War II) and that such areas should be opened up for multiple uses, that is, not only for development—roads, houses, mining, lumbering, grazing—but for public recreation—boating, skiing, bus touring, resorts, golfing. Designated wilderness areas would be off-limits to nearly everyone except backpackers. What Stegner starts out by saying is that although this is a recreation report, he is not going to address possible wilderness uses, but the value of the wilderness *idea.*

"Something," he writes, "will have gone out of us as a people if we ever let the remaining wilderness be destroyed; if we permit the last virgin forests to be turned into comic books and plastic cigarette cases." If we drive the few remaining wild species into extinction, pollute the last clean air, dirty the last clean rivers, and push our paved roads through the "last of the silence," then "never again will Americans be free in their own country from the noise, the exhausts, the stinks of human and automotive waste." Having wilderness there, simply there, is good for our spiritual health. "We . . . need that wild country available to us, even if we never do more than drive to its edge and look in. For it can be a means of reassuring ourselves of our sanity as creatures, a part of the geography of hope."[21]

The letter came into the hands of Stewart Udall, who at the time, 1962, was the Secretary of the Interior. He was so impressed by it that he

40

set aside his speech for a wilderness conference and instead simply read aloud Stegner's letter. The letter came to be published several times and ended up as a sort of anthem of preservation which spread around the world. In 1961, a year before the letter was composed, Udall had appointed a reluctant Stegner as an assistant to the Secretary and gave him as his first job to survey and report on a number of areas that were being considered for designation as National Parks. Stegner served for four months, and his last few weeks were spent in the Library of Congress doing research and preparing an outline for a book by Udall. Stegner had suggested the project and various possibilities for development, and he wrote a sample chapter for what became *The Quiet Crisis*.[22] Even in his role as assistant to the Secretary of the Interior, he was able to bring his art to bear on his concern for preservation.

In addition to his many articles, Stegner celebrated his friend Bernard  **41** DeVoto's contributions to the struggle by writing his biography, *The Uneasy Chair* (1974) and editing his letters.[23] He edited *This Is Dinosaur: Echo Park and Its Magic Rivers* (1955), which was largely responsible for preventing the construction of the Echo Park dam, and, with his son Page, wrote about our complex and generally destructive relationship with our continent in *American Places* (1981).[24] Then in 1987 he published a collection of lectures at the University of Michigan called *The American West as Living Space*, which were largely concerned with the problems of conservation.[25]

But beyond even these things, in a final triumph of his art as an expression of his beliefs, he was able to bring together the two strands of his life, his devotion to the writing of fiction and his devotion to the preservation of the environment. He once told Ansel Adams, the famed landscape photographer with whom he served on the Sierra Club board of directors and whom he greatly admired, "I do wish I was able to bring my art [referring here to his novels and short stories] and my advocacy for conservation together as successfully as you have."[26] But he did— more subtly, perhaps, but it is still there. We find this combination in many of the stories and in nearly every novel he was to write, most explicitly in *A Shooting Star* in mid-career in 1961, to his last novel, *Crossing to Safety*, in 1987. And what was extremely important to him was that he did so without perverting his fiction by making it a vehicle for overtly preaching a message.

However, even long before that turning point when he became an activist, his fiction often revealed the values and attitudes which became the foundation for his environmental activities. Looking back on his very first novel, *On a Darkling Plain* (1940), we can see that he exposes the myth of Rugged Individualism as the basis for having settled the West and endorses the importance of social cooperation. In *The Big Rock Candy Mountain* (1943) he tackles the American Dream, finding it far more damaging than does Dreiser in *An American Tragedy* or Fitzgerald in *The Great Gatsby*. Almost alone among major writers of our time, he realized that the dream has not only twisted our lives and corroded our values, it has despoiled the very land that has given us such hope. And that hope, as represented by the frontier, is what gave the West such a symbolic role in representing the dream and has made the perpetuation of the mythic West possible.

42

Eight years after publishing his first activist article in 1953, Stegner published his fifth novel, *A Shooting Star*. In it, the heroine's brother, for no other apparent reason than greed (he seems to have plenty of money), wants to take the family land and convert it to an upscale housing development, whereas the heroine, Sabrina, wants to donate it for a park. And the developer as a villain appears once again in *All the Little Live Things* (1967), but this time as a buffoon who has no idea what his bulldozers are doing to the green foothills. The novel, perhaps the most environmentally conscious of all his fictions, concerns the value of life, of all life, if left naturally to flourish without our attempts to dominate it with our chemicals and machines.

His Pulitzer-Prize-winning novel, *Angle of Repose* (1971), takes him back to Dutton, Powell, and another colleague of Powell's, Clarence King, and the days of the Geological Survey in the 1870s. The fictional Oliver Ward, patterned after another real participant in the Survey, is a civil engineer whose grand project is to build an irrigation canal in Idaho to bring water to the high desert. Partly because of the difficulty and expense of creating the canal and partly because of his integrity, which will not allow him to mislead his investors, Ward fails. In all of this, Stegner is telling the archetypal story of easterners who have come to the West to make their fortune, but with that story there is also a subtext about the lack of water in the West, a dramatization of the doctrine right out of John Wesley Powell's *Report on the Lands of the Arid Regions* (1879).

Stegner thought of himself as essentially a novelist, and although he wrote in many different genres—history, biography, travel articles, literary criticism, and short stories—writing novels was, he felt, his vocation. And he was an ambitious man—it was through his novels that he felt that he would make a reputation. But after the initial article prompted by DeVoto and his subsequent service on the National Parks Advisory Board and the boards of the Sierra Club and Wilderness Society, he felt a deep obligation to write in service of his environmental convictions as often as he could make time for. It was David Brower, the Director of the Sierra Club, who talked him into editing *This Is Dinosaur*. It was so successful in marshaling public opinion and convincing Congress to abandon the Echo Park dam that Brower was continually after Stegner to write more. "He had," Brower would say admiringly, "a way with words."[27] But Stegner was first and foremost a novelist, and Brower hit a nerve when he called one time to talk him into another project, telling him that he was only wasting his time on mere "stories" when the fate of the world hung in the balance. Stegner's anger was partly in response to Brower's apparent contempt for the art of creative writing, but it also, no doubt, was prompted in part by guilt.

Wallace Stegner was a man with an active conscience. While he would make a number of significant contributions to the cause throughout the latter part of his career, including the famous "Wilderness Letter," he was torn on the one side by the feeling that he could do more and on the other by his devotion to the art of fiction. He reflected that internal conflict in a letter to Tom Watkins of the Wilderness Society, who was preparing an article about Stegner's environmental contributions:

> I have not been an effective or even eager activist.
> In all the issues that matter, there are dozens of people—
> David Brower, Ed Wayburn, Howard Zahniser, the hard
> nosed tough, and durable types . . .—who have had an

immediate, practical, effective usefulness. I never have. . . .
Actually I would like, and would always have liked, nothing
better than to stay home and write novels and histories. . . . I
am a paper tiger, Watkins, typewritten on both sides. Get that
in somewhere.[28]

Typewritten, yes, but a voice, nevertheless, that will persist in our culture, not only in several dozen essays, but in a dozen novels, most of which are still in print. Near the end of his novel *All the Little Live Things,* bringing to bear his literary skill to define our place in nature in one of his most poignant passages, he has the dying Marian tell the grief-stricken Joe Allston:

**44**    Don't feel bad. I'm glad you love me, but I hope you and Ruth
won't grieve. It's right there should be death in the world, it's
as natural as being born. We're all part of a big life pool, and
we owe the world the space we fill and the chemicals we're
made of. Once we admit it's not an abstraction, but something
we do personally owe, it shouldn't be hard.[29]

Wallace Stegner was not just a Pulitzer Prize and National Book Award–winning novelist, he was an artist with a conscience, an artist with important ideas for our time about humankind and its relations to the land around it. That he had such a variety of weapons in his arsenal—as accomplished writer of fiction and nonfiction, as historian, as active outdoorsman, as amateur naturalist and geologist, and as teacher—made him almost unique in the pantheon of environmental heroes. Just stop for a moment to think how his role as teacher of writing during his twenty-five years at Stanford connected with his environmentalism; look at the many students of his who have been connected with the land and with a strong sense of place: Larry McMurtry in Texas, Wendell Berry in Kentucky, Edward Abbey in New Mexico and the Southwest, Ken Kesey in Oregon, James Houston in California, and Ernest Gaines in Louisiana.

Other writers have made their reputations by shocking us, by rebelling, by suicidal excesses, by scoffing at every positive element in American life. Stegner never took the cheap path to fame. Certainly, he, himself, was not above harsh criticism of certain behaviors or attitudes in his society. But he was an artist wherein the man and his work were of one piece constructed on the bedrock of integrity. The secret of Wallace Stegner is that he never felt sorry for himself, never indulged himself at the expense of others, but cared deeply for those around him, for his country, its land and its people.

# Notes

1. Wallace Stegner, "The Making of Paths," in *Marking the Sparrow's Fall: Wallace Stegner's American West,* ed. Page Stegner (New York: Henry Holt, 1998), 14. The first year that the family went out from town to the homestead, Wallace's brother Cecil was with them, but thereafter, he had a job during the summers with the grocery store in town.

2. Wallace Stegner, *Wolf Willow* (New York: Viking Press, 1955), 278.

3. Ibid., 29.

4. Wallace Stegner, "Child of the Far Frontier," in *Marking,* 5.

5. Stegner has written about this in many places, among them "Thoughts in a Dry Land" and "Living Dry," both collected in *Where the Bluebird Sings to the Lemonade Springs: Living and Writing in the West* (New York: Random House, 1992).

6. Wallace Stegner, *All the Little Live Things* (New York: Viking Press, 1967).

7. "Wilderness Letter." This piece has been reprinted many times, most recently in *Marking the Sparrow's Fall,* 116.

8. (Also called "Buglesong"), *The Collected Stories of Wallace Stegner* (New York: Random House, 1990), 13–20.

9. See, for example, "The War Between the Rough Riders and the Bird Watchers," *Sierra Club Bulletin,* May 1959, 4–11; "Variations on a Theme by Crevecoeur," in *Where the Bluebird Sings,* 99–116 (on Rugged Individualism); and "If the Sagebrush Rebels Win, Everybody Loses," *The Living Wilderness,* Summer 1981, 30–35.

10. *Utah Libraries* 18 (Fall 1975): 7–21.

11. Wallace Stegner, *The Big Rock Candy Mountain* (New York: Duell, Sloan and Pearce, 1943).

12. Wallace Stegner, *Beyond the Hundredth Meridian: John Wesley Powell and the Second Opening of the West* (Boston: Houghton Mifflin, 1954).

13. "Literary by Accident," *Utah Libraries* 18 (Fall 1975): 12.

14. Stegner moved to Salt Lake City when he was twelve, in 1921, and lived there until he graduated from the University of Utah in 1930.

15. Interview with Wallace Stegner by the author, May 7, 1987.

16. Wallace Stegner, "One Fourth of a Nation: Public Land and Itching Fingers," *Reporter*, May 1953, 25–29.

17. "Battle for the Wilderness," *New Republic* 130 (February 15, 1954): 13–15; "We Are Destroying Our National Parks," *Sports Illustrated* 3 (June 13, 1955): 28–29, 44–46.

18. Collected in *Where the Bluebird Sings*, 117–32.

19. Wallace Stegner, "Lake Powell," *Holiday* 39 (May 1966): 64–68, 148–51.

20. Stegner, *Marking the Sparrow's Fall*, 110.

21. "Wilderness Letter," in *Marking the Sparrow's Fall*, 112, 117.

22. Interview with Stewart Udall by author, May 22, 1989.

23. Wallace Stegner, *The Uneasy Chair: A Biography of Bernard DeVoto* (Garden City, N.Y.: Doubleday, 1974); *Letters of Bernard DeVoto*, ed. Wallace Stegner (Garden City, N.Y.: Doubleday, 1975).

24. Wallace Stegner and Page Stegner, *American Places* (New York: E. P. Dutton, 1981).

25. Wallace Stegner, *The American West as Living Space* (Ann Arbor: University of Michigan Press, 1987), containing "Living Dry," "Striking the Rock," and "Variations on a Theme by Crevecoeur," which were later also published in *Where the Bluebird Sings*.

26. A conversation between Wallace Stegner and Ansel Adams, on video, n.d., Stanford University Library Special Collections.

27. Interview of David Brower by the author, June 19, 1989.

28. T. H. Watkins, "Typewritten on Both Sides: The Conservation Career of Wallace Stegner," *Audubon*, September 1987, 88–90+.

29. Stegner, *All the Little Live Things*, 287.

# "The VaNe Sisters" and Nabokov's "subtle and loving" Readers

**C**onsidering that Vladimir Nabokov's 1951 story "The Vane Sisters" was not published until 1959, making it the last of his short fictions to see print,[1] and that the story was his favorite, the relative paucity of critical attention to it seems as enigmatic as Nabokov's own choices in narratives and friends. The current dismissal of the seven-part text may have stemmed from readers' responses to the author's revelation that the last paragraph of the story is an acrostic, the epitome of a punning, language-obsessed writer's tricks. Once we can "read" the last paragraph acrostically, we might assume that we "know" the story. Yet what is the full import of the message, "icicles by cynthia; meter from me sybil"? We may "know" that the acrostic ties the last segment of the narrative back to its opening, which is a rich description of icy and sinister beauty, marred with the reddish shadow of a parking meter shaft. In "knowing" that, however, what do we understand?

Readers then and now have failed to see that "The Vane Sisters" is about much more than a narrator's strangely distanced recognition of the death of Cynthia Vane. As Nabokov wrote sadly to Katharine White, after she rejected the story for the *New Yorker* in 1951, "I am really very disappointed that you, such

47

a subtle and loving reader, should not have seen the inner scheme of my story."[2]

In Nabokov's comment lies part of the problem of interpretation. By focusing on craft, marking "The Vane Sisters" as still another tour de force of technique, the author failed to note one of the real accomplishments of his 1951 narrative. Nabokov himself repeatedly trained his critics to look for technical brilliance. Yet as Brian Boyd comments, although Nabokov was often thrilled by "writers breaking free of conventions and finding new ways of seeing and telling," he also consistently "valued new subjects, the agonies of childbirth in *Anna Karenin* or the miseries of childhood in *Bleak House*."[3] What Nabokov accomplished, in part, in "The Vane Sisters" was a deft indictment of the supercilious and often merciless treatment that members of the American intellectual elite—male college professors—were capable of meting out to their lovers—women who were, in some cases, their undergraduate students. Today we would call it sexual harassment.

**48**

On campuses throughout the United States, women graduate students hold informal meetings to discuss what they politely term the "chilly" climate in academe.

On many campuses, women graduate students hold even less formal meetings to discuss which professors are "safe" to take classes with. Tales of the Americanist who French kisses new women students at the fall potluck alternate with stories of the medievalist who gropes for students' thighs as he sings bawdy ballads, accompanying himself on the lute.

On one campus, the administration finally unearths some misuse of funds to justify firing a tenured male professor who had not only had sex with undergraduate female students (in his office) but also put at least one of those women in touch with men who would pay her for intercourse.

On another highly regarded campus, an aging full professor is forced to retire and is denied the customary "emeritus" standing because of his frightening, persistent pursuit of a woman doctoral student less than half his age.

On another campus, a woman graduate student arranges for her brother, a Marine, to meet her after her seminar, pretending he is her lover, in order to still her married professor's requests that she go with him for coffee or dinner. After weeks of saying NO, and more weeks of being escorted home by her brother, the woman student complains to the professor's wife. Her grade in seminar is two levels lower than her customary mark.

On still another prestigious campus, the suicide of a beautiful ethnic minority woman, rumored to having been involved with a middle-aged professor in her major field, goes uninvestigated; on another, a beautiful undergraduate student marries the abusive yet loving older professor, once his divorce is final, only to find that his abuse grows worse as time passes.    **49**

Nabokov's icicles, in both the opening scene and the concluding acrostic of his penetrating story, suggest what readers today have come to admit about powerful, sometimes unscrupulous, university teachers. Resonant of the lower regions of Dante's inferno, the ice of the landscape, and the narrator's pointless fascination with the icicles and their reluctant drops, takes the reader immediately into an abstract realm: Nabokov's technique of placing the tragic stories of Sybil and Cynthia Vane within a matrix of intellectualized pursuits divorces their lives—and deaths—from reality. As was characteristic of response to Nabokov's writing, like other of his stories and novels, "The Vane Sisters" was seldom critiqued thematically. In 1951, or in 1959 when the story appeared, few readers would have noticed its feminist political emphasis—largely because such emphasis, like the term *sexual harassment*, did not yet exist.

There remains, however, Nabokov's very disappointed letter to Katharine White, with its closing sentence in which he laments that her usual loving and subtle reading ability had failed her. It seemed logical to Nabokov that a woman would have been his best reader for this particular story. When he wrote "The Vane Sisters" in February and March of 1951, he had only recently begun teaching the course in European fiction at Cornell University that was to be a large, popular class for the next decade. He had not been teaching in the United States institution for very long (and was still lamenting the scant note-taking of his undergraduate students). His wife, Vera, wrote to Katharine White at the beginning of that spring semester, "He has never had so little time for writing. In this respect it is probably the worst year of his life and though he derives much pleasure from his big course and from the students' reaction, the necessity to neglect his writing often makes him feel miserable."[4] One surmises that other things about the system added to that misery and led the writer and his beloved Vera to keep themselves somewhat distant from much of the university community. It seems reasonable that an American version of academe, with all its possibly ugly sexual machinations, disappointed both of them.

The subject matter would have kept many readers of "The Vane Sisters" from ready identification with the issue of sexual harassment. Given a "difficult" seven-part story, named to recall several previous European and Russian stories about a family of women, the oblique opening that describes a self-satisfied professor spending his energy watching for drops of melted water to fall from icicles is hardly riveting. His calling his observations "trivial" does not excuse his pastime, nor does his reference to the icicles as "a family." That he can spend time observing "a family of brilliant icicles" immediately after a title that includes the word *sister* deserves our attention but may not attract it. Lush descriptions of sphericals, drops, and circles suggest—with the wordplay characteristic of Nabokovian intrigue—that this may be a fiction about nothingness rather than about women in families, and the suggestion seems hammered home with the closing sentence to the long paragraph, when the nameless narrator thinks himself in such harmony with nature (and pleased with his major accomplishment of this section, finding the water droplet he has been looking for) that he describes himself as being "in a state of raw awareness," "one big eyeball rolling in the world's socket" (619).

Run that by me again, Nabokov. This is a story written in English, so we cannot blame some inept translation from the Russian for the cloudiness of the image. What *is* the import of being one big eyeball, quickly loosened from any transcendental association by being placed "in the world's socket," a physical impossibility. (One is forced to digress and ask, If the world is itself a socket, then what is *its* location? This is hardly Nabokovian metaphysics at its easiest.) The gerund *rolling* is another troublesome word. For the narrator, a man supposedly in control of his actions and his emotions (judging as we must from the description early in the text), the only choice Nabokov gives us—to be a rolling eyeball— prompts queasiness from the reader, or if not queasiness, an impermanence at least of that all-important vision, all-important to the perspective of the narrator of any work.

As good readers, we are trained to seek permanence, clearheadedness, stability, as writers from Charles Dickens through Henry James have instructed us. But the crux of Nabokov's "The Vane Sisters" is that the narrating consciousness, the professor of French who has been the teacher of the suicide Sybil Vane, Cynthia's younger sister, is untrustworthy. He is, in fact, something of a fool.

Many critics, including Brian Boyd, agree on this characterization. Gennady Barabtarlo shows that much about the story aims to "explode" the "trustworthiness" of the narrator,[5] and he and Charles Nicol emphasize Nabokov's tactic of undermining the character of the first-person narrator "by accumulation of subtle detail."[6] Douglas Fowler alerts readers that they must observe "the graying, mirroring, adjacent planes of objective and subjective 'realities,'"[7] polarities which Cynthia's life view and the narrator's represent. Foundational is Nabokov's own statement in his 1951 letter to White, stating that the professor of French who narrates the story is "priggish," "a sometimes obtuse scholar and a rather callous observer of the superficial planes of life."[8] The reader has already seen the "scholar" in action as he hunts for a dripping icicle, his current project. Language heavy with irony derides that interest: "I walked up, and I walked down, and I walked straight into a delicately dying sky, and finally the sequence of observed and observant things brought me, at my usual eating time, to a street so distant from my usual eating place that I decided to try a restaurant which stood on the fringe of the town" (620).

The nursery rhyme cadence of his "quest" underscores the scholar's obviously trivial pursuit, just as the pompous language tries to invest his simple need to eat and his resulting choice of restaurant with searing importance.

Proof of his "rather callous" response to life is even more vividly portrayed through his inability to see the tragedy in Sybil's suicide. Not only does he early dismiss Cynthia's concern about her younger sister's involvement with D., the happily married professor, but he trivializes Sybil's actual death by pointing out her inaccurate French in the touching suicide note she appends to her examination paper. His lack of interest in Sybil is subsumed in his tentative fascination with D., even as he describes his young colleague as a monster: D. feels no remorse at passing through the site of Sybil's death. Forgiving him that death, the narrator rather describes him as "still young, still brash, still shifty, still married to the gentle, exquisitely pretty woman who had never learned or suspected anything about his disastrous affair with Cynthia's hysterical young sister" (620–21). In his choice of those two words–*disastrous* and *hysterical*—Nabokov provides insight into his narrator's mind, explaining in effect the way he has found to excuse the manipulative lover, D.

Nabokov's epistemological slanting leads the reader to assume things that the author himself does not. The first assumption is that affairs with students are legitimate, even innocent, if they succeed. When they are "disastrous," however, as this one was, evidently the student is to blame, particularly if the student, a young female, is "hysterical." Circular in its reasoning or lack of same, the narrator's implied argument is that Sybil was the prototypical "hysterical" woman because she killed herself over the end of the love relationship. To care about another person is, here, to be abnormal. To be marked as woman, with the womb that gives the adjective *hysterical* its only true meaning, is to be inherently fragile, emotional, caring enough to die for passion. And to be on the other side of the gender line, to have no womb and therefore be capable of reason rather than emotion or passion, seemingly gives the male observer the right to use such reductionary shorthand to describe what happened in the relationship between Sybil and D.

The brilliance in Nabokov's rendering of D., and of his double-like

52

professorial colleague, the unnamed French professor, is that each man understands that affairs—especially affairs with undergraduate students —are based on power rather than on love. These men live in the real and all-too-gendered world. They need have neither contrition nor grief over the death of a young, relatively inept student (inept because she cannot even do well on a French exam), no matter what the causative factors in her choice of suicide. What is important is that D. has kept any knowledge of Sybil's death, or his relationship with her, from his "gentle, exquisitely pretty" wife. What is equally important is keeping in place the facade of appropriate behavior (or acknowledging that appropriate behavior is a casual love relationship that naturally ends, with both parties going separate ways and continuing the lives they had previously led). Passion is irrelevant to this scheme of things; it simply doesn't count.

The irony at the heart of the narrator's shorthand description of "what happened" is that he has no idea what happened. What he knows is that Cynthia "suddenly summoned" him to Boston to "make me swear" to talk with D. (and get him "kicked out") about his affair with her sister because she was so concerned about Sybil that she knew her life was in danger (621). Again, Nabokov's language as filtered through the narrator's consciousness belies his own casual response. Clearly, Cynthia is terribly worried about her sister, and her urgency, like her set of moral imperatives, shows that she understands the acts D. is capable of. When the narrator is assured that D. is leaving town to work outside academe, his assumption is "out of sight, out of mind." Surely a trivial love affair will end with distance, and Sybil is, in effect, saved by D.'s planned move.

All the false assumptions that ground the conversations between the narrator and Cynthia and between the narrator and D. are reinscribed with the closing sentence Nabokov chooses to end the paragraph that repeats them. The narrator is relieved, bluntly, that "the whole matter, which had threatened to become one of those hopelessly entangled situations that drag on for years, with peripheral sets of well-meaning friends endlessly discussing it in universal secrecy—and even founding, among themselves, new intimacies upon its alien woes—came to an abrupt end" (621).

Against this background of countless "hopelessly entangled situations"—male professor with female student, or older male with younger woman, or married man with unmarried woman, or married man with married woman—the chiaroscuro of other illicit relationships piles in whorls of secrecy, facades of innocence, and polite assumptions. The cool acceptance of these "situations" marks the narrator and D. as like participants in the steady, false world of human passions. And it is to that false academic world that Sybil, true to her name, conflating a course grade with her lover's name, speaks in her suicide note: "Death was not better than D minus, but definitely better than Life minus D" (622).

Like the narrator, unfortunately, the reader too accepts the devaluing of Sybil's passion. Here Nabokov shows the reason he has limited the narrative to one teller, the seriously flawed scholar-professor. Everything the reader knows about Sybil comes through his eyes—from her high heels and fur coat to her casually "dumped" suitcase (621). In fact, and with some curiosity, the professor watches her closely as she takes her exam, wondering whether D. has already "dumped" her.

At crux here is the temperamental difference between the Vane sisters—Sybil and Cynthia—and their professor-as-observer. Both passionate women become the classic objects of the male gaze, a gaze unable to "see" their inner selves and ultimately content with the facticity of what can be observed. Nabokov's narrative method underscores the terrible limitation of such a gendered gaze and provides the reason for the extensive descriptions of both women in the story.

Ironically, the physical description of the young and admittedly beautiful Sybil affects the reader as negative, again because the observer makes her into some tawdry female object. Even though she is "childishly slight in close-fitting grey," wearing a "small, small-flowered hat with a little hyaline veil" over her "carefully waved dark hair," Sybil seems unappealing. Her skin, for example, is scarred from a skin disease, and although she has tried to cover the marks with a tan, the narrrator notes that her attempt has only "pathetically masked" her flaws, and the tan has "hardened her features" (621). Worse, she has "painted everything that could be painted." That her eyelids are "darkened" and her lips "chapped"—details that, combined with her full makeup, might suggest the ravages of tears—go nearly unnoticed by the professorial observing eye.

**54**

What the narrator emphasizes in his account of Sybil's taking her French exam is his own bothersome work in grading the examination papers. To the students who inquire, he explains that it will take a week for him "to read the stuff" (621). And once started on "the ugly copybooks" and their "chaos of scripts," he comes to Sybil's paper only because he has misalphabetized the exam books, placing the Vane exam close to the front of the class. His negative descriptions of Sybil continue as he reads her paper, noting that she used "several demon hands" by changing from a hard pencil to a darker lead to ink, work that he continuously judges as he reads: "little of permanent value," "even poorer than I had expected," and (an apparently final negative) an impression on the page that bore "some traces of lipstick" (621–22). Like the meandering paragraphs of the narrator's quest for a melted drop of icicle which opened the story, the long description of Sybil's search for a readable **55** "lead" brings the metaphor of "the hour of lead" to the reader's mind. Even before she reaches the only legible part of her writing, when she borrows a pen to inscribe her suicide note, signaling that the only important thing she wants her professor to know is why she is going to her death, Nabokov's observer-narrator has written Sybil off. He has no respect for her situation, her person, or her knowledge, and his language and attitude clearly convey that disrespect to the reader.

To give him credit, once he does read the suicide note he recognizes it for what it is and calls Cynthia. "I lost no time in ringing up Cynthia" (622), he states in his usual self-praising diction. But the description of his taking Cynthia (at her request) the examination book is once more Nabokovian irony at its best. He seems unable even to *recognize* Cynthia's obviously distraught behavior. In this scene, of a disorienting and unwieldy grief, the narrator is at his most blind. He paints Cynthia as someone finding inappropriate humor in her sister's death message ("Just like her!" [622]) and implicitly criticizes her for making them highballs to drink. He describes ornately her clinging to the examination book as she studied the "death message," a notebook now "splashed with soda water and tears" and subsequently "limp" (622). The important point about Cynthia's clutching the notebook that includes the suicide note is that she cannot give up the one tangible marker of her sister's choice. She is reassured by the evidence of sanity in Sybil's behavior—her wry choice of "telling" the very man who had been entrusted with saving her, as if Sybil would not have known of Cynthia's role in her situation, particularly after D. has broken off with her, is characteristic. Even though the narrator points out the inaccuracies of Sybil's French, the reader understands, as does Cynthia, that even that lapse was intentional. Sybil has damned the professoriate with its own tools.

Despite the narrator's comment about "rather tasteless trivialities," Cynthia is visibly grieved—the narrator mentions her boundless tears, "the heaving surface of her grief"—but he seems not to understand her need to show him the chaste bed in which Sybil chose to die. The "chilly little bedroom" is remarkable for its lack of innocence (in the narrator's telling), even though he draws our attention to the purity of the "tender, inessential body" (622) that was taken from the bed, dead, early that morning. The choice of the word "inessential" adds to the enigma of what Sybil's death means, and it also foreshadows the furthering of the wry plot. With his strangely competitive eye, the narrator adds to the debacle of the scene not only of Sybil's death but of Cynthia's bereavement, the line that "D. must have known [Sybil's body] down to its last velvet detail" (622). Considering the unappealing physical description of Sybil the narrator chose to give earlier, Nabokov's choice of the modifier "velvet" is both gently tactile and conclusively ironic.

The opening paragraph of Part 3 continues to show how obtuse the narrator has been about the effect on Cynthia of Sybil's death. When he takes up with the older Vane sister (because she has moved to New York and he now goes there for research purposes), he comments that Cynthia "for some odd reason . . . had taken what people . . . term a 'cold water' flat" (623). The connection between Sybil's chilly bedroom and Cynthia's need to be stripped of physical comfort, just as the connection between her moving from one city to another to divest herself of her guilt at being unable to free her younger sister from her passion for D., goes unnoticed. Plain and simple, it matters little to the narrator why Cynthia has moved to New York. What is significant is that he now has someone to meet when he travels there, a partner in his own sexual liaison.

As he had in his description of Sybil, the narrator consistently undermines Cynthia's evident charms. He notes that he finds her less than attractive though "other men thought [her looks] striking" (623). Much like Sybil, Cynthia has the vivacious manner (or might one say "hysterical" manner?), the "frank, frightened blue" eyes, and the "zest" for using cosmetics. But in his strangely mixed sentences of description, the narrator betrays his unease at her sexuality—besides himself, he calculates that she has three lovers, all of whom he disapproves; she does not shave her legs; and she seldom bathes. One might, of course, find her sexuality—identified with tactile and sensory imagery—appealing.

The narrator's relationship with Cynthia is the crucial—and humanizing—one of the story. In the 1951 letter, Nabokov describes the plot of the story: the "hero" "unwittingly passes through the enchanting and touching 'aura' of Cynthia, whom he continues to see (when talking about her) in terms of skin, hair, manners."[9] But even when he is intimately involved with a woman, the stolid observer-narrator "knows" his beloved only through the observable traits that might make her valuable in the eyes of other men. He is able to give us little information about the essential qualities of Cynthia Vane. Nabokov, in the letter to White, does give the reader such information when he says that Cynthia has a "forgiving, gentle doe-soul" and that her part in besting the narrator in the convoluted denouement of the narrative was essentially a gift, what the author called "this gift of an iridescent day (giving him something akin to the picture he had liked, to the only small thing he had liked about her)."[10]

It is, in fact, the midpoint of the story before the narrator mentions what really fascinates him about Cynthia, which is her ability as an artist. A painter of "delightful, gay" scenes, she created what he calls "honest and poetical pictures" (624). His favorite of her works was a scene of sky and tree called "'Seen Through a Windshield'—a windshield partly covered with rime, with a brilliant trickle (from an imaginary car roof) across its transparent part." At this image, suggesting both the icy brilliance of the story's opening and the flawed perspective of the narrator as he places himself behind the iced-over pane of glass (the pane that sug-

**57**

gests the sisters' patronymic), Nabokov turns the story to its second narrative course, that of the assumed bifurcation between the worlds of the living and the dead.

Cynthia believes that Sybil is affecting her from the other world; she correspondingly sends D. mementos from her dead sister at irregular, and one supposes disconcerting, intervals. Cynthia "showed a ridiculous fondness for spiritualism" (626), according to our narrator; and Cynthia felt the power of the recently dead in her everyday life. Cynthia is superstitious about being superstitious, and so the narrator's disapproval of her behavior leads the reader to devalue her as the story moves toward its satisfying end. In the midst of what becomes pages-long vituperation of Cynthia Vane and her assortment of friends, the narrator admits that she has a great understanding of people, and he does present this gem of a metaphor to describe Cynthia's relationship with her younger sibling. He quotes her: "Sybil's personality, she said, had a rainbow edge as if a little out of focus" (625). The reader imagines the narrator overlooking the glory of "rainbow edge" to concentrate on the blurred "focus," but despite his disapproval, the reader accepts Cynthia as a purveyor of beauty, color, and insight.

Increasingly in those long paragraphs of harsh description of Cynthia, her beliefs, and her friends, Nabokov moves to the language and imagery of art, the stage, and literature. The narrator's tone of scientific rationalism gives way to a more personal, more creative use of language, which culminates in the acrostic message itself: *icicles by cynthia, meter from me Sybil* (631). As the language shows, it is Sybil who authors the message, Sybil (helpless and hysterical younger sister) who takes not only the plot but the language of the story into her own hands. The power the men assume to be theirs is as evanescent as anything in Cynthia's imaginary. The last unexpected meeting between the narrator and D. is carefully planned and arranged; only because the Vane sisters know the men so well can the plot be organized so precisely. Douglas Fowler is right, the "moral life of Nabokov's characters typically shows no moral development at all."[11] Had either D. or the narrator grown or changed, the Vane sisters would not have been able to predict so accurately their responses to the contrived situation.

Lest the reader be drawn into the narrator's mind-set once more, however, Nabokov gives the second half of his story a new plotline, one that charts the relationship between the narrator and Cynthia. A mirror image of the supposed affair between D. and Sybil, this relationship is described in the language of the narrator, from his churlish and uncharitable perspective. What is familiar is the degradation of the woman partner and the self-puffery of the man. With wicked irony, Nabokov shapes the dialogue between the narrator and Cynthia to lead to a climactic breakup. His ironic handling of the situation shows convincingly that the narrator has no understanding of what their relationship has been or what Cynthia is like as a person. After pages of splenetic description of his lover, her belief in spiritualism, and her eccentric friends, the narrator notes that he one day writes her an innocently querulous note, what he calls "a perfectly harmless and, on the whole, well-meant note, in which I poked a little Latin fun at some of her guests" (628). **59**

He then describes Cynthia's "hysteric" response. They meet accidentally at the library, and he writes with great bewilderment: "Suddenly, with no provocation on my part, she blazed out at me with vulgar vehemence, using poisonous words" (628–29). The facade of appropriate behavior, which needed to be in place in the public environs of the library, is shattered with indescribable abruptness. Conveniently forgetting his hurtful, intellectually amusing, and "perfectly harmless" letter, the narrator rests easy that Cynthia has become, like her sister, hysterical. After all, he gave her "no provocation." He is most assuredly as innocent as D., who gave Sybil the same lack of provocation to think he was in love with her. But more distressing than the suddenness of Cynthia's attack was its unladylike tone. As he emphasizes, Cynthia did not speak to him; rather, she "blazed out." And she did not couch her complaints in brilliant or intellectual language. Instead, she used "poisonous words" and—worse— "vulgar vehemence" (628–29). Anything but the commonplace, the vulgar, our sophisticated university professor says. Anything but passionate speech. Anything but passion.

In a later sentence, he repeats the gist of Cynthia's tirade. What was this vulgarity that she was forcing him to hear? Only that he, the complacent and amusing professor, who was careful and clever enough to insult her friends in Latin, was "a prig and a snob" (629). And that rather than seeing into the hearts of people, he saw only "the gestures and disguises" they wore.

Like the acrostic message, which takes power away from the visibly powerful and realigns relationships, Cynthia's speech sets the relationship to rights. Clearly, she has finished with the narrator. Their breakup is long overdue. But Nabokov's greatest irony comes now, at the end of the paragraph, when the narrator takes his ruffled feathers home and concludes that the relationship must end: as he tells his reader, "I decided to stop seeing her altogether" (629).

Nabokov ends the story with the narrator's account of his dream-filled night, months later, after he has learned from D. that Cynthia has died (of a bad heart, whether metaphoric or literal). Expecting that her aura will suffuse his dream, he is somewhat disappointed that she seems nowhere evident. But as he writes down what he remembers from the night, his language creates the acrostic that gives him the ultimate news: that his entire quest, his meeting with D., his learning of Cynthia's death, and his need to speculate on what the lives of the Vane sisters had meant—particularly to his own—was the contrivance of both the women which he, and D., had seen as objects of pity and scorn.

In 1966, Nabokov grouped "The Vane Sisters" with three other short stories in a collection he titled *Nabokov's Quartet*. Preceded by "An Affair of Honor" from the 1920s and "Lik" from the 1930s, "The Vane Sisters" appears third in the book, even though in chronological order, it should be last. A 1930s story, "The Visit to the Museum," closes the collection. In his foreword to the book, Nabokov commented on the unity of the stories as they attempt to counter the tendency of literature to romanticize.[12] In the case of "An Affair of Honor," the men intent on dueling with each other over the wife and lover they each desire realize the value of their own lives and run out on the encounter. Shame can be borne more easily than death. Their values differ from those of Sybil and Cynthia, and the privileging of the women's understanding of passion comes through more clearly in this arrangement of the four stories than when "The Vane Sisters" is read separately.

"Lik" and "The Visit to the Museum" both challenge known concepts of "reality." Even though Nabokov did not want the latter story compared with Franz Kafka's work, it of course plays with many of the same concepts: inexplicable physical change, appearance versus reality, the mutable consciousness. In many ways, "The Vane Sisters" continues those challenges to realism, but it vests even more energy in the role of the narrator. It is through the storyteller's eyes that any story exists. The reality of the fiction depends in large part on the way aspects of the story are envisioned, narrated, and resolved. Readers have difficulty with both Sybil's and Cynthia's appearance and character because of the narrow vision of the superior male narrator. More than the other three stories included here, "The Vane Sisters" demands some knowledge of gender roles, social expectations for men and women, and cultural pressure to conform to those social expectations. It becomes a story of the 1950s—if not of the 1990s—in its theme and content, even without our consciousness of its date of composition.

**61**

Nabokov was not known for his feminist views, nor am I suggesting that he has here adopted the posture of a feminist. My suggestion is, rather, as indicated in the strangely capitalized "VaNe" of this essay's title, that Vladimir Nabokov saw in his own marginalized position in an American university an analogue with the woman's position in a heterosexual love relationship. VN provides the genesis, orthographically, of the patronymic of the sisters' family. There is a great deal of Nabokov in the characterization of Cynthia Vane which he describes to Katharine White as "forgiving, gentle doe-soul."

My suggestion is, in short, that Nabokov might have realized his essential goodness, which might translate within academe as femininity, when his creative genius seemed to be besieged by the highly rational intellectualism of his university colleagues. In his search for a metaphoric equivalent for the conflict he felt in his identity—a university professor more in tune with the instinctive and the spiritual than with the scholarly—he came upon "The Vane Sisters," and in his account of the supposedly victimized women who cleverly and remorselessly and still innocently had the last word, he spoke his own last word to what sometimes seemed inimical forces. That the *New Yorker* would not publish this late tale, filled with personal vindication and written with as much careful verve and finesse as anything he had penned, both surprised and hurt the all-too-vulnerable author.

I make this suggestion in the same playful spirit with which Nabokov writes the foreword to *Nabokov's Quartet*. There he describes with clear joy the way the story works: "The narrator of 'The Vane Sisters' is supposed to be unaware that his last paragraph has been used acrostically by two dead girls to assert their mysterious participation in the story. This particular trick can be tried only once in a thousand years of fiction. Whether it has come off is another question."[13] By 1966 fully cognizant that, of course, the trick had come off and that he remained a supreme master of fiction—Russian, American, European—Nabokov modestly, slyly, placed his fictional tongue-in-cheek and demanded that readers pay attention to the skill they might see "only once in a thousand years of fiction." Mikhail Epstein calls Nabokov "a great master of the endgame,"[14] but it is important to remember that he was not only that but a man with a great mastery of knowledge about the inner worlds of human life.

**62**

# Notes

1. "The Vane Sisters," in *The Stories of Vladimir Nabokov* (New York: Vintage, 1995), 619–31. This is one of the few stories Nabokov wrote originally in English (see his list, p. xvii of same edition). Page numbers for citations are given in the text.

2. Vladimir Nabokov, *Selected Letters, 1940–1977*, ed. Dmitri Nabokov and Matthew J. Bruccoli (New York: Harcourt Brace Jovanovich/Bruccoli Clark Layman, 1989), 117.

3. Brian Boyd, *Vladimir Nabokov: The American Years* (Princeton: Princeton University Press, 1991), 197–98.

4. Quoted ibid., 192.

5. Gennady Barabtarlo, *Aerial View: Essays on Nabokov's Art and Metaphysics* (New York: Peter Lang, 1993), 95.

6. Charles Nicol and Gennady Barabtarlo, eds., *A Small Alpine Form: Studies in Nabokov's Short Fiction* (New York: Garland, 1993), xii.

7. Douglas Fowler, *Reading Nabokov* (Ithaca: Cornell University Press, 1974), 202.

8. Nabokov, *Selected Letters*, 117.

9. Ibid.

10. Ibid.

11. Fowler, *Reading Nabokov*, 56.

12. Vladimir Nabokov, Foreword to *Nabokov's Quartet* (New York: Phaedra, 1966), n.p.

13. Ibid.

14. Mikhail Epstein, "Goodbye to Objects, Or, The Nabokovian in Nabokov," in *A Small Alpine Form*, ed. Nichol and Barabtarlo, 217–24.

# Morality and Its Alternatives

## *The Damnation of Theron Ware*

The remarkable parallels between Harold Frederic and Kate Chopin have struck many readers, especially in connection with the authors' best-known novels: *The Damnation of Theron Ware* and *The Awakening*.[1] Published, respectively, in 1896 and 1899, the two novels were all but forgotten, along with the very names of their authors, until the latter part of our century, when both Frederic and Chopin, and especially the novels named, were suddenly rediscovered and began to enjoy a major vogue. Chopin is now pretty firmly ensconced in the canon; Frederic, though he is not likely to relapse into his erstwhile obscurity, has not kept the same reputational pace.[2] We can only speculate on the reasons for this difference, but it seems safe to say that the popularity of *The Awakening* has been buoyed by its feminist matter—which is not to deny the book's inherent artistic excellence. But *Theron Ware* is an artistic masterpiece too, and, in an age when women's studies have begun to blend into gender studies that also address the role of men, one might expect the Frederic novel to have achieved parity with *The Awakening*, at least as a study of cultural history.[3] This would be especially plausible in light of the striking similarities between the basic plots of the two works, for in *Theron Ware* the titular male protagonist experiences a spiritual and erotic awakening strikingly like that of Chopin's Edna Pontellier. Even the imagery and texture of the two books are uncannily alike. Except for the pronoun genders, it would be hard to identify which book the following passages come from:

> It was apparent . . . from the very first moment of waking next morning, that both he and the world had changed overnight. The metamorphosis, in the harsh toils of which he had been blindly laboring so long, was accomplished. He stood forth, so to speak, in a new skin, and looked about him, with perceptions of quite an altered kind, upon what seemed in every way a fresh existence. (*Theron Ware* 204)

> She felt like some new-born creature, opening its eyes in a familiar world that it had never known. (*The Awakening* 109)[4]     **65**

Equally arresting, among concrete textual similarities, is the role of music: performances of piano works by Frederic Chopin, by crucially influential characters, enter the two novels as determining events. (Incidentally, the play on the two authors' surnames is itself uncanny.)

We are concerned in this essay with Frederic's writing, not Chopin's; the foregoing comparisons are intended simply to isolate the question why Frederic's masterpiece has not caught on as Chopin's has. A reason suggests itself, one connected less with the preoccupations of readers than with the inherent nature of Frederic's fiction. During the years of his obscurity, historians of literature classified him (when they took note of him at all) as a regionalist and a realist, interested mainly in casting a cold eye on his native area, the Mohawk Valley of upstate New York. Good critics now recognize, as reviews and memorials did around the time of his death in 1898, that the very essence of Frederic's work is its lack of classifiable essence, a radical opalescence of attitude.[5] For one thing, his settings range far beyond American locales. A recurrent thread of theme and situation can be detected in his novels: as Carey McWilliams puts it, "the chaos that results when an untrained, uneducated, and unsophisticated person escapes from a provincial society and suddenly finds himself an heir to the culture, lore and wisdom of the ages."⁶ But to recognize this recurring motif does not take us far toward understanding Frederic, since he repeatedly insists on creating and then canceling impressions and effects. Moreover, it is sometimes hard to say just what a particular novel by Frederic is essentially about; *Theron Ware*, for example, is a congeries of modes and themes: a study of religious sociology; an interior drama of values; a version of the conflict between individual freedom and societal, or environmental, constrictions; an exploration of ideas (science versus art; religion and myth; the competing demands of beauty, truth, and morality); an examination of local ethnic mores as embodied in Roman Catholics (Irish and Italian) and in various denominations of Anglo-Saxon Protestantism. And even this modal variety is not the chief obstacle to pinning Frederic down; more important are the richness and subtlety of his ironies, which make it difficult to locate confidently his core values and vision.

The indeterminacy resulting from all this, however, is exactly suited to the task of exploring certain questions of values. My main focus in this essay will be on one of the most urgent of these questions: the competing claims of morality and of a radically antinomian personal freedom. In engaging this question as he does in *Theron Ware*, Frederic of necessity skates over some dangerous ideological thin ice. We are accustomed to hearing novelists such as Sinclair Lewis hailed for their courage in exposing the shoddy values of American businessmen, medical doctors, and religious charlatans; but as regards his reception by the liberal intellectual community nothing could be safer than these satirical exposés. What is at issue for Lewis and his enlightened readers in works such as *Babbit, Arrowsmith,* and *Elmer Gantry* is not the value of morality in itself but how morality can be redeemed from false versions of it.⁷ The "illumination" attained by Theron Ware is a more truly explosive matter, whether judged by liberal or conservative ethical standards.

For the convenience of those who have not read *The Damnation of Theron Ware,* or have not read it recently, a short summary of the novel is perhaps in order.

Theron Ware is a promising young Methodist minister, serving in upstate New York. He and his engaging young wife, Alice, are expecting a choice reassignment to a fashionable and worldly congregation, but in-

66

stead they are reassigned to the town of Octavius, where the Methodist congregation is narrow-minded and mean-spirited. (Alice is forbidden even to wear flowers on her hat.) One day, Theron sees a procession of Irish laborers carrying home one of their fellows, who has been mortally injured by a fall from a tree. Out of fascinated curiosity, Theron follows the crowd to the victim's shanty. Heretofore unacquainted with the Irish, and accustomed to think of them stereotypically as boorishly uncultured and politically suspect, Theron is surprised and impressed by the solemn beauty of the Catholic last rites, as administered by the parish priest, Father Forbes. Also present at the ceremony is a beautiful, elegantly dressed young woman named Celia Madden, daughter of the wealthy Irish immigrant mill-owner who employs the men. She takes Theron under her wing, explaining the ceremony to him.

Theron cultivates the acquaintance with Celia and Father Forbes, along with an old friend of the priest's, a Dr. Ledsmar. Father Forbes, Theron soon discovers, is an extensively learned man and a religious modernist who discourses easily on the mythic roots of religion, including Christianity. Celia emerges as an accomplished musician, a worshiper of beauty, a thoroughly Pre-Raphaelite aesthete (opulent red hair included). Dr. Ledsmar is her antithesis, a learned, cynical, and misogynistic atheist.

Dazzled by this constellation of glamour and advanced intellectual sophistication, Theron yearns to become part of it and to leave behind the straitened values of his provincial congregation, with whose leaders his relations have become uneasy. A turning point occurs when his church is visited by a Sister Soulsby and her husband-assistant, who have abandoned their shady pasts for the more respectable, if still hucksterish, career of professional revivalist fund-raisers. The Soulsbys are spectacularly successful in raising money for Theron's church, but even more important for Theron is some friendly advice given him by the affable and attractive Sister Soulsby. She urges him not to think of leaving the ministry but rather to pursue his own ends while cannily trimming his sails to his congregation's biases. To neutralize Theron's pangs of conscience over this program, she outlines the essence of her philosophy: the world contains sheep and goats, but they are not to be separated before the Last

**67**

Judgment. In the meantime people need not draw the line between good and bad too overscrupulously in judging either others or themselves.

Theron takes this advice, becoming an adept if not very sincere preacher and leader of his flock. Meanwhile, his pull toward Celia's aesthetic and hedonist "Greek" values, as she calls them, is strengthened by two powerful incidents. The first is a visit he pays to the flamboyantly sybaritic quarters she has furnished for herself in an isolated quarter of her father's large house. Here she all but literally seduces him by playing Chopin's piano music, sharing with him cigarettes and wine (normally forbidden to Theron), and changing into dishabille. The second incident occurs during a summer camp meeting of the Methodists, from which Theron slips away to join the less inhibited, and more beery, Irish-Catholic picnic being held in another part of the woods. He and Celia have an intense tête-à-tête conversation which ends in her bestowing on him a tender kiss.

Theron's imagination is now thoroughly inflamed; he is convinced that Celia is in love with him. Learning that she and Father Forbes are about to travel together by train to New York City and suspecting that the two are having an affair, he determines to shadow them. (He is not very skillful at this; we will learn later that Celia spotted him at the beginning of the trip.) By this point, Theron has begun to hear warnings about the change in his personality, but he ignores them as ill-founded. He is denounced as contemptible by an ailing brother of Celia and also by a former friend, Gorringe, who has developed a sympathetic crush on Alice, the wife Theron has begun to neglect and patronize. The reader learns that Father Forbes and Dr. Ledsmar have begun to write Theron off, for their different reasons.

As he trails the priest and Celia to New York City, Theron fantasizes about a future life of pleasurable luxury with Celia. He accosts her in her New York hotel room, expecting that she will be eager to run off with him and, because she is a wealthy woman, to support him. In fact, however, she and Father Forbes have traveled to New York on the innocent and serious business of retrieving another of Celia's brothers from a scrape. Pressed relentlessly by the infatuated Theron, she is forced to tell him that she and her friends, who were once drawn to him, now regard him as a "bore." Her kiss, she explains, had been a sad valedictory gesture. Devastated, Theron leaves the hotel. He next appears, after an alcoholic bender lasting for days, at the Soulsbys' New York house. Sister Soulsby listens to his despairing plaints and reassures him that all is not lost. The Soulsbys take him and Alice out of town for several months of psychological rehabilitation, after which Theron and his wife are to migrate to Seattle, where he is to go into the real estate business. Our last glimpse of him shows Theron still fantasizing, this time about a political career in which he will spellbind crowds as he had once done from the pulpit.

Frederic's fiction, especially his novels, represents a variety of modes for which there can be few parallels among important writers. This variety may very well spring from the same shifting basis in "relativity" that Charlotte Porter, an early reviewer, found in *Theron Ware*. Austin Briggs **69** Jr. makes the point forcefully: "Here indeed is a snarl of possibilities. . . . Sister Soulsby's advice to Theron . . . that the sheep and the goats are to be separated at Judgment Day 'and not a minute sooner' must be applied by the reader from the very start of the book."[8] In fact, as Briggs points out, there is some evidence that Frederic at one point considered calling the novel *Snarl*—presumably in the sense of "a tangled labyrinth of ambiguities and ironies that cross each other endlessly."[9] If we do not recognize this "confounding of affects" (to borrow a phrase Goethe once used about Kleist) as Frederic's central strategy in *Theron Ware*, we may well half-dismiss the novel as interesting but ultimately chaotic. This is especially likely to happen because so many of the confounded affects touch moral and psychological nerves that are almost always reflexively activated, both by literature itself and in literary criticism. A host of examples spring to mind, some of them obvious and often noted, others less so.

For example, when Theron comes to believe that he can no longer, in good conscience, serve as a Methodist minister, our reflex response is to underwrite this decision as a milestone he has reached on the road to personal integrity. But Sister Soulsby's contrary advice, that he stay in the ministry while adopting a policy of benign, "good" fraud, proceeds—or so it seems to many readers, myself included—from her capacity for

humane sympathy, a genuine concern on her part for the Wares' fulfillment and happiness. Although she is not very scrupulous, and indeed
believes that scrupulosity is a wasteful expenditure of spiritual energy, she
seems to have weighed thoughtfully the relative claims of conscience and
of general personal well-being. Nor, at least in her private relationships,
does she have much if any of the selfish absorption in herself or the re-
pellent deviousness we tend to associate with mere machiavels or pragmatic opportunists. The novel's confounding of affects, insistently exemplified in her, is reflected in the wide difference of opinion about her
among readers.[10]

Celia Madden, an authentic rebel against the church's long history of
misogyny and morbid asceticism, is nevertheless a near-essential pillar of
the local Catholic church and community. She admits to being a
Catholic for purely aesthetic reasons, but then it is difficult to separate
doctrine from aesthetic effect in Catholicism, at least as it is portrayed in
*Theron Ware*. It is hard not to be captivated by the beauty and freedom
Celia aspires to in her life and surroundings, encapsulated during the
memorable scene where she performs some of Chopin's noblest music.
(Some eight compositions are specifically identified and described not
only expressively but accurately.) With only a slight shift of perspective,
however, she can be seen as a comically jejune disciple of a Pater-Swin-
burne-Wilde aestheticism that, even at its best and most serious, invites
irreverent parody. (Oscar Wilde did, in fact, have Frederic's novel sent to
him during his imprisonment.[11]) Celia's antipathy for Dr. Ledsmar, as a
cold-blooded scientific rationalist, is convincing enough to have inspired
comparisons with Nathaniel Hawthorne's Rappaccini figures.[12] On the
other hand, his contempt for her has an epigrammatic bite that authors
tend to reserve for the censure of truly deplorable characters:

> She is not worth talking about—a mere bundle of egotism, ig-
> norance, and red-headed immodesty. If she were even a type,
> she might be worth considering, but she is simply an abnormal
> sport, with a small brain addled by notions that she is like Hy-
> patia, and a large impudence rendered intolerable by the fact

70

that she has money. Her father is said to be a decent man. He ought to have her whipped. (224)

Ledsmar's gratuitous misogyny, toward Celia and all her sex, will tip the scales in her favor for most readers, but in any case it would be a mistake to regard the positioning of these two characters in the novel as simply an antithesis. More important is the adverse judgment that, their mutual differences notwithstanding, both of them ultimately pass on Theron Ware; in their disillusionment, she calls him a bore and he gives Theron's name to a lizard. Similarly, the two-sidedness of Sister Soulsby is blended into the narrative and its symbolic characterization in such a way that she and her views, in certain limited contexts part of an antithesis between morality and expedience, ultimately become part of a richer mixture of ideas and affects. For example, the pragmatist Sister Soulsby and the idealist Celia Madden both register an affinity to Chopin's music, Sister Soulsby by setting familiar old hymns to his melodies.

This method, of creating polarities (as they seem at first) that later dissolve into unities or (more often) fragment kaleidoscopically, is the heart of Frederic's novelistic strategy in *Theron Ware*. Our reflexes invite us to consider Theron's wife, Alice, as the dull, domestic alternative to Theron's aesthetic and spiritual emancipation as embodied in Celia. That polarity does operate in certain episodes and contexts, but Alice is also a kind of twin to Celia, both of them representing, at different stages in Theron's life, the allure of femininity, the spice of nonconformity, and—summing up all this—the glamour of money, not to mention more particular details such as the importance of the piano to both women.[13] In other ways, too, Alice breaks free from her place in the archetype of Husband-Wife-Temptress, for example in her apparently innocent but somewhat ambiguous crush on lawyer Gorringe. For that matter, Gorringe himself breaks away from reflex patterns; his sly worldliness is no match for the monetary sleight of hand of his "pious" fellow trustees of the church or for Sister Soulsby's monetary machinations. The faintly disreputable air Gorringe exudes when we first meet him mutates into a romantic aura because of his early disappointment in love, and his anger at Theron's treatment of Alice makes him almost an emblem of chivalry.

There are other anomalies. Nowhere is it suggested that Father Forbes, for all his freethinking tendencies, is remiss in his pastoral duties, although he can sometimes take a casual attitude toward them, as when he allows parishioners to wait in an anteroom while he entertains his guests, at his leisure, over a gourmet dinner. The novel makes a strong case for the glories of art, but Dr. Ledsmar has some pungent things to say about art as decadence. (The Jews, he argues, after surviving for millennia exactly because they rejected art, as typified in graven images, are in danger of going the way of other ancient religions now that they have assumed a prominent place among the modern world's creative artists.) The treatment of the Irish lies somewhere between the earnest and the ludicrous. In accordance with Frederic's lifelong championing of the Irish, *Theron Ware* systematically explodes stereotypical views of them, but the bartenders at the Irish Catholic picnic are hard-pressed to keep up with the demand for beer. What are we to make of Father Forbes's oracular prediction, on that occasion, that the Irish will come to dominate American culture when, as he claims is happening, they forsake Celtic whiskey in favor of Teutonic lager? Indeed, the entire geographical setting of the novel, though obviously dictated by Frederic's having grown up in the region, seems almost grotesque in light of the spiritual drama enacted there. When, in *Tender Is the Night,* Scott Fitzgerald wants to banish the fallen Dick Diver to the obscurest end of the earth, he loses him in upstate New York, not far from *Theron Ware* country. Celia has worked bravely to make a part of her father's house a haven of Hellenism, but even she recognizes the odds against her: "I suppose if an old Greek could see it, it would make him sick, but it represents what *I* mean by being a Greek. It is as near as an Irishman can get to it" (193). All this is as if the setting of *The Oresteia,* or *Faust,* or *The Brothers Karamazov* were relocated in Terre Haute or Kalamazoo.

The leavening of farcical comedy that runs through *Theron Ware* is, or should be, apparent. But the most jarringly anomalous incident in the novel propels us in the opposite direction, suggesting tragedy and inviting severe moral commentary. It is curiously significant that this incident is treated with an almost throwaway casualness. Celia's father, Jeremiah Madden, owner of the local wagon works and the wealthiest man in the town of Octavius, is probably the most sympathetically portrayed character in the entire novel. A man of homely, unaffected tastes, he is capable of deep fellow-feeling, especially toward those of his countrymen, buried in the older of the two local cemeteries, who barely survived the horrors of the potato famine only to die soon after emigrating to America. Yet it is Madden who assigned to his ill-fated workman MacEvoy, by trade a wheelwright, the unfamiliar task of trimming an elm tree in front of Madden's mansion, thereby occasioning the laborer's death. We are given brief glimpses of the suddenly bereaved widow and mother MacEvoy and of her resentment, which the gorgeously dressed Celia describes to Theron as if she were a little surprised at all the fuss:

73

> it was . . . because MacEvoy was one of our workmen, and really came by his death through father sending him up to trim a tree. Ann MacEvoy will never forgive us that, the longest day she lives. Did you notice her? She wouldn't speak to me. After you came out, I tried to tell her that we would look out for her and the children, but all she would say to me was: "An' fwat would a wheelwright, an' him the father of a family, be doin' up a tree?" (46)

This breezy response to the tragedy is overwhelmed, for the purposes of the story and of Theron's impressions, by the aesthetic and cultural keynotes of the scene: the dazzling presence of Celia, elegant in her spring dress and hat, set off by an exquisitely designed parasol; the solemn incense-laden beauty of the rite of extreme unction; Father Forbes's learned postmortem disquisition on the ancient Persian origins of the ceremony (and, incidentally, of baptism too); and the priest's playfully rueful admission of being exasperated at the eagerness of his parishioners to call the priest before the doctor, even for the most trivial indispositions. The episode ends as Theron and Celia reach her house, the site of the accidental death; but this connection is ignored by everyone, including the author, amid the details of the house's elegance and of the halo effect produced on Celia's complexion by the sun filtered through the aforementioned parasol.

In almost any other novel one can think of or imagine, an episode such as this, with its blithe submersion of grimness and moral guilt beneath a casual wash of sensuousness, would be savagely satirical. Even in that landmark of aestheticism, Wilde's *Picture of Dorian Gray*, the Sybil Vane episode, wherein Dorian spurns Sybil and drives her to suicide when she opts for real life in preference to her thespian art, is freighted with moral seriousness, by way of eliciting at least a temporary feeling of deep remorse on Dorian's part. No such moral weight, however, is given to the death of MacEvoy in *The Damnation of Theron Ware*. The episode functions solely to mark the first instilling in Theron of his new thirst for beauty and learning.

**74**    I dwell on the grimmer aspects of the MacEvoy episode, arresting exactly because Frederic gives them so little overt emphasis, because the episode epitomizes the double vision of values—aesthetic and moral—that, perhaps more than any other of the novel's confounding of affects, gives *Theron Ware* its disturbing resonance as philosophical speculation. This dimension of the novel, which lends it a depth and breadth of application far transcending mere local color realism, is the only thing that accounts for certain portentous phrases that both early reviewers and more recent critics have applied to the book. Reviewing *Theron Ware* in 1896, Charlotte Porter alluded to the shifting "element of relativity" in the book;[14] in the same year, an anonymous reviewer in *The Critic* found overtones in *Theron Ware* of "mysterious, impersonal, Titanic forces."[15] O'Donnell and Franchere echo this phrase as describing the real dynamics of which Celia, Father Forbes, and Dr. Ledsmar are the vehicles, and they also assert that Frederic brings to his provincially set story a consideration of "abstract, universally disruptive world-ideas" and "inscrutable forces."[16] Austin Briggs argues that, although the novel is a "classic statement" of late nineteenth-century beliefs and values, "there should be no doubt that Frederic sees the education of Theron Ware in a universal perspective."[17] "Titanic"? "Universally disruptive"? "Inscrutable"? "Universal perspective"? Many critics, clearly, locate us in deep waters—and they are right.

The only theme in the book, it seems to me, that accounts for such extravagant language is the antinomian theme, a term I am using in a psychological sense deriving, but different, from its original theological application. This extended, psychological sense did not emerge out of nowhere in the fin de siècle, "decadent" period. At least a century earlier, most emphatically in the works of William Blake, the root, theological notion that one is delivered from the constraints of the moral law by a redemptive, superabundant grace far beyond questions of personal desert modulated into a more universal, more secular, and more psychological form. This evolved form of antinomianism postulates that the good life (in this context, the ambiguity in the word *good* is of the essence) can best be lived by relaxing the clenched-teeth rigors of moral conscience and redirecting one's spiritual energies toward self-realization and the closely related ideal of the pursuit of beauty. The heart of Shelley's argument in **75** *A Defence of Poetry*, which elevates an inspiring dynamic of art above mere doctrine as a means of promoting happiness and thus improving the world, is along the same antinomian lines. So is Keats's notion of the "pleasure thermometer" as expressed in *Endymion*, and so are the attempts by Coleridge and Byron, in poems like *Christabel* and *Manfred*, to transmute moral guilt into psychological guilt. In their different ways, the vatic pronunciamentos of Emerson, as well as Hawthorne's anatomy, in *The Scarlet Letter*, of the toll taken by moral guilt on psychological health, take us along the same path. Matthew Arnold's condemnation of Philistinism in *Culture and Anarchy*, and his plea that the imbalance between Hellenism and Hebraism in Victorian culture be rectified, not only is pertinent but seems to have directly inspired at least one passage in *The Damnation of Theron Ware:* "I divide people up into two classes, you know," Celia explains to Theron, "Greeks and Jews. . . . It is the only true division there is. . . . [Among the Greeks] the Philistine was as unknown, as extinct, as the dodo!" (194).[18]

The fin de siècle, "decadent" turn toward aestheticism as a force programmatically deployed against moralism was merely the culminating wave of a tide that had been rising for a century. Indeed, one could argue that the antinomian aestheticism we associate with Pater, Swinburne, Huysmans, Wilde, and Beardsley tended to cancel out its own message, exactly because the new mode was propagated at the end of the century in a tone so sensational and aggressively exotic as to constitute, very nearly, a satire on itself. For that matter, the anticipations we have noted from earlier in the century are almost all in a similar, if not so flamboyant, mode of the vatic or visionary or prophetic. By contrast, in *Theron Ware* Harold Frederic explored the antinomian theme in a tone, prose style, and geographical setting that are more straightforwardly realistic, sometimes almost to the point of banality.

As a result, the conflict as presented in *Theron Ware*—between morality and abandon, between the respective imperatives of the good and of the beautiful—is presented raw, as it were, without the distancing afforded by visionary heightening or "decadent" posturing aimed at shock or éclat. Moreover, overwhelmingly strong cases can be made, in interpreting *Theron Ware,* on either side of the issue of conscience versus freedom. It hardly seems necessary to adduce evidence showing Theron's fatuity and callousness; except for Sister Soulsby, every major character in the book levels devastating criticism at him in the closing chapters, and the drunken debauch after his last interview with Celia and Father Forbes reduces him to a figure of farce. His essential littleness, his utter failure to achieve true "illumination," is ironically underlined by his grandiose vision of himself, at the very end, as a charismatic figure still exerting his sway over the public. This from the man whom Celia, expressing the consensus of his erstwhile role models, had dismissed as a "bore."

From a different perspective, however, the awakening in Theron of exciting new feelings and ideas cannot be dismissed as meretricious. He has good reason for wanting to escape the spiteful narrowness of his Methodist congregation; we cannot feel that he is misguided in opting instead for the values epitomized in Celia's wondrous musicianship and in Father Forbes's breadth of learning. The private concert of Chopin's music Celia performs for Theron, along with the author's movingly impressionistic—and at the same time accurate—description of each piece on the program, largely redeems whatever may be overly purple in the setting. Celia's professed creed, with its rejection of "moral bugbears," does not convict her of mere irresponsibility; the trip she takes to New York City, with Father Forbes's cooperation, is for a serious purpose, and she has nursed her dying brother Michael so assiduously that the priest fears for her own health. Both Forbes and Celia possess a genuine largeness of spirit that transcends mere attitudinizing. Her withering appraisal of what the ancient church elders—"those brutes they call the Fathers," "your miserable Jeromes and Augustines and Cyrils"—did to Christianity (258, 240) is closely in line with feminist thought from Christine de Pizan and Chaucer's Wife of Bath to present-day historians of women's cultural roles. That Theron feels drawn to Celia, and to Father Forbes, is to his credit. Sister Soulsby's playing down of the role of "conscience" in her unminced-words discourse with Theron (170) may ring false to some readers, but surely we breathe fresher air when we move from the Methodists' encampment to the Catholic picnic, where the show of stockings by ladies on swings is a topic for casual conversation and where, in Theron's words, "I suppose that in this whole huge crowd there isn't a single person who will mention the subject of his soul to any other person all day long" (239). This sentiment builds on an earlier recognition by him: "Evidently there was an intellectual world, a world of culture and grace, of lofty thoughts and the inspiring communion of real knowledge, where creeds were not of importance, and where men asked one another, not 'Is your soul saved?' but 'Is your mind well furnished?'" (132). We cannot take all these animated passages as sardonic satire intended simply to expose the folly of self-deceiving high-mindedness.

Still, the high-mindedness does clash with the picture of Theron as contemptible. To say that Frederic confounds affects in the novel may be useful as description, but does the description help us understand the novel's strategies—other than to remind us, truistically, that most things can be understood in more than one way? I would suggest that the recurrent strategy by which the novel's affects cancel one another out are variants, presented indirectly, of its exploration of the antinomian theme. In *Theron Ware* Frederic has rendered, with almost unique success, and primarily through his double-takes on matters involving values, the perennial problem that emerges when antinomian spiritual energizing clashes head-on with morality, when two perfectly valid senses of *good* collide.

The important point to recognize is that the conflict *is* head-on, is irresolvable. Only rarely in literature (though much more frequently in life) is the conflict apprehended in this way. (Mann's *Death in Venice* is one of the rare instances.) It is common enough to read works in which the protagonist is implicitly admired for daring to drink the new wine of freedom, but in most such works what has been left behind is a suffocating, deadly constraint of spirit—as in Edith Wharton's *Ethan Frome* or, less starkly, in *The Age of Innocence*. Almost as often—in literature, that is—attempts to find a heady new freedom are grimly exposed as foolish and destructive irresponsibility, a blind defiance of the imperatives on which depends all that is authentic and truly humane, as in unsympathetic takes on Emma Bovary. The conflict is perfectly realized in the agonizing dilemma faced by Maggie Tulliver in Eliot's *The Mill on the Floss*, when Maggie has to choose between her need for passionate love and her obligation to morality as embodied in the selfless, gentle cousin with whose fiancé she is running away.

Maggie chooses self-renunciation. Morality trumps her need for pleasurable human happiness, as it tends to do in literary works, by default, whenever the quest for freedom involves a genuine conflict, not with mere stultifying custom but with the imperatives of sound conscience—whenever, that is, self-realization conflicts with duty. In *Theron Ware* Frederic presents both sides in the conflict as imperatives from which there is no appeal and then leaves the conflict unresolved instead of tilting the balance of imperatives in one direction or the other. What is especially remarkable is that this avoidance of definitive judgment does not arise from invertebrate relativism or even from a sense of the complexity of life and people. It is *utterly* wrong for Theron to ignore the beckonings of a new and larger world; the demands of spiritual freedom are absolute, undeflectable. It is also *utterly* wrong to give pain—specifically, in Theron's case, the actual and potential pain suffered by his wife, Alice; one cannot trade away one's soul even in return for the most authentic beauty.

Few good storytellers of the past few centuries, and probably even fewer in our own time, have considered themselves moralists, except—as they often insist—to the extent that morality means a duty to be faithful to the truth, to the way the world and people really are. To falsify these things is, for the artist, the only pertinent mode of immorality. When morality is thus understood as a function of truth—a perfectly valid way of thinking, most of us would agree—authors can silently bypass judgments about moral values in the plainer, behavioral sense. That is, authors are freed up to assume that their readers, or at least the right-minded and enlightened among them, will share basic criteria of right and wrong behavior, good and evil behavior, even when—indeed especially when—such values conflict with the vulgar consensus. But the extent to which such judgments are reflex or powerfully conditioned is not sufficiently appreciated. No one likes to have his or her car stolen, but I have been told by a Hollywood screen writer that, if a movie opened with a scene showing a teenage boy stealing a car, the intent would almost certainly be to establish the boy immediately as a sympathetic character. On a larger scale, in fiction of the last two centuries, the pursuit of monetary wealth by a character is an almost certain sign of moral delinquency in that character, whether wealth is a key theme in the narrative or not— despite the fact that virtually every actual person in the world wants and tries to have more money than he or she has. (Who, other than Jane Austen and Henry James among novelists of the last two centuries, has felt free to portray wealth without attaching a stigma to those who possess it?)

**79**

At the same time, authors and the presumably humane among their readers are prone, again by reflex, to sympathize deeply with characters who try to liberate themselves from the narrowness of their lives. Indeed, there are few more exhilarating motifs than this one. The trouble is that authors often stack the deck by identifying the narrowness to be escaped with a meretricious version of morality—a "so-called" morality like that of Hawthorne's puritans or the merely conventional respectability of Wharton's New York social registrants. And when the deck is not stacked by the author, so that we are forced to recognize that soul-expanding freedom can sometimes be achieved only by giving pain to relatively innocent bystanders, the moral imperative not to give pain wins out by reflexive default. We shock ourselves and other people if we do not respond this way. The result of such situations in fiction is often tragic suffering, as, for example, with Anna Karenina. We are almost never encouraged to feel that the giving of pain can be justified, as a toll worth exacting in the interests of gaining personal freedom. When Henrik Ibsen's Nora Helmer goes off on her own, leaving her husband and children to fend for themselves, we dwell less on any new happiness that may lie in wait for Nora than on the painful effort her prospective reeducation will demand of her and on her function as a pioneer in advancing the cause of women. We must see her action as a moral choice; we would feel uneasy if we simply envisioned for her a condition of exhilarated happiness.

In saying that authors usually stack the deck, I do not mean to imply that they are less than honest, except perhaps in the aggregate. An artist painting a springtime landscape is not obligated to remind us that winter also exists. Authors writing tragedy are not obligated to remind us that some people live happy lives. A composer writing a funeral march need not include a passage acknowledging that birth is a joyous miracle (even assuming that a piece of music can make such suggestions). Similarly, a story about psychic liberation need neither portray it as a self-deceiving sham nor celebrate it as an absolute good. *The Damnation of Theron Ware* does both these things, however, and that is why it is so fascinating and disturbing. It impresses on us the irresistible appeal of beauty and freedom, the radical goodness of these things; it also impresses on us the peremptory authority that morality—authentic morality, not mere sham imitations of it—rightly wields over us. And it impresses on us the utter incompatibility, in many vital situations, of these two dynamic systems in the human psyche. In writing a novel that does so much, Harold Frederic deserves credit for creating a work of high art that is also a tour de force. It is excruciatingly hard for us to come to terms with this novel, for it sets in motion the deepest, though also the most contradictory, of our value systems. And as a broad by-product, *Theron Ware* brings home to us how strongly, in reading almost all other fiction, we are at the mercy of reflex responses conditioned by the tacit conventions both of literature and of polite critical discourse.

# Notes

1. *The Damnation of Theron Ware* was published in England under the title *Illumination*. Frederic apparently preferred the latter title. The irony of employing alternative titles suggesting, respectively, the conditions of darkness and of light is appropriate for this novel, as we shall see. The text cited and quoted in this article is Harold Frederic, *The Damnation of Theron Ware*, with an introduction by Scott Donaldson and a note on the text by Stanton Garner (New York: Penguin Books USA, 1986). This edition reprints the authoritative text: *The Damnation of Theron Ware or Illumination*, edited by Charlayne Dodge and Stanton Garner, vol. 3 of the Harold Frederic Edition (Lincoln: University of Nebraska Press, 1985).

2. A recent, and therefore especially comprehensive, tracking of the ebbs and flows of Frederic's reputation is in the preface to Robert M. Myers, *Reluctant Expatriate: The Life of Harold Frederic*, Contributions to the Study of World Literature, no. 59 (Westport, Conn.: Greenwood Press, 1995), xi–xiv.

3. *"Theron Ware* is a powerful masterpiece"—Stanton Garner, *Harold Frederic*, University of Minnesota Pamphlets on American Writers, no. 83 (Minneapolis: University of Minnesota Press, 1969), 38; the novel is "one of the great achievements of American letters"—Austin Briggs Jr., *The Novels of Harold Frederic* (Ithaca: Cornell University Press, 1969), 139. Such claims are not uncommon in critical appraisals of *Theron Ware.* When it was published, it enjoyed enthusiastic, and almost unanimous, critical acclaim, as well as popular success; see, for example, Briggs, *Novels of Harold Frederic,* 1–2, 97; and Donaldson, in *Theron Ware,* xvii–xviii. Many commentators and biographers are at pains to insist that, his prolific output notwithstanding (he wrote some fifteen books, in addition to a vast amount of writing as London correspondent for the *New York Times*), Frederic wrote with an artist's meticulous care, after thorough research; see, for example, Thomas F. O'Donnell and Hoyt C. Franchere, *Harold Frederic,* Twayne's United States Authors Series (New Haven: College and University Press, 1961), 62, 157; and Donaldson, in *Theron Ware,* xiii. A letter Frederic wrote to Thomas H. Huxley on December 21, 1892, while disclaiming advanced expertise, attests the wide research Frederic conducted in ancient religion and anthropology, material he drew on in *Theron Ware.* This novel occupied him over a period of five years and required research not only on the antiquarian subjects mentioned but also on biology, genetics, Methodism, theology, philosophy, and music—all of which are touched upon, in significant detail, in the novel. See Donaldson, in *Theron Ware,* xiii; and Volume 1 of the Harold Frederic Edition: *The Correspondence of Harold Frederic,* ed. George E. Fortenberry, Stanton Garner, Robert W. Woodward, and Charlayne Dodge (Fort Worth: Texas Christian University Press, 1977), 323–26, 389.

4. Kate Chopin, *The Awakening,* Norton Critical Editions, 2d ed. (New York, 1994). This authoritative text reprints the 1899 first edition.

5. One reason for the eclipse of Frederic's reputation was Vernon Louis Parrington's sour view of him in *Main Currents in American Thought,* 3 vols. (New York: Har-

court, Brace, 1927–30), 3:288, cited in O'Donnell and Franchere, *Harold Frederic,* 76. Parrington makes Frederic sound like a regional realist and embittered social critic. O'Donnell and Franchere point out, however (152–53), that Parrington was examining early work by Frederic and that he might have judged differently had he lived to complete his book. Like Frederic's contemporaries, more recent critics have tended to insist that, despite his attunement to many currents of his time—or, perhaps, exactly because he was attuned to so many of them—he is unclassifiable as a realist, naturalist, romancer, local colorist, or in any other familiar literary category or movement of his time; see Briggs, *Novels of Harold Frederic,* 11; O'Donnell and Franchere, 144, 160; and Donaldson, in *Theron Ware,* xvi.

6. Carey McWilliams, "Harold Frederic: 'A Country Boy of Genius,'" *University of California Chronicle* 35 (1933): 30; quoted in Briggs, *Novels of Harold Frederic,* 13.

7. On the influence of *Theron Ware* on Lewis's *Elmer Gantry* and the relative merits of the two books, see Briggs, *Novels of Harold Frederic,* 122 and footnote. Briggs also cites opinions on the subject by Mark Schorer and Charles V. Genthe.

8. Ibid., 115n, 116.

9. Ibid., 116n.

10. As we have seen, Briggs lends a sympathetic ear to Sister Soulsby. On the other hand, Garner sees her as a "Mephistopheles" and her tutelage as "pernicious" (*Harold Frederick,* 34–35).

11. Ironically, it was also read, and endorsed, by Prime Minister Gladstone; see Briggs, *Novels of Harold Frederic,* 102–3.

12. See, for example, ibid., 130–31.

13. On the parallels between Theron's responses to Celia and Alice, see Donaldson, in *Theron Ware,* 23; and Briggs, *Novels of Harold Frederic,* 118.

14. Charlotte Porter, "Notes on Recent Fiction," *Poet-Lore* 8 (1896): 460. The review is signed "C," identified by Briggs, *Novels of Harold Frederic,* 115n, as Charlotte Porter.

15. *Critic* n.s., 25 (1896): 310, cited in O'Donnell and Franchere, *Harold Frederic,* 110, 172.

16. O'Donnell and Franchere, *Harold Frederic,* 112.

17. Briggs, *Novels of Harold Frederic,* 129.

18. Myers, *Reluctant Expatriate,* 125, discusses the influence of Matthew Arnold on Frederic. He cites also John O. Lyons, "Hebraism, Hellenism, and Harold Frederic's *Theron Ware,*" *Arnoldian* 6 (1979): 7–15.

# Lessons of the Bear

**or** Eugene Henderson, eponymous hero of Saul Bellow's *Hen-*   **83**
*derson the Rain King,* given his needs and purposes, the crucial
event was the trip to Africa. This is made clear at the very beginning: "When I think of my condition at the age of fifty-five,
when I bought the ticket, all is grief."[1] Henderson, like so many
of Bellow's protagonists, is a quester, a searcher after his place in
life's designs. Where Augie March demands "a fate worth suffering for,"[2] Henderson is driven by an imperious inner voice, a
pure hunger only intensified by the absence of object: *"I want, I
want,"* it says (12, 14, 24, 28, 32, etc.).

But Henderson stands out among these other Bellow
questers not so much for his success as for the detailed attention
to his instruction. The success is made clear at the very beginning: "However, the world which I thought so mighty an op-
pressor has removed its wrath from me" (3). *Herzog,* in this regard, follows a nearly identical path—crisis and the resolution
of crisis announced at the very beginning, with the novel to follow devoted to the period between, the process of the resolution. So too with *The Dean's December,* where Albert Corde, like
Eugene Henderson, finds a "sense of improvement" at the end
of his journey.[3]

A central question, by such structures, is clarified—what

happens to effect the happy outcome? What lessons enable the stricken Henderson to "burst the spirit's sleep" (225)? Who are his teachers? What wisdom does he learn? Bellow's heroes are in general remarkably susceptible to teachers, quick to subscribe to wisdom served up by others far and near. Moses Herzog calls one of these tutors (Simkin, an attorney) "a Reality-Instructor," adding that he seems to "bring them out."⁴ Augie March also attracts such figures—he describes Mintouchian as "another of those persons who persistently arise before me with life counsels and illumination."⁵ Tommy Wilhelm, from *Seize the Day*, could speak for all of these, and for Henderson, when he calls himself "a sucker for people who talk about the deeper things of life."⁶

Of course not all (not half) these gurus are wise, or honest (Tamkin, from *Seize the Day*), or even sane (Basteshaw, from *Augie March*). And the protagonists themselves, the suckers, have a penchant for dispensing counsel only slightly less evident than their eagerness to hear it. Augie March, for example, on board the doomed *Sam MacManus*, becomes the "ship's confidant." "I passed out advice in moderate amounts," he says.⁷ Charlie Citrine, from *Humboldt's Gift*, is less restrained: "I had business on behalf of the entire human race."⁸

Henderson is right at home in this company. He has many instructors, but chief among them is Dahfu, king of the Wariri. No other "Reality-Instructor" in a Bellow novel gets so much attention for his views, which are at several points presented in summary form:

> And what he was engrossed by was a belief in the transformation of human material, that you could work either way, either from the rind to the core or from the core to the rind; the flesh influencing the mind, the mind influencing the flesh, back again in the mind, back once more to the flesh. The process as he saw it was utterly dynamic. (236)

This system of mutually influential relationships has its roots in Dahfu's empirical perceptions: "He started with the elementary observation, which many people had made before him, that mountain people were mountain-like, plains people plains-like, water people water-like, cattle people . . . cattle-like" (237). Dahfu himself waxes eloquent on the subject: "the psyche is a polyglot, for if it converts fear into symptoms it also converts hope. There are cheeks or whole faces of hope, feet of respect, hands of justice, brows of serenity, and so forth" (238). Kenneth Trachtenberg, in *More Die of Heartbreak,* advances a similar notion, explicitly adding the temporal dimension, the influence of a Zeitgeist: "Outer forces inject themselves into us, penetrating the very nervous system. When the individual discovers them inside his own head, their appearance seems to him entirely natural and what these forces say he can truly understand, just as Hitler and the population of Germany spoke a common language."[9]

Dahfu's course of instruction centers on a lioness, Atti, who is housed beneath the palace. In this use of animals he resembles other mentors from Bellow's novels. Augie March is at one point deeply involved with Caligula, a "washout" eagle who ends up in an Indiana zoo, while Charley Citrine attempts to deal with a bat-wielding, gun-toting Rinaldo Cantabile by recalling "Konrad Lorenz's discussion of wolves."[10] In *The Dean's December* there is the elegant birthday party in the Sorokin high-rise for the Great Dane, Dolphie, where the pampered dog seems "the Great Beast of the Apocalypse" to Albert Corde.[11]

Dahfu's pedagogy centers on imitative exercises. Henderson is encouraged to act the lion—"Be the beast!" urges Dahfu—to emulate Atti's posture, glare, and roar (267). The purpose is of course acquisitive. Henderson is to do as Dahfu himself has done, as his ancestors did before him: "Each absorbed lion into himself" (265). At several points Dahfu makes explicit the importance of his involvement with Atti. "Atti and I influence each other," he tells his pupil. "I wish you to become a party to this" (228). Such a program, of course, is based in turn on the fundamental belief in the malleability of human material, in personality as constructed, in character as a feat of accomplishment. "It is all a matter of having a desirable model in the cortex," Dahfu preaches. "For the noble self-conception is everything" (268).

Actually, this last point adds something to the basic notion, or at least shifts the balance. For if the relationship of flesh and spirit is in fact "utterly dynamic," with each influencing the other, it nevertheless seems

**85**

clear that the emphasis falls on the creative aspects of mind, of imagination. "Imagination," Dahfu says, "imagination, imagination! It converts
to actual. It sustains, it alters, it redeems! . . . What Homo sapiens imagines, he may slowly convert himself to" (271). In this credo too, as in so
many others, Dahfu joins other Bellow heroes. Often patronized by associates near and far, male and female, as dreamy, ineffectual, finally
childlike figures, they most often mount apologias founded on the claims
of the imagination. Dean Corde, for example, regarded with contempt
by Alec Witt, Dewey Spangler, the Romanian colonel in charge of the
hospital, and his brother-in-law Zaehner, among others, finally articulates a defense (in thought only, characteristically, just as Moses Herzog
defends himself by addressing imaginary letters):

**86**      Literal! What you didn't pass through your soul didn't even
exist, that was what made the literal literal. Thus he had taken
it upon himself [in magazine articles much decried by his de-
tractors] to pass Chicago through his own soul. A mass of
data, terrible, murderous. It was no easy matter to put such
things through. But there was no other way for reality to happen. Reality didn't exist "out there." It began to be real only
when the soul found its underlying truth.[12]

Dahfu, despite his position as king, is regarded as just such an ab-
stracted goof by Horko and the Bunam, representatives of Realpolitik
among the Wariri. He's their king, they reason; he has a job to do. Not
only his involvement with Henderson, but the whole enterprise with the
lion Atti, his search for the "underlying truth" of his own soul, they regard as dangerous irresponsibility, another instance of an Aeneas figure
dallying with Dido while Rome waits to be founded.

Dahfu and Henderson, then, despite their obvious differences, are
portrayed by Bellow as brothers at an essential level, comrades in exile
from the world-historical mainstream. It even turns out, just as his
course of instruction with Atti opens, that Henderson is already no
stranger to the influence of animals. (It turns out, unsurprisingly, that
such influences may be other than deliberately cultivated, are perhaps

more often than not unconscious.) Dahfu soon suspects as much, though he cannot identify the species. "'However,' he said, 'it is another animal you strongly remind me of. But of which?'" (266).

The answer would seem to be clear. Henderson is a pig farmer, and has been one for some time: "When I came back from the war it was with the thought of becoming a pig farmer, which maybe illustrates what I thought of life in general" (20). He follows through on these plans, and his life soon becomes deeply involved with pigs:

> I took all the handsome old farm buildings . . . and I filled them up with pigs, a pig kingdom, with pig houses on the lawn and in the flower-garden. The greenhouse, too—I let them root out the old bulbs. Statues from Florence and Salzburg were turned over. The place stank of swill and pigs and the mashes cooking, and dung. (20–21)

The result of this occupation, of such surroundings, is predictable, given Dahfu's scheme, and Henderson is explicit about it. On one occasion he tells his first wife, Frances, that the pigs are not to be harmed: "You'd better not hurt them. Those animals have become a part of me" (270). As Dahfu with his lion, so Henderson with his pigs—or so poor Henderson thinks. The thought does not please him, and he offers no assistance when Dahfu wonders what animal is responsible for the physical and behavioral characteristics he senses in his pupil. "I hesitated to come clean with Dahfu and to ask him right out bluntly whether he could see their influence" (270). Instead, he conducts his own examination: "I felt my jowls, my snout; I did not dare to look down at what had happened to me. Hams, tripes, a whole cauldron full of them. Trunk, a fat cylinder. It seemed to me that I couldn't even breathe without grunting" (270).

There is, however, another possibility, though Henderson does not recollect it at the time. Pigs, it turns out, are not the only animals to play a significant role in his life. Not until his flight home to Connecticut, accompanied by the lion cub he takes to be Dahfu's descendant, does he remember his prior association, antedating even that of the pigs, with the

circus animal Smolak, an elderly brown bear. Then, too late for his conversations with Dahfu, it occurs to him to wonder if his tutor perhaps
sensed the influence of Smolak, rather than that of the pigs:

> So before pigs ever came on my horizon, I received a deep im-
> pression from a bear. So if corporeal things are an image of the
> spiritual and visible objects are renderings of invisible ones,
> and if Smolak and I were outcasts together, two humorists be-
> fore the crowd, but brothers in our souls—I enbeared by him,
> and he probably humanized by me—I didn't come to the pigs
> as a tabula rasa. It only stands to reason. Something deep al-
> ready was inscribed on me. In the end, I wonder if Dahfu
> would have found this out for himself. (338–39)[13]

Bellow goes to some lengths to point out the consequences of this discovery. During the African self-examination, for example, Henderson
was specifically distressed by his "grunting," taken as a vivid sign of
porcine influence. He later repeats this concern in a letter to his wife,
Lily: "Otherwise, I seem to have benefited physically here, except that I
have a persistent grunt. I wonder if this is new, or did you ever notice it
at home?" Then, near the end of the book, in a passage praising the benefits of memory, Henderson observes that "pigs don't have a monopoly
on grunting" (336). This refers specifically to the recollection of his involvement with Smolak; his fuller account makes specific reference to the
fact that Smolak "grunted and cried to me" (338) as man and bear rode a
roller coaster together.

The important task, given such a structure, a quest happily concluded,
a program of instruction based on the conscious emulation and unconscious influence of various animal models, is to characterize the content
of the lessons—the effect of Dahfu's lion, the "deep impression" of the
carnival bear. In general, it turns out that the influence of Atti is primarily behavioral, while that of Smolak is essentially attitudinal. One teaches
Henderson a style of action, a mode of becoming; the other models a
perspective, a way to be. In the case of Atti, her desirable qualities are

enumerated by Dahfu. She is above all unavoidable. This is vital, says Dahfu, because Henderson has "accomplished momentous avoidances." Atti will render them impossible: "She will burnish you. She will force the present moment upon you" (260).

The vivid, unavoidable event experienced as wake-up call, as summons to action, is a recurrent element in Bellow's novels. Artur Sammler, for example, watching a pickpocket ply his trade on a bus, is both fascinated and repelled. It is "a powerful event," and Sammler exits the bus "with the benefit of an enlarged vision."[14] For Henderson himself there is the sudden death of his serving lady, Miss Lenox, which is the immediate, precipitating cause of the trip to Africa. In the small room of paltry junk which is all Miss Lenox leaves behind, Henderson is struck by a sense of limited time:

**89**

> The last little room of dirt is waiting. Without windows. So
> for God's sake make a move, Henderson, put forth effort. You,
> too, will die of this pestilence. Death will annihilate you and
> nothing will remain, and there will be nothing left but junk.
> (40)

Henderson's "move" on this occasion initiates the novel's major narrative: "So Miss Lenox went to the cemetery, and I went to Idlewild and took a plane" (40).

Atti, then, will "force the present moment" upon her pupil. But there is nothing of Henderson's frenzy about her activity. "Lions are experiencers," says Dahfu. "But not in haste. They experience with deliberate luxury" (260). In addition, there are specific lessons in the physical movements of the lion: "Now, watch the way she walks. Beautiful? You said it! Furthermore this is uninstructed, specie-beauty. . . . Oh, Henderson, watch how she is rhythmical in behavior" (262).

The import of these exercises is at times generalized by Dahfu: "By means of the lion try to distinguish the states that are given and the states that are made. Observe that Atti is all lion. Does not take issue with the inherent. Is one hundred per cent within the given" (263). Such emphasis on "the inherent" and "the given" might appear to be at odds both with the general emphasis on human malleability and the specific stress laid on the altering and redeeming powers of imagination. It seems likely, however, that Bellow intends "the inherent" as circumscribing (and thereby even focusing, potentiating) rather than negating imagination's powers of transformation. The point would seem to be that "the states that are made" are most satisfactory, most fully achievable, when they are developments, devoted nurturings, of "the states that are given." At one point, confronting the stare of the Bunam, Henderson hears an interior voice that articulates such a view in emphatic terms: *"So now do not soften, oh no, brother, intensify rather what you are. This is the one and only ticket— intensify"* (187).

So much for the influence of Atti. Henderson's interactions with her

are certainly intense, but they are brief. Atti's primary association is with Dahfu. Henderson's have been with Smolak, and Smolak is a very different beast. Where Atti is a powerful and impressive animal, Smolak is a "ditched old creature . . . almost green with time and down to his last teeth, like the pits of dates" (338). Where the lion moves with the rhythmic grace of uninstructed "specie-beauty," Smolak is a pathetic "trained bear," too much instructed and by such degraded tutelage exiled from every specifically ursine power. He once rode a bicycle, but now, outfitted "in a cap and bib, he drank from a baby bottle while he stood on his hind legs" (338). The contrast is conspicuous—if Atti is at home in the given, Smolak is abandoned in the made. Where Atti is frightening, Smolak is himself frightened.

Smolak's association with Henderson centers in the roller-coaster rides they endure together, twice a day, for the entertainment of customers at an Ontario amusement park:

> By a common bond of despair we embraced, cheek to cheek, as all support seemed to leave us and we started down the perpendicular drop. I was pressed into his long-suffering, age-worn, tragic, and discolored coat as he grunted and cried to me. At times the animal would wet himself. (338)

These differences between the two animals and the contexts of their ties to human associates are certainly striking, but it turns out that their underlying similarities are in some ways even more fundamental. In the first place, both relationships exist on the margins of their respective social orders. The man and the animal, in their association, are "outcasts together" (338)—the relationship of Dahfu and Atti is actively opposed and openly disapproved, while Henderson and Smolak, high on the careening roller coaster, are united in terror while "the Canadian hicks were rejoicing underneath with red faces" (339). The meaningful unions are consummated, the saving lessons communicated, in despised and dangerous spaces outside convention's pale. The quest takes the hero *away*, not only geographically, spatially, but also socially.

Another shared quality is even more fundamental. Henderson, as his narration reaches its close, interrupts his account of Smolak for a general statement that applies as well to Dahfu and Atti, and to his own relationships to Dahfu, to Lily, and to Romilayu: "Once more. Whatever gains I ever made were always due to love and nothing else" (339). It is clear, to begin again with Smolak, that man and bear felt a love for one another. They were, says Henderson, "very close" (338). On their frightening roller-coaster rides they "hugged each other . . . with something greater than terror": **91**

> I shut my eyes in his wretched, time-abused fur. He held me in
> his arms and gave me comfort. And the great thing is that he
> didn't blame me. He had seen too much of life, and some-
> where in his huge head he had worked it out that for creatures
> there is nothing that ever runs unmingled. (339)

Similar proclamations of love are found throughout the novel. Just after his ascent to the Sungo position, Henderson is nearly overcome by affection for Dahfu: "I was grateful to him. I was his friend, then. In fact, at this moment, I loved the guy" (193). Later, noting the evident feeling of Atti for Dahfu, Henderson puts his observations into much the same words: "On her own animal level it was clear beyond any need of interpretation that she loved the guy. Loved him! With animal love. I loved him too" (227). Finally, he is no less explicit about Dahfu's reciprocal love for Atti: "He fell in love with his lioness at first sight—coup de foudre" (258).

The lessons, then, are many. Both animals live fully in their own condition. As Atti does not "take issue with the inherent," so Smolak endures his own situation, and does not blame Henderson. Both, like Dahfu trapped in his problematic kingship, accept the paradoxical being that is forever a becoming, the creaturely life mixed in bizarre fashion of states given and states made. And finally, most important, every fruitful association is rooted in love.

The novel closes with Henderson's return. He calls his wife, hears her voice, "speaking about love" (332), boards and exits various planes in Khartoum, Athens, Rome, Paris, and London, acquires a Persian child headed for Nevada, and ends his account (appropriately) in Newfoundland. While the plane refuels, the renewed Sungo on the lam circles it again and again at a gallop, carrying the child in his arms. The cold, bracing air is "a remedy," and the child is "medicine applied" (340). Even the stilled propellers are beautiful, to his newly appreciative eye. New morning, Newfoundland, New World, Thanksgiving just ahead—a full-bore Adamic ending. No matter that the plans for medical school seem as wacky as ever (and must in any event be postponed "until next semester" [334], given the November return), that the man happily running in circles in Newfoundland remains in many ways similar to the Henderson who seemed to Dahfu to "rush through the world too hard"(188). What is new is the attitude, the buoyant happiness, the stilling of the querulous voice.

The closing scene, on close examination, is a remarkably precise replaying of the carnival episode from long ago, the remembering of which Henderson counts as "a great favor" (336). Henderson in Newfoundland has taken the place of Smolak in Ontario. He holds the Persian child as he was himself held by the bear, hugging him "close to my chest" (340) just as before Smolak "held me in his arms and gave me comfort" (339). Man and child now circle the parked plane while "Dark faces were looking from within" (341), just as man and bear once revolved on the roller coaster "while the Canadian hicks were rejoicing underneath with red faces" (339). Outside conventional restraints, isolated in their union and united by love, orbiting in motion about stilled others, restless man, abused animal, and orphan child work a mutual solace and redemption. Lessons of the lion, lessons of the bear, all gains "due to love and nothing else" (339)—a simple regimen, it would seem, but in the full light of its apprehension prayers for rain are answered, the restless traveler turns toward home, long night's journey reaches day.

# Notes

1. Saul Bellow, *Henderson the Rain King* (New York: Viking, 1959), 3. Subsequent references are noted in the text. Although I made no extensive use of prior scholarship in preparing this article, I did read much of it, and found Kathleen King's "Bellow the Allegory King: Animal Imagery in *Henderson the Rain King*," *Saul Bellow Journal* 7 (1988): 44–50, and Michael Bellamy's "Bellow's More-or-Less Human Bestiaries: *Augie March* and *Henderson the Rain King*," *Ball State University Forum* 23 (1982): 12–22 especially rewarding. Ted Billy's "The Road of Excess: Saul Bellow's *Henderson the Rain King*," *Saul Bellow Journal* 3 (1983): 8–17 centers on concerns different from mine (Bellow's use of Blake) but is nevertheless a pertinent and unusually convincing study. I am grateful to my former student Rhett Stephens for bibliographic searches undertaken on my behalf.

2. Saul Bellow, *The Adventures of Augie March* (New York: Viking, 1953), 503.

3. Saul Bellow, *The Dean's December* (New York: Harper & Row, 1982), 283.

4. Saul Bellow, *Herzog* (New York: Viking, 1964), 30.

5. Bellow, *Augie March*, 478.

6. Saul Bellow, *Seize the Day* (New York: Viking, 1956), 69.

7. Bellow, *Augie March*, 493, 494.

8. Saul Bellow, *Humboldt's Gift* (New York: Viking, 1975), 396.

9. Saul Bellow, *More Die of Heartbreak* (New York: William Morrow, 1987), 22.

10. Bellow, *Augie March*, p. 363; Bellow, *Humboldt's Gift*, 81.

11. Bellow, *Dean's December*, 294.

12. Ibid., 266.

13. Here, at the introduction of bears, two points might be added. One, more general, is that bears have a prominent and widespread mythological presence. Ainu *kamui*, Korean Tangun, Hindu Jambhavan, Finnish *karhulaulunäytelmä* just start the list. Elisha is violently served by bears (2 Kings 2:23–24); Marian Engels's *Bear* (1976) is a marvelous and mythically resonant novel. No claim of "influence" is advanced,

of course, beyond the obvious observation that Bellow is a widely read man. Second, more specific, is that bears appear in other Bellow novels: Herzog shrinks from appearing as a "tame bear" at Easthampton parties (*Herzog*, 23), Asa Leventhal, in *The Victim*, frets about being shut up like "a bear in a winter hole" (Saul Bellow, *The Victim* [New York: Vanguard, 1947], 98), and Maurice Venice, studying Tommy Wilhelm's screen test, notes his "bearlike" walk (*Seize the Day*, 23).

14. Saul Bellow, *Mr. Sammler's Planet* (New York: Viking, 1970), 11–12.

# Hawthorne's "Mad, Merry Stream of Human Life"

## *The Roman Carnival as Apocalypse in* The Marble Faun

The Roman Carnival that Hawthorne wrote about in his letters **95** and Italian notebooks of 1858 and 1859 and used strategically as the climactic scene in his last completed novel, *The Marble Faun* (1860), boasts a storied and colorful past.

The origins of the famous Carnival at Rome associated with pre-Lenten activities were in the pagan rites of the pre-Christian era. From early times pagan communities in Babylonia, Egypt, Greece, Rome, and perhaps others unrecorded, staged "parades, masquerades, pageants, and other forms of revelry" whose origins lay in fertility rites associated with the arrival of spring and the rebirth of vegetation.¹ Early examples of such festivals were celebrations of Osiris in Egypt and of Dionysus in the Athens of the sixth century B.C., the latter of which, as historical record reveals, saw the first use of floats for spring festivals.² During the era of the Roman Empire, the main carnivals in Rome, whose origins were folk celebrations and the Greek Mysteries of Dionysis, were the Bacchanalia, honoring the god of wine and revelry; the Saturnalia, in honor of the god of agriculture; and the Lupercalia, a festival of fertility rites held to celebrate the pastoral god Lupercus.

Since all of these carnivals were the outgrowth of folk and pagan traditions, when Christianity gained a foothold in the

Roman Empire, the Catholic church was powerless to stop them and ultimately had to adopt them, especially the Saturnalia, as part of Christian religious celebrations, albeit in reformed modes. Immediate church
influence was seen in the Feast of Fools, which included a mock mass,
and the Feast of the Ass, which "retained pagan rites and was at times
very bawdy."³ Gradually, however, the church's influence overtook many
of the Carnival proceedings, and they were transformed into a single extended celebration closely associated with Lent, the eight-day celebration beginning the Tuesday before Shrove (or Fat) Tuesday and concluding on that notable day before Lent itself began. In fact, the word
*carnival* itself possibly derives from Medieval Latin *carnem levare* or *car-
nelevarium* (*caro* meaning flesh and *levare* to put aside), thus referring to
abstinence from meat during the forty days of the Christian Lenten season each year.⁴

**96**

During medieval times the church so controlled the Roman Carnival
that it lost much of its festive flavor, but fifteenth-century Renaissance
Rome saw the return of carnival "high-jinks and horrors of ancient
times."⁵ Pietro Barbo, or Pope Paul II (1464–71), took such delight in the
celebration that he set up horse races and other varieties of races in the
spirit of good, clean fun: races for children, young Christians, middle-
aged men, senior citizens, buffaloes, and donkeys. These races, or *corsi*,
extended from the pope's Palazzo Venezia at the south end and proceeded north along the city section of the Via Flaminia, which in time
assumed the name Via del Corso. The Corso is the longest and straightest street in old Rome, extending about a mile from the Palazzo Venezia
to the Piazza del Popolo; thus despite its narrowness, it was most suited
to the prolonged races. As the festival continued over the years, however,
Pope Paul II allowed the races to degenerate into what Sir Rennell Rodd
calls "unseemly contests" that included races by hunchbacks and other
disabled persons, Jews (who were tormented by the crowd along the
route), and naked old men—all of whom were pursued by mounted
troopers. In later years the horse races became riderless.⁶

After the Renaissance, the Carnival began to decline in magnitude
and deviltry. It was only up to the time of the mid-seventeenth century,
Mikhail Bakhtin observes, that people "were *direct participants* in carni-

valistic acts and in a carnival sense of the world."[7] As the city of Rome expanded, rowdiness prevailed to the extent that it grew "impossible any longer to abandon the main thoroughfare of the capital city to a week of misrule."[8] As we know from Hawthorne's remarks in 1858–59, the Carnival was long past its prime then, and it continued to decline until by the beginning of the twentieth century it hardly resembled its storied past. Present-day remnants exist mainly on Shrove Tuesday, which is the day carnival-goers in costume flock to the city's piazzas as part of pre-Lenten activities.

Along with Hawthorne's extensive commentary on the Carnival in the late 1850s, other writers have recorded their observations of the spectacle. John Evelyn, while in Rome in the winter and spring of 1645, took in the "impertinences" of the Carnival, finding the area "swarming with whores, buffoones & all manner of rabble."[9] Goethe, who lived along the Corso from November 1786 to April 1788, comments extensively on the Carnival in his *Italian Journey* of 1788. He lambastes the Carnival for its inability to "make an altogether agreeable impression: it will neither please . . . [the] eye nor appeal to . . . emotions"; moreover, "the noise is deafening, and the end of each day unsatisfactory."[10] Closer to Hawthorne's time, and reacting much less negatively to the event, Charles Dickens describes the Carnival in *Pictures from Italy* (1846), focusing on the "bewitching madness" of the costumes and painting a graphic picture of the balconies on almost every house decked out as viewing boxes for the parade—the balconies so haphazard in their architectural placement that, Dickens says, "if year after year, and season after season, it had rained balconies, hailed balconies, snowed balconies, blown balconies, they could scarcely have come into existence in a more disorderly manner."[11]

Shortly after Hawthorne's Italian sojourn, in 1873, Henry James witnessed the Carnival and, in *Italian Hours,* discusses it more in a political context. He states that the Carnival was a more joyous occasion before the recent political unification of Italy.[12] "The fashion of public revelry has woefully fallen out of step. . . . Now that Italy is made the Carnival is unmade."[13] He says that a traveler, once used to the fully papal Rome and returning now, "must have immediately noticed that something momentous had happened—something hostile to the elements of picture and color and style" (136–37). The Carnival scene, in a Corso always well trafficked but now "a perpetual crush" (137), is not pretty—it's "degenerated" (139): the women wear ugly masks of wire, and flour and lime shower down on celebrants and bystanders alike, tossed by people on the balconies above. James himself experienced the dumping of a "half a bushel of flour on my too-philosophic head" (139). Leaving the scene and attempting to skirt around the perimeter of Rome to avoid the Corso, "his ears full of flour," he discovers that "do what you will you can't really elude the Carnival" (139–40). James concludes that "the Carnival had received its death-blow in my imagination" (139).

Generally sharing James's views some thirty-five years later, William Dean Howells witnessed the Carnival in 1908 in its twilight years. He remarks, "It was the eve of the last sad day of such shrunken and faded carnival as is still left to Rome," and notices a few children in holiday costumes and young girls in a cab "safely masked against identification and venting in the sense of wild escape, the joyous spirits kept in restraint all the rest of the year."[14]

Francis Wey describes the Carnival of the 1880s in detail, including the political background of recent events when Rome was annexed to the rest of Italy. His depiction of the scene in the Corso, with "hailstones of plaster" pelting the revelers, is vivid. He echoes James's lime- and flour-covered image, and his elaborate description of the gaiety, especially on Shrove Tuesday, is one of the most detailed in print. In a meaningful comment that embraces to some degree the feelings of both Hawthorne and Kenyon in *The Marble Faun*, and more certainly the philosophy of Carnival voiced by Mikhail Bakhtin, Wey concludes, "If you were alone, you would lose your sense of isolation, for everybody accosts you, and, making merry with you or at you, offers himself as a butt for your whims."[15]

Finally, Sir Rennell Rodd in *Rome of the Renaissance and Today* (1932) describes the Carnival of the 1870s as follows: "All the Balconies were draped and filled with merry companies. Elaborately decorated cars with allegorical groups and carriages filled with masqueraders drove up and down in continuous procession." Everyone in the streets was costumed, "and the prudent provided themselves with wire masks because not only were flowers and sweetmeats thrown from the balconies, but a lively battle was maintained with little pellets of lime-whitened clay about the size of a pen, called coriandoli, which gave a stinging blow on the face." At the end of the week of revelry, "everyone lighted a taper and the whole length of the Corso glittered with little flames. The revel continued till midnight. Then the church bells rang. The sound of merriment died away. It was Lent, and weeks of abstinence and penitence ensued."[16]

Following his service as U.S. consul to Liverpool, England, Nathaniel Hawthorne and Sophia, their three children, and governess Ada Shepard visited France briefly and then traveled on to Italy, where they were to live for a total of seventeen months. They resided in Rome from January to June 1858, in Florence from June to October, then back in Rome **99** for a second sojourn that extended from October until May of 1859. Thus Hawthorne was in Rome during two of the annual pre-Lenten Carnivals, and he availed himself of both of them.

In keeping with his ambivalent feelings about Rome in general, Hawthorne unsurprisingly developed a like-dislike attitude toward the Carnival, as reflected in his letters, notebooks, and *The Marble Faun* itself. His negative reaction to the first Carnival he witnessed, in 1858, was caused in large part, it seems, by the wet, gloomy weather that held for the duration of the celebration.[17] On February 9, 1858, Hawthorne comments in his notebooks on the preparation for the Carnival, noting "bouquets . . . bounteously for sale, in the shops and at the street corners . . . and reservoirs of ammunition in the shape of sugar-plums and little pellets of paste or chalk." But he questions "whether the Romans themselves take any great interest in the Carnival: The balconies along the Corso are almost entirely taken by English, Americans, or other foreigners."[18] A few days later (February 13, 1858) he writes a long, detailed description of the Carnival and all its trappings. He records being hit in the eye with a sugarplum "made up of lime—or bad flour at best—with oats or worthless seeds as a nucleus" (64). Disappointed with the whole affair, he comments dispiritedly that the Carnival has simply grown old and tiresome and seems to appeal more to foreigners (especially Americans and the

British) than to Italians themselves. He notes that the Roman bystanders were not even smiling and appeared to be having anything but a good time. He quips, "The whole affair is not worth this page or two," concluding, "I never in my life knew a shallower joke than the Carnival of Rome" (70).

The next day, February 14, 1858, he takes younger daughter Rose with him along the fringes of the Carnival vicinity up on the Pincian Hill's "safe heights" above the Piazza del Popolo, where they watch the festivities before descending to the Corso. He sees revelers arrested for throwing lime at will and observes that the jollity of the Carnival "does not extend an inch beyond the line of the Corso," where it "flows along in a narrow stream." Beyond that one sees "nothing but the ordinary Roman gravity" (76). The day following, February 15, he notes that several people were killed in the Corso, either trampled by the racing horses or by the dragoons clearing the racecourse (78–79). Two days later, on the last afternoon and evening of the Carnival, he and Rose again attend the festivities together and stand at the edge of the crowd, while Sophia, Una, and Julian occupy a hired balcony above the Corso. In the midst of showers of falling confetti, Rose catches a bouquet while Hawthorne is hit with a cabbage-like object, undoubtedly informing his comment in the *Notebooks* that the Carnival is most enjoyed by those under twenty (83). However unimpressed is he with the event, however, he nevertheless muses over the possibility that "I could make quite a brilliant sketch of it, without widely departing from truth" (83).

Interestingly, the next year, 1859, after his several months in Florence, Hawthorne's reactions to the Carnival are much more sanguine.[19] Describing preparations for the Carnival on February 27, he remarks in his notebook about the bright sunshine as opposed to the rain and gloom of the previous year. After enumerating all the necessary supplies for the Carnival that fill the shops (especially the "masks of wire, pasteboard, silk, or cloth, some of beautiful features, others hideous; fantastic, currish, asinine, huge-nosed, or otherwise monstrous" (496–97), he concedes, getting caught up in the spirit of it all, "I could have bandied confetti and nosegays as readily and riotously as any urchin there. But my black hat and grave Talma would have been too good a mark for the combatants" (499). A few days later, March 4, in a letter to his publisher William D. Ticknor, he writes with surprising levity: "We are now in the height of the Carnival, and the young people find it great fun. To say the Truth, so do I; but I suppose I should have enjoyed it still better at twenty."[20] In the remaining days of the 1859 Carnival he records in his *Notebooks* that he enjoys the festivities "better . . . than could have been expected" and witnesses the events "principally in the street, as a mere looker-on (which does not let one into the mystery of the fun) and twice from the balcony whence I threw confetti and partly understood why the young people like it so much" (499). Yet he is also puzzled by something elusive about the spirit and gist of the Carnival—something about its mystery: when he tries to isolate and focus on any one humorous masquerader for detailed description and comment, the figure tends to slip out of his hands and vanish; still, he remarks that "there really was fun in **101** the spectacle as it flitted by" (500).

In a similar observation, when he and Una attend the next day, March 8, and sit in Mrs. (Mary Elizabeth Benjamin) Motley's balcony in the Corso, he writes that the passing "spectacle is strangely like a dream, in respect to the difficulty of retaining it in the mind and solidifying it into a description" (501). But he still enjoys it enough that he does his part "to pelt all the people in cylinder hats with handfulls of confetti" (501). He is also complimentary of the behavior of the throng, as opposed to the unruly way similar crowds would act in England or America. He marvels at "how people can let loose all their mirthful propensities without unchaining their mischievous ones" (502).

On the closing day of the 1859 festival, after eight "playdays," as he designates them, Hawthorne again observes the celebration from both the street level and Mrs. Motley's balcony. Standing on the street among the crowd, he takes pains to describe the lower-class bystanders around him: the women, "generally broad and sturdy figures," wearing large silver or steel bodkins in their hair (503). This last day, ominously, is sunless, rendering the costumes and decorations drab and shabby looking. Yet Hawthorne's appraisal of the event remains positive: it might appear a depressing spectacle to the bystander, but even if one should take "the slightest share in it, you become aware that it has a fascination" (503–4).

He then describes in detail the closing ritual of the last night—the "Mocollo"—as the revelers crowd the Corso with lighted tapers, or Roman candles, in hand shouting, "Senza Moccolo," and the participants try hard to extinguish the candles of those around them.[21] As the lights flicker and die, gaslights, which Hawthorne refers to as the "fixed stars" of the "transitory splendors of human life," are illuminated and over-power the scattered mocolli (504). So the Carnival ends, with Hawthorne curiously admitting that he is "glad that it is over" (504). His journal entry on the next morning reads, ironically, "but, to-day, we have waked up in the sad and sober season of Lent" (505).

Carnival, then, was a phenomenon that played on Hawthorne's mind and creative imagination while he was in Italy, as indeed it did over his entire career as a writer. We recall the carnivalized revelers in "The May-Pole of Merrymount," the unruly spectacle of the "parade" that rides Major Molineaux out of town to waves of raucous laughter in "My Kins-man, Major Molineaux," the boisterous, grotesque Black Sabbath cele-bration in "Young Goodman Brown," the joyous political parade passing along Pyncheon Street under the arched window in *The House of the Seven Gables,* the colorful election day festivities in *The Scarlet Letter,* and the pastoral frolics of the main characters in the bucolic fields of Blithedale Farm in *The Blithedale Romance*—all instances of what Nina Baym refers to as the "Walpurgisnacht" scenes that appear throughout Hawthorne's fiction.[22]

It was thus out of an act of self-effacement or calculated understate-ment that Hawthorne wrote to his publisher and friend James T. Fields from Leamington on February 11, 1860, "received your letter from Flo-rence, and conclude that you are now in Rome, and probably enjoying the Carnival—a *tame* description of which, by the by, I have introduced into my Romance."[23] Hawthorne's denoting the Carnival scenes of *The Marble Faun* a "tame" description, of course, has to be taken with a grain of salt, for chapters 48 and 49, "A Scene in the Corso," and "A Frolic of the Carnival," are the key climactic chapters of the novel in which we discern the fates of all four major characters: the two Americans, Kenyon and Hilda, and the two Italians, Donatello and Miriam. Further, there are significant foreshadowings of the Carnival chapters in the novel, episodes in which the main characters are caught up in rare displays of joy and abandon in this otherwise dark tale.

Such instances include three chapters early in the novel and two just before the Carnival scene. Chapters 8, "The Suburban Villa," 9, "The Faun and Nymph," and 10, "The Sylvan Dance," all take place in the woods of the Villa Borghese and depict Donatello and Miriam caught up in lighthearted frolicking and sporting repartee until, in the midst of their mirthful sylvan dance, Miriam is suddenly confronted by the sinister figure of the model. Then late in the book, just before the Carnival episode, chapters 46 and 47 depict Kenyon's pleasant stroll on the Campagna and an unexpected happy encounter with Miriam and Donatello, both of whom are already dressed in costume for the Carnival: Donatello as a young peasant in "short blue jacket, the small-clothes buttoned at the **103** knee, and buckled shoes" and Miriam "in one of those brilliant costumes, largely kindled up with scarlet, and decorated with gold embroidery, in which the contadinas array themselves on feast-days."[24] It is a significant scene in which Kenyon finds the fragmented statue of the Venus figure that Miriam and Donatello had discovered two days earlier. In a fleeting moment, before the weight of Miriam's and Donatello's fates settles on them oppressively, Miriam exhorts, "Ah, Donatello, let us live a little longer the life of these last few days! It is so bright, so airy, so childlike, so without either past or future! Here, on the wild Campagna, you seem to have found, both for yourself and me, the life that belonged to you in early youth; the sweet, irresponsible life which you inherited from your mythic ancestry, the Fauns of Monte Beni. Our stern and black reality will come upon us speedily enough. But, first, a brief time more of this strange happiness!" (428).

For the last time, it appears to Kenyon that Donatello has regained "some of the sweet and delightful characteristics of the antique Faun. . . . There were slight, careless graces, pleasant and simple peculiarities, that had been obliterated by the heavy grief" incurred by hurtling the model to his death off the Tarpeian Rock, with Miriam's tacit consent (433–34). This scene on the Campagna, of course, with its lighthearted yet soon chastened emotions directly presages the Carnival scene, which follows

immediately. And it is here that Miriam instructs Kenyon how to become reunited with Hilda, who has been ominously missing for several
days (and we know is being held for questioning by authorities about the
murder of the model/monk). Miriam advises Kenyon, "The day after to-
morrow . . . an hour before sunset, go to the Corso, and stand in front of
the fifth house on your left, beyond the Antonine Column. You will learn
tidings of a friend!" (435). And then the "happy . . . flitting moment" on
the Campagna passes and Miriam and Donatello—momentarily having
been "sylvan Faun" and "Nymph of grove or fountain"— depart, a "re-
morseful Man and Woman, linked by a marriage-bond of crime," setting
forth "towards an inevitable goal" (435).

Thus many elements of *The Marble Faun* lead into chapters 48–49, set
during the Carnival itself. On the appointed day during the celebration,
Kenyon shows up on the Corso an hour earlier than Miriam instructed,
hoping to find Hilda. He discovers the "merriment of this famous festival . . . in full progress." The Corso "was peopled with hundreds of fantastic shapes, some of which probably represented the mirth of ancient
times, surviving through all manner of calamity, ever since the days of the
Roman Empire. For a few afternoons of early Spring, this mouldy gayety
strays into the sunshine; all the remainder of the year, it seems to be shut
up in the catacombs or some other sepulchral store-house of the past"
(436).

Briefly, what happens in these two chapters, "A Scene in the Corso"
and "A Frolic of the Carnival," is that Kenyon becomes caught up in the
throng of revelers and all the trappings of the festival as he awaits sight
of Hilda. In contrast to his state of anxiety and melancholy, the scene
about him is resplendent with gay colors and beautiful flowers and other
decorations. Hawthorne tells us that had Kenyon been of lighter mood
and able to see it all with his "clear, natural eye-sight, he might have
found both merriment and splendour in it" (438). Bushel baskets of bouquets were for sale at every street corner, the Corso itself a "spectacle . . .
picturesque" as from every window and many balconies along "that noble
street, stretching into the interminable distance" hung "gay and gorgeous

carpets, bright silks, scarlet cloths with rich golden fringes, and Gobelin tapestry, still lustrous with varied hues" (438), and in every window were "the faces of women, rosy girls, and children, all kindled into brisk and mirthful expression by the incidents in the street below" (439). Fake sugar plums of lime and oat kernel were thrown up from the streets and sometimes down from the balconies, while "a gentler warfare of flowers was carried on, principally between knights and ladies." These bouquets, we are told, in former times were pretty and fresh; however, the present nosegays, hastily bundled by "sordid hands," are made up chiefly of ordinary flowers. Further, the current-day flowers are recycled, being picked up out of the streets wilted and muddy and quickly resold, "defiled as they all are with the wicked filth of Rome" (440). Originally gathered by young people out of the nearby fields or their own gardens, they were "flung . . . with true aim, at the one, or few, whom they regarded with a sentiment of shy partiality at least, if not with love. . . . What more appropriate mode of suggesting her tender secret could a maiden find than by the soft hit of a rosebud against a young man's cheek" (440).

 While waiting and watching amid the hurly-burly of the day, Kenyon catches sight of Miriam and Donatello, in their costumes worn on the Campagna, but this time each with face concealed behind "an impenetrable black mask" (443). Shortly afterward, the two figures, hand in hand, reappear out of the crowd and all three clasp hands momentarily in forming an ephemeral "linked circle of three" before they part, uttering "Farewell" in unison (448). Donatello and Miriam are almost immediately detained by Roman officials, and at the same time, symbolically, Kenyon is hit by two missiles—a cauliflower, "flung by a young man from a passing carriage" (451), and a rose-bud "so fresh that it seemed that moment gathered" tossed by Hilda, dressed all in white domino, from a balcony occupied by an English family. Hilda smiles down on Kenyon with "a gleam of delicate mirthfulness in her eyes," which Kenyon "had seen there only two or three times, in the course of their acquaintance, but thought it the most bewitching and fairy-like of all Hilda's expressions" (451). That night, Hilda returns to her quarters in her "Virgin's shrine," relights the lamp that had been extinguished during her absence and now which "burned as brightly" as if it had never been cold, and the next morning is greeted by the one faithful dove that had not deserted her ethereal mistress during her absence (454). The Carnival scene, in short, is one of joy and gloom, as Rita Gollin has observed: "The moment of Donatello's arrest is the moment Hilda is released from confinement."[25]

When approaching the meaning of these two chapters that constitute the crucial Carnival scene in the novel, it is fruitful to look closely first at the language that Hawthorne uses in describing the dynamic of the Carnival.[26] His phrases are very telling, many of them reflecting on Kenyon's mixed attitude toward the festivities occurring all around him. Hawthorne writes of the "merriment of this famous festival" (436) in which some of the "fantastic shapes represented the mirth of ancient times" (436). The present Carnival, however, exudes a "mouldy gayety" and is an institution of mere "shallow influence" with "flagging mirth," a "worn-out festival" (436–37). It is a "grotesque and airy riot" (437) to be enjoyed by youth, but to Kenyon it seems but "the emptiest of mockeries" (437). It is "a spectacle . . . fantastic and extravagant" (441), a "wild frolic" (451), "the tumult of life" (453), "a crowd of masquers rioting" (453), and an "obtrusive uproar" (454). The engulfing water images are especially pertinent to Kenyon's character and immediate situation: the Carnival is a "mad, merry stream of human life" (439), "a tempestuous sea," as the crowd sweeps over the spot where Kenyon, Donatello, and Miriam hurriedly exchanged their few parting words—(448), a "turbulent stream of wayfarers" (448), a "whirlpool of nonsense" (450), and an "eddying throng" (450). The Carnival, then, is as a stream or confluence of forces that threatened to engulf Kenyon but appear to divide and flow around him rather than pull him into their vortex. Kenyon is only partially the "active participant" that Bakhtin identifies as essential to the nature of carnival.[27]

Much of the Carnival scene is imbued with a surrealistic aura, as Kenyon, described by Udo Natterman as a "sullen outsider in the Carnival,"[28] with his dark mood and what Hawthorne describes as a "troubled face" (445), is accosted by the swarming revelers. The irony and juxtaposition of the conflicting images is striking. We are told:

Fantastic figures, with bulbous heads, the circumference of a bushel, grinned enormously in his face. Harlequins struck him with their wooden swords, and appeared to expect his immediate transformation into some jollier shape. A little, long-tailed, horned fiend sidled up to him, and suddenly blew at him through a tube, enveloping our poor friend in a whole harvest of winged seeds. A biped, with an ass's snout, brayed close to his ear, ending his discordant uproar with a peal of human laughter. Five strapping damsels (so, at least, their petticoats bespoke them, in spite of an awful freedom in the flourish of their legs) joined hands and danced around him, inviting him by their gestures to perform a horn-pipe in the midst. Released from these gay persecutors, a clown in motley rapped him on the back with a blown bladder, in which a **107** handful of dried peas rattled horribly. (445)

As if there were not sufficient harassment, Kenyon finds that his "merry martyrdom was not half over":

There came along a gigantic female figure, seven feet high, at least, and taking up a third of the street's breadth with the preposterously swelling sphere of her crinoline skirts. Singling out the sculptor, she began to make a ponderous assault upon his heart, throwing amorous glances at him out of her great, goggle-eyes, offering him a vast bouquet of sunflowers and nettles, and soliciting his pity by all sorts of pathetic and passionate dumb-show. Her suit meeting no favour, the rejected Titaness made a gesture of despair and rage; then suddenly drawing a huge pistol, she took aim right at the obdurate sculptor's breast, and pulled the trigger. The shot took effect, (for the abominable plaything went off by a spring, like a boy's pop-gun,) covering Kenyon with a cloud of lime-dust, under shelter of which the revengeful damsel strode away.

Hereupon, a whole host of absurd figures surrounded him, pretending to sympathize in his mishap. Clowns and parti-colored harlequins; orang-outans; bear-headed, bull-headed, and dog-headed individuals; faces that would have been human, but for their enormous noses; one terrific creature with a visage right in the center of his breast; and all other imaginable kinds of monstrosity and exaggeration. These apparitions appeared to be investigating the case, after the fashion of a coroner's jury, poking their pasteboard countenances close to the sculptor's, with an unchangeable grin that gave still more ludicrous effect to the comic alarm and horrour of their gestures. Just then, a figure came by, in a gray wig and rusty gown, with an ink-horn at his button-hole, and a pen behind his ear; he announced himself as a notary, and offered to make the last will and testament of the assassinated man. This solemn duty, however, was interrupted by a surgeon, who brandished a lancet, three feet long, and proposed to him to let him blood. (446)

The phantasmagoric scene is not unlike scenarios found in modern and postmodern writers such as Franz Kafka, Kurt Vonnegut, Robert Coover, Donald Barthelme, and John Barth, especially in contrasting the joyous masquerading to Kenyon's soul-struck despair and disjointed presence from the whole mad scene. "The affair was so like a feverish dream," we are told, that "Kenyon resigned himself to let it take its course" (446). Earlier, before Kenyon had been personally bombarded, the scene of the "spectacle so fantastic and extravagant" is said to affect him "like a thin dream, through the dim, extravagant material of which he could discern more substantial objects, while too much under its control to start forth broad awake" (441–42). Kenyon is also said to react with "dreamy eyes" to the "riotous interchange of nosegays and confetti . . . while the procession passed" (443). Gollin has already perceptively identified and explained the dreamlike nature of Kenyon's experience. She writes that more "explicitly dream-like" than the earlier "sylvan dance" scenes of chapter 9, the Carnival scene "is a trope for the dance of life."[29] Gollin also observes that throughout the novel "dreams define the way characters respond to experiences and the way they appear to others.

Miriam, Donatello, and the model all appear to be as strange and ambiguous as dream phantoms that go through metamorphoses yet remain
recognizable." Kenyon's getting struck by the cauliflower, Gollin avers,
"suggests [his] summons by mundane reality, and the rosebud his opportunity for love."[30]

Does the Carnival process hold out any hope for Kenyon?[31] Many
scholars think not. Baym refers to "the end of Kenyon's feverish season
in purgatory." Reading *The Marble Faun* as an "elegy for art," she interprets the ending as "a gesture of heartsickness and despair, of hopes denied, effort repudiated. The novel is like the Venus statue that three of
the main characters discover in the Campagna, "created by Hawthorne's
imagination, then discolored, disfigured, and shattered by his prudence,
his conscience, his fatigue, his sense of futility."[32] Natterman dwells on
Kenyon's (and Hilda's) inability to adapt to the foreign environment,
commenting that for both of the American characters there is the reality of the "slightly hostile quality of the foreign environment"; fittingly,
at the Carnival "Kenyon is symbolically shot with lime dust and hit by a
cauliflower used as a missile."[33] Gollin is one of the few who is less pes-
simistic in her interpretation, concluding that in Hilda's presence, despite
the noise and confusion of the Carnival, Kenyon finds his "perplexing
dream is dispelled."[34] But if we reflect on *The Marble Faun* in the mode
of carnivalized literature, as defined and articulated by Mikhail Bakhtin,
Hawthorne does indeed (as in Gollin's reading) imply some hope. To
Bakhtin the basic elements of carnivalized experience as reflected in novels informed by that tradition are that everyone participates in the carnival act, normal laws, prohibitions, and restrictions are suspended, and "a
free and familiar attitude spreads over everything."[35] Moreover, as is evident in the distorted, costumed figures milling along the Corso in *The
Marble Faun*, Bakhtin emphasizes the role of ambivalent images in carnivalized literature: there are dualities, polar opposites, paired images,
opposites, everything seemingly in reverse appearance and order (126), all
of which prompt him to observe that because "a carnivalistic" life is "life
drawn out of its *usual* rut, it is to some degree 'life turned inside out,' 'the
reverse side of the world'" (122). Marty Roth amplifies Bakhtin's statement by observing that "the distinctive markers of carnivalesque art are

less likely to be intoxication and drunkenness than the trope of the world upside down, destructive laughter, feasting, or the image of the grotesque body."[36] Indeed, except for the feasting, these traits certainly characterize the Carnival scene in *The Marble Faun*.

This is not to say, however, that *The Marble Faun* as a whole is what Bakhtin categorizes as "carnivalized literature." For one thing, while the world of the Roman Carnival is one of dualities, opposites, and reversal of mores and norms, the same does not fully apply to life outside the frame of this annual revelry. Hawthorne, in contrast to Bakhtin, does not advocate a topsy-turvy world order that overturns the accepted "official" values system, or else we would find Kenyon giving himself wholeheartedly to his pursuit of art rather than yielding to Hilda's influence and the comforts of the hearth. Another major feature of Bakhtinian carnival is not so evident in Hawthorne's novel either—or at best is only selectively applicable in what occurs. Bakhtin speaks of carnivalized literature, through the inversions mentioned above, as evoking a dialogized rather than a monologized dynamic. In his view, "All *distance* between people is suspended, and a special carnival category goes into effect: *free and familiar contact among people*. This is a very important aspect of a carnival sense of the world. People who in life are separated by impenetrable hierarchical barriers enter into free familiar contact on the carnival square."[37] The differences between Bakhtin and Hawthorne are, of course, obvious. What Bakhtin describes may be true of Rabelais's as well as Dostoevsky's works, the two writers about whom Bakhtin has mainly written and holds up as examples of carnivalization, but it does not ring true of Hawthorne in the overall context of his fiction despite certain carnivalized scenes and episodes scattered throughout his works. Again, we think of the scene Hawthorne describes in his *Notebooks* of standing on the pavement of the Corso among the working-class people, whom he describes in restrained uncomplimentary terms: the dowdy women with "generally broad and sturdy figures."[38] This is not to insist that there is no measure of "togetherness" in *The Marble Faun*. Carnival does suggest influences that can be lasting. Miriam and Donatello are caught up together in what Norris Yates describes as the "wild Bacchic dance of the Carnival,"[39] but it is a tragic dance after all. And Kenyon is drawn into the melee whether he desires it or not and refuses to give himself over to it wholeheartedly.[40] Whereas Bakhtin's idea of carnival is one of exhilarating, liberating experience, Hawthorne's "American Carnival," as Roth astutely points out, "usually has dark and forbidding features."[41] Further, it offers no true, lasting alternative for monologism. As Roth says, "One condition of Carnival is a release of oceanic feeling, a suspension of the sense of self."[42] In the carnival of Hawthorne's novel we see Kenyon momentarily "linked" to a "circle of three" (448) with Donatello and Miriam; he is so passive overall in the midst of this "mad, merry stream of life" (439) that he simply "resign[s] himself" to "let it take its course" (446). The "eddying throng of the Corso" (450), the "whirlpool of nonsense" (450), the "tempestuous sea," the "turbulent stream of wayfarers" (448) may engulf almost everyone in their way, including Dontello and Miriam and even in a sense Hilda, who appears in her white domino **111** costume on the balcony above Kenyon "full of tender joy" and with "a gleam of delicate mirthfulness in her eyes" (451). Meaningfully, Hawthorne writes of Hilda, "That soft, mirthful smile," which Kenyon had seen only two or three times since he has known her, "caused her to melt, as it were, into the wild frolic of the Carnival, and become not so strange and alien to the scene, as her unexpected apparition must otherwise have made her" (451). But not so the "distant," dreamy-eyed Kenyon standing below, who largely eludes immersion in the scene.

As Roth emphasizes, however, "Carnival is unthinkable without mood alteration,[43] and although Kenyon's mood remains unaltered until the end of the scene, when he is hit by Hilda's rose, it is obviously changed at that juncture and appears to be sustained, as we see a few days later, when he jests to Hilda about a tabby cat lying on an altar in the Pantheon assuming that she is "an object of worship" (458). The "anxious and unquiet spectator" of a "darker mood," with the "sad and contracted brow" and "troubled face," is released from his doldrums by the appearance of the carnivalistic figure of Hilda clad in white domino. And while in chapter 50 Kenyon capitulates on his notion of the fortunate fall and asks Hilda to be his "guide... counsellor ... [and] inmost friend" and to "guide... [him] home," they both will return to that home at least somewhat transformed by their experiences.[44] And all of their experiences, like those of Donatello and Miriam, appear to coalesce in the apocalyptic (in the sense of revelatory) Carnival chapters. Carnival took a front and center position among Hawthorne's own associations with Rome and thus ineluctably became an integral, climactic part of *The Marble Faun,* his last finished novel.

## Notes

1. *New Columbia Encyclopaedia,* 4th ed., *s.v.* "carnival."

2. Ibid.

3. Ibid.

4. See *New Encyclopoedia Britannica,* 15th ed., *s.v.* "carnival"; *The Encyclopedia Americana: International Ed., 1997, s.v.* "Carnival."

5. Hsio-Yun Chu and Jan Z. Pervil, *Let's Go Rome: 1998* (New York: St. Martin's Press), 13.

6. Rennell Rodd, *Rome of the Renaissance and Today* (London: Macmillan, 1932), 40–41. It was not until some two hundred years later, in 1688, that Pope Clement IX ended the Jew races, but the horse races continued until the end of the nineteenth century. See John Varriano, *Literary Companion to Rome* (New York: St. Martin's Griffin, 1991), 126.

7. Mikhail Bakhtin, *Problems of Dostoevsky's Poetics,* ed. and trans. Carl Emerson (Minneapolis: University of Minnesota Press, 1984), 131.

8. Rodd, *Rome,* 41.

9. *The Diary of John Evelyn,* ed. E. S. de Beer (London: Oxford University Press, 1959), 196.

10. J. W. Goethe, *Italian Journey (1786–1788)* (New York: Pantheon Books, 1962), 445–46. See also Goethe, *Das Romische Carnival* (Berlin: Weimar and Gotha, 1789).

11. Charles Dickens, *Pictures from Italy* (Oxford: Oxford University Press, 1987), 371, 372.

12. In 1870, after a plebiscite, Rome was annexed by the Kingdom of Italy. In 1871 the capital was transferred from Florence to Rome, and the government "set about transforming the city into a modern metropolis" (*New Catholic Encyclopedia,* 1967, *s.v.* "Rome").

13. Henry James, "A Roman Holiday," in *Italian Hours* (Boston: Houghton Mifflin, 1909), 136. James's parting shot, interestingly, was somewhat more positive: viewing the Carnival on the climactic Shrove Tuesday, he pronounces the Corso "altogether carnivalesque" (152). Subsequent references are noted parenthetically in the text.

14. William Dean Howells, *Roman Holidays and Others* (New York: Harper & Brothers, 1908), 167.

15. Francis Wey, *Rome* (New York: D. Appleton, 1888), 428–29.

16. Rodd, *Rome,* 41.

17. Julian Hawthorne later confirmed that "the weather was bad nearly all the time, and my father's point of view was correspondingly unsympathetic." Julian's own description of both Carnivals that occurred while the Hawthornes were in Italy is informative. See *Hawthorne and His Circle* (New York: Harper & Brothers, 1903), 277–91; the quotation appears on p. 277.

18. Nathaniel Hawthorne, *The French and Italian Notebooks,* ed. Thomas Woodson. *The Centenary Edition of the Works of Nathaniel Hawthorne,* ed. William Charvat et al. (Columbus: Ohio State University Press, 1980), 14:64. Hereafter cited as *Notebooks,* or by page numbers, in the text.

19. Again, see Julian Hawthorne, who observes: "This mood [in 1859], we see, is far more gentle and sympathetic than the former one; there is sunshine within as well as without; and, indeed, I remember with what glee my father took part in the frolic, as well as looked on at it; he laughed and pelted and was pelted; he walked down the Corso and back again; he drove to and fro in a carriage; he mounted to Mr. [John Lothrop] Motley's balcony and took long shots at the crowd below. The sombre spirit of criticism had ceased, for a time, to haunt him" (*Hawthorne and His Circle,* 286–87).

20. Nathaniel Hawthorne, *The Letters, 1857–1864,* ed. Thomas Woodson, *Centenary Edition,* 17:164.

21. This is the night of the Carnival that Bakhtin describes as the embodiment of the ambivalent "image of fire" in carnival. It is a fire that "simultaneously destroys and renews the world" (*Problems of Dostoevsky's Poetics,* 126). At the end of the carnival "hell"—a special structure such as a vehicle covered with carnival trappings—was "triumphantly set on fire." Each participant, as he or she tries to put out the candle, cries *"Sia ammazzato"* ("Death to thee").

22. Nina Baym, *"The Marble Faun:* Hawthorne's Elegy for Art," *New England Quarterly* 44 (1971): 374.

23. Hawthorne, *Letters,* 229 (emphasis added).

24. Nathaniel Hawthorne, *The Marble Faun, The Centenary Edition,* 4:426. All citations of the novel are to this edition and are noted parenthetically in the text.

25. Rita Gollin, *Nathaniel Hawthorne and the Truth of Dreams* (Baton Rouge: Louisiana State University Press, 1979), 184.

26. Bakhtin's summation of the nature, or "problem," of carnival is that "its essence, its deep roots in the primordial order and the primordial thinking of man, its development under conditions of class society, its extraordinary life force and its undying fascination . . . is one of the most complex and most interesting problems in the history of culture" (*Problems of Dostoevsky's Poetics,* 122).

27. Ibid., 122.

28. Udo Natterman, "Dread and Desire: 'Europe' in Hawthorne's *The Marble Faun,*" *Essays in Literature* 21 (Spring 1994): 61.

29. Gollin, *Nathaniel Hawthorne,* 183.

30. Ibid., 184. Baym and Natterman interpret the cauliflower incident differently. Baym reads it as perhaps Hawthorne himself casting the blow on Kenyon as an "expression of contempt for the sculptor's pitiful weakness" ("*Marble Faun*," 375). To Natterman Kenyon's being hit by both the cauliflower and lime dust is a sign of the "slightly hostile quality" of the foreign country toward travelers ("Dread and Desire," 62).

31. The psychological dimensions of Kenyon's Carnival experience are the focus of Nina Baym's article "*The Marble Faun:* Hawthorne's Elegy for Art." Baym's point is that Donatello and Miriam become such "figures of fantasy" in the last third of the book (almost always appearing in costumes) that "they are not 'themselves' any longer, but rather are phantoms in Kenyon's consciousness." They become "less whole characters than fragments of Kenyon's suddenly exploded psyche" (372). The Carnival, according to Baym, "represents the final capitulation" of Kenyon, for without Hilda he "will surely go mad," so "ludicrously inadequate" is he for the profession of artist that he has chosen to pursue. Baym insightfully interprets the grotesqueness of the Carnival: "The psyche in a state of anarchic turbulence throws up into the light of consciousness a myriad of horrible fears and fantasies, grotesque and terrifying figures out of the world of dreams, mostly with sexual import" (374).

Norris Yates, the first scholar to pursue the masked dance trope in Hawthorne's fiction, refers to the masked dance in *The Marble Faun* as "both an escape and a penitential rite" ("Ritual and Reality: Mask and Dance Motifs in Hawthorne's Fiction," *Philological Quarterly* 34 [1955]: 70). Certainly in their "final celebration [during the Carnival], Miriam and Donatello are whirled along in a saturnalia of penitence" (69).

32. Baym, "*Marble Faun,*" 375, 376.

33. Natterman, "Dread and Desire," 62.

34. Gollin, *Nathaniel Hawthorne*, 184.

35. Bakhtin, *Problems of Dostoevsky's Poetics*, 122, 123.

36. Marty Roth, "Carnival, Creativity, and the Sublimation of Drunkenness," *Mosaic: A Journal for the Interdisciplinary Study of Literature* 30 (1997): 8.

37. Bakhtin, *Problems of Dostoevsky's Poetics*, 123.

38. Hawthorne, *Notebooks*, 503.

39. Yates, "Ritual and Reality," 69.

40. As John Wegner points out, Kenyon is the only character who, by the novel's end, associates freely with all three of the other major characters. See "Contemporary Inspiration for Kenyon in *The Marble Faun*," *Nathaniel Hawthorne Review* 23 (1997): 26–38.

41. Roth, "Carnival, Creativity," 14.

42. Ibid., 4.

43. Ibid.

44. Thus I believe Baym goes too far in stating that the Carnival "fail[s] utterly" in providing a catharsis for Kenyon ("*Marble Faun*," 374).

114

# El Otro Sud

## Willa Cather and Cormac McCarthy

**F**or the past couple of years I have become increasingly interested    **115**
in the fiction of Cormac McCarthy, who may well be America's
greatest living novelist. But McCarthy is always compared with
William Faulkner; it occurred to me to think about him together with Willa Cather only when a student of mine happened to remark that, like Cather, McCarthy began in the
South, moved west, and wrote about the old Southwest. Suddenly I had my obsession—*el otro sud,* the other South. Not the
place one is born but the place the stringent longings of one's
imagination make one come to.

The patterns of Cather's and McCarthy's lives are somewhat
different. Born near Winchester, Virginia, Willa Cather moved
to Nebraska in 1883 at the age of nine. Though she retained
powerful memories of Virginia, and though near the end of her
life she came full circle, to set her final novel, *Sapphira and the
Slave Girl,* in her childhood and her birthplace, for many years
Cather considered her move to Nebraska to have been an absolute, self-obliterating transformation. "Blotted out," as she put
it in *My Antonia,*[1] she began life anew on the prairie. When
eventually she discovered her major fictive ground, it was not as
a Southern but as a Midwestern writer—and a writer, furthermore, in whose work one does not ever see a definitive or per-

manent transition from Midwestern to Southwestern settings, from
Nebraska to Nevada or Arizona. McCarthy, in contrast, grew up in
Knoxville, Tennessee (though he was born and lived his first four years in
Rhode Island), attended the University of Tennessee, and located his first
four novels—*The Orchard Keeper, Outer Dark, Child of God,* and *Suttree*—
among the outcasts, criminals, and degenerates in his highly fevered ver-
sion of Appalachia. Only in early middle age did he move to El Paso,
Texas, teach himself Spanish, and begin the great Southwest novels:
*Blood Meridian,* published in 1985, and the Border Trilogy, *All the Pretty
Horses, The Crossing,* and—published in spring 1998—*Cities of the Plain.*
McCarthy's oeuvre divides neatly midway through; he has been first a
Southern, then a Southwestern writer. The pattern of Cather's career,
like the pattern of her residings, is far more various.

116      What, then, do these vastly different writers have in common, beyond
the mere fact that each moved from the South to the Mid- or Southwest? What ground, specifically, does *Death Comes for the Archbishop*
share with *Blood Meridian* and what with *The Crossing?* This essay will be
in two sections, each exploring one specific aspect of this question. First,
I look at the shared historical moment of the two historical novels, *Death
Comes for the Archbishop* and *Blood Meridian.* Then, switching to *The
Crossing,* I explore what I perceive to be the writers' still deeper affinities,
in their passionate concerns with God, the desert, and the telling of stories.

> *You wouldn't think that a man would run plumb*
> *out of country out here, would ye?*
>
> —Cormac McCarthy, *Blood Meridian*

Near the end of *Death Comes for the Archbishop,* Archbishop Jean Latour is on his way back to Santa Fe from a visit to Eusabio, the Navajo
chieftain whose son has recently died. He is accompanied by Eusabio, a
character introduced only late in the novel, whose way of being in the
world is far different from anything the narrative has hitherto described.
Latour remarks, "When they left the rock or tree or sand dune that had
sheltered them for the night, the Navajo was careful to obliterate every

trace of their temporary occupation. He buried the embers of the fire and the remnants of food, unpiled any stones he had piled together, filled up the holes he had scooped in the sand."[2] Cather goes on to generalize about Native Americans:

> It was as if the great country were asleep, and they wished to carry on their lives without awakening it; or as if the spirits of earth and air and water were things not to antagonize and arouse. When they hunted, it was with the same discretion; an Indian hunt was never a slaughter. They ravaged neither the rivers nor the forest, and if they irrigated, they took as little water as would serve their needs. The land and all that it bore they treated with consideration; not attempting to improve it, they never desecrated it. (234)

**117**

In Eusabio's actions one sees what Lawrence Buell calls "the environmental imagination."[3] Unlike the novel's missionary protagonists, bearers of the Word and builders of the empire, he behaves with the conviction, as Suellen Campbell puts it, that "humans are neither better nor worse than other creatures (animals, plants, bacteria, rocks, rivers) but simply equal to everything else in the natural world."[4] Cather's generalizations about Native Americans' attempting not "to 'master' nature, to arrange and re-create" but rather to accommodate "themselves to the scene in which they found themselves . . . from an inherited caution and respect" (234) are borne out by Paula Gunn Allen, who writes in "The Sacred Hoop" that non-Christian tribal people "acknowledge the essential harmony of all things and see all things as being of equal value in the scheme of things," that they "allow animals, vegetables, and minerals (the entire biota, in short) the same or even greater privileges than humans."[5] Or, as Cather remarks:

> Father Latour judged that, just as it was the white man's way to assert himself in any landscape, to change it, make it over a little (at least to leave some mark of memorial of his sojourn),

it was the Indian's way to pass through a country without disturbing anything; to pass and leave no trace, like fish through the water, or birds through the air. (233)

Perhaps this is why I have been so haunted for years by the image that occurs immediately after the passages quoted above. As Father Latour and Eusabio approach Albuquerque, suddenly "two Zuñi runners sped by them, going somewhere East on 'Indian business.' They saluted Eusabio by gestures with the open palm, but did not stop. They coursed over the sand with the fleetness of young antelope, their bodies disappearing and reappearing among the sand dunes, like the shadows that eagles cast in their strong, unhurried flight" (235).

To vanish without a trace—from the novel (for this is the only time the Zuñi are ever mentioned), from the world—and not to want to leave a trace: the image haunts me because to me, as to virtually all the characters in the fiction of Willa Cather and Cormac McCarthy, these things are practically inconceivable. Poignantly, the passages about Eusabio and the Zuñi runners occur right at the end of section 7 of the novel, "The Great Diocese," and lead immediately into section 8, "Gold under Pike's Peak"; it is as if Cather no sooner articulates this harmonious, biocentric relationship with the land than it gives way to the exigencies of expansion and acquisition. Father Vaillant leaves Santa Fe to minister to the miners in the Colorado gold rush—and to buy land for the church. The bishop stays behind to fulfill his lifelong ambition, also a kind of gold rush; as he says to Father Vaillant about the "rugged wall of rock" he discovers, which is "not green like the surrounding hills, but yellow, a strong golden ochre, very much like the gold of the sunlight": "that hill, Blanchet, is my Cathedral" (241). But slight as they are, the few sentences about Eusabio and the Zuñis exert enormous weight, for they critique the whole imperial enterprise that is the subject of both *Death Comes for the Archbishop* and *Blood Meridian*.

Though Cather and McCarthy interpret the situation in diametrically opposing ways, *Death Comes for the Archbishop* shares its precise historical moment with *Blood Meridian* in what Michael Paul Rogin calls "the

American 1848," when America's victory in the Mexican War and the ratification of the Treaty of Guadalupe Hidalgo constituted "an ironic triumph for 'Manifest Destiny,' an ominous fulfillment for the impulses of American nationalism."[6] In 1848 Father Ferrand travels to Rome to beg that the French Jesuit Jean Marie Latour, rather than a Mexican priest, be appointed vicar—later bishop—of the vast, newly won territory of New Mexico, "cradle of the Faith in the New World" (6). It is the year, as well, that McCarthy's protagonist, called simply "the kid," nearly dies in a barroom brawl and, "finally divested of all that he has been," begins the sojourn that will take him to the desert as an Indian scalper and bounty hunter, defined by his "taste for mindless violence".[7] *Death Comes for the Archbishop* also extends a historical sweep similar in extent to that of *Blood Meridian*. Both novels set their protagonists in almost ceaseless motion—the kid, killing; the bishop, preaching—and reveal through their characters' travels a multicultural situation of incredible complexity, in which Anglo, Mexican, and Native American forces contend in the volatile Southwest. By the time of Latour's death in 1888, he has lived, in Cather's rather too rosy phrasing, "to see two great wrongs righted; [he has] seen the end of black slavery, and [he has] seen the Navajos restored to their own country" (292) after the bitter years of their ill-conceived exile to the Bosque Redondo. Though McCarthy's kid does not live to see it, the novel's epilogue similarly reaches forward to close the century and ends with a brilliant image of the fate of American wilderness: a man, a fence-poster, "progressed over the plain by means of holes which he was making in the ground . . . as if each round and perfect hole owed its existence to the one before it" (337).

In his recent book *Willa Cather and the Myth of American Migration*, Joseph Urgo discusses the thoroughly political context of *Death Comes for the Archbishop*, specifically the ways in which Latour's founding of the diocese of Santa Fe acts along with the "scouts and soldiers"[8] to wrest temporal and religious power away from Mexico—and from the Native Americans—and to consolidate the United States presence in the newly acquired territories. "All day I am an American in speech and thought," Jean Latour writes his brother,

—yes, in heart, too. The kindness of the American traders, and especially of the military officers at the Fort, commands more than a superficial loyalty. I mean to help the officers at their task here. I can assist them more than they realize. The Church can do more than the Fort to make these poor Mexicans 'good Americans.' And it is for the people's good; there is no other way in which they can better their condition. (35–36)

*Death Comes for the Archbishop* is so serene in its telling, and the religious faith that informs it so ardent and luminous, that it is easy to overlook the degree to which religion is a business in the novel and serves capitalistic and militaristic aims. Sometimes, as in the story of the Mexican slave Sada, for whom Latour opens the church one midnight to pray but whose abuses cannot be questioned because, Latour tells Vaillant, it would be "inexpedient" to antagonize her Protestant owners (216), the choice for empire over justice and the attempt to mitigate that choice through pious acts are profoundly disturbing. For several reasons it is true, as Urgo says, that "the novel is not a simple act of nationalistic"— or, I would add, religious—"apologia" (180). First, the narrative is rich with interpolated legends, fables, and stories from several white and non-white traditions; to this extent it enthusiastically embraces a vivid multicultural heterogeneity. Also, especially near the end, as in the passages about Eusabio and the Zuñi runners, what strikes me as a longing for other, non-nationalistic ways of dwelling with the land surfaces poignantly. But the novel is far more celebratory than not, of empire yoked with Christian redemption. Even the desert itself, described in the prologue as hellish in ways far worse than "thirst . . . [or] Indian massacres" (7), soon transforms in nature and turns out to support the colonial project, time and again miraculously preserving the missionary priests.

Urgo comments that "the world, in Cather's texts, operates not of its own volition but by the will of its perceivers. . . . Meaning is not inherent but is discovered or applied by acts of signification" (181). This raises an interesting question. It is true that the novel reveals multiple forms of cultural "mythmaking" (182), multiple ways of perceiving meaning—just a few examples, all religious, are legends of the subterranean snake of the Pecos Indians, the Navajo Shiprock and sacred Canyon de Chelly, the miraculous appearances of the Virgin of Guadalupe to Juan Diego and of the Holy Family to Junípero Serra. But it is also true that some of these tales are held to be "myths" and others to be "miracles"; that is, some are seen as cultural formations, others as divinely authorized truths, preexisting and independent of the will of any perceiver. Furthermore, the non-Christian sources are Christianized—and thereby brought into the fold of what the novel holds as truth—wherever possible. *Death Comes for the Archbishop* both presents and participates in the syncretistic process of cultural privileging and appropriation that has played so rich a part in the history of religions, as in Cather's transformation of the regained Navajo lands to "an Indian Garden of Eden" (297), or—an especially interesting example—Cather's use of the miracle of the Virgin of **121** Guadalupe.

Gloria Anzaldúa points out in *Borderlands/La Frontera: The New Mestiza* that the Virgin of Guadalupe, whose miraculous appearance to a peon, Juan Diego, in 1531 Father Vaillant hears about with such rapture from a poor Mexican priest near the beginning of the novel, has a long and multicultural history. "*La Virgen de Guadalupe's* Indian name is *Coatlalopeuh*," Anzaldúa writes: "She is the central deity connecting us to our Indian ancestry." Originally, Coatlalopeuh descended from "Mesoamerican fertility and Earth goddesses," from the terrifying Coatlicue and the gentler Tonantsi. She was driven underground, however, by the later "male-dominated Azteca-Mexica culture," which divided "her who had been complete, who possessed both upper . . . and underworld . . . aspects" back once again into light and dark.[9] Then,

> after the Conquest, the Spaniards and their Church continued to split Tonantsi/*Guadalupe*. . . . They desexed *Guadalupe*, taking *Coatlalopeuh*, the serpent/sexuality, out of her. . . . They went even further; they made all Indian deities and religious practices the work of the devil.
>
> Thus *Tonantsi* became *Guadalupe*, the chaste protective mother, the defender of the Mexican people. (27–28)

In 1660, the church named her Mother of God, synonymous with the Virgin Mary. She became *"la Santa Patrona de los mexicano"* (30) and is still, according to Anzaldúa, "the single most potent religious, political and cultural image of the Chicano/*mexicano"* (31). But the pre-Christian, Native American elements of this history do not make their way into *Death Comes for the Archbishop;* drawing on multicultural sources, the book at the same time obscures them. At moments—as, preeminently, in the passages about Eusabio and the Zuñi runners—the book hovers outside its belief system. But finally, meaning exists in the world, and that meaning is Christian. "The Miracles of the Church," Latour tells Vaillant in a beautiful but deeply ambiguous passage, "seem to me to rest . . . upon our perceptions being made finer, so that for a moment our eyes can see and our ears can hear what is there about us always" (50).

122       *Blood Meridian* could not be more different in its idea of truth. It is informed not by the calm, radiant light of eternity but by "the very life of the darkness" (epigraph). Like *Death Comes for the Archbishop, Blood Meridian* is largely drawn from actual events and characters,[10] and its tale of the kid's involvement with Judge Holden and the Glanton gang exposes as if by parable the violence of the American heritage, the sheer bloodlust that operates beneath expansionist political rhetoric. The west-ering sun that shines so gloriously in the prologue to *Death Comes for the Archbishop,* setting like the Church Triumphant with a "peculiar quality of climax— of splendid finish" (4), becomes for McCarthy "the Evening Redness in the West," and that redness is not caused by any cathedral's "much multiplied candlelight" (4). It is caused by the blood of Manifest Destiny: blood that soaks the ground, blood of the murdered in great pools, that

> set up into a sort of pudding crossed everywhere with the tracks of wolves or dogs . . . [that] lay in dark tongues on the floor and . . . grouted the flagstones and ran in the vestibule where the stones were cupped from the feet of the faithful and their fathers before them and threaded its way down the steps and dripped from the stones among the dark red tracks of . . . scavengers. (60)

"The way of the world," says the judge, "is to bloom and to flower and die but in the affairs of men there is no waning and the noon of his expression signals the onset of night. His spirit is exhausted at the peak of its achievement. His meridian is at once his darkening and the evening of his day" (146–47). The American Southwest, "the American 1848," is that meridian.

In *Death Comes for the Archbishop*, violence and suffering, indeed dramatic action, are kept almost entirely offstage. Many conflicts and deaths occur during the course of Latour's calm, steady missionary labor,[11] but even the most extensive of the conflicts—Latour's struggle to wrest control of the parish of Taos from Padre Martínez—and the most gruesome of the deaths—Buck Scales's hanging or Friar Baltazar's plunge from the Acoma cliff—are reported at a distance and serenely. *Blood Meridian*, in contrast, overwhelms its reader with violence; bodies outrage and are outraged incessantly, and the deaths are always foregrounded. Men, women, children, animals: all are repeatedly and characteristically "slathered and dripping with blood," as the Glanton gang moves from village to village, "hacking at the dying and decapitating those who knelt for mercy" (39). There is nothing McCarthy will not write, nothing his warriors will not do:

> There were in the camp a number of Mexican slaves and these ran forth calling out in Spanish and were brained or shot and one of the Delawares emerged from the smoke with a naked infant dangling in each hand and squatted at a ring of midden stones and swung them by the heels each in turn and bashed their heads against the stones so that the brains burst forth through the fontanel in a bloody spew and humans on fire came shrieking forth like berserkers and the riders hacked them down with their enormous knives and a young woman ran up and embraced the bloodied forefeet of Glanton's warhorse. . . .
>
> The dead lay awash in the shallows like the victims of some disaster at sea and they were strewn along the salt foreshore in

a havoc of blood and entrails. Riders . . . moved among the
dead harvesting the long black locks with their knives and
leaving their victims rawskulled and strange in their bloody
cauls. . . . Men were wading about in the red waters hacking
aimlessly at the dead and some lay coupled to the bludgeoned
bodies of young women dead or dying on the beach. One of
the Delawares passed with a collection of heads like some
strange vendor bound for market. (156–57)

In the descent into murder and depravity that is *Blood Meridian*, ordinary life is kept offstage. Only Buck Scales, the subhuman serial killer
from *Death Comes for the Archbishop*, could inhabit the world of the
bounty-hunting Glanton gang, of Judge Holden the hairless genius who
rapes, murders, and cannibalizes children, of the kid with his "taste for
mindless violence" (3). Only the women sweeping the streets of one tiny
Mexican village in *Blood Meridian*, glimpsed for a moment as the gang
rides by, could inhabit the world of Vaillant and Latour, where soup
recipes, church bells, and white mules named Contento and Angelica fill
the space of need and where instead of McCarthy's landscape—of
blood-drenched mud, skull-tracked sand, and "mountains on the sudden
skyline stark and black and livid like a land of some other order . . . whose
true geology was not stone but fear" (47)—the desert becomes a "bright
[edge] of the world," whose air is "something soft and wild and free,
something that . . . lightened the heart, softly, softly picked the lock, slid
the bolts, and released the prisoned spirit of man into the wind, into the
blue and gold, into the morning, into the morning!" (275–76).

Jane Tompkins remarks in *West of Everything* that the desert makes
death the issue: "Life must be seen from the point of view of death."[12]
Both Cather's and McCarthy's titles suggest that too—though again, utterly differently. *Death Comes for the Archbishop*, whose title is drawn from
Holbein's *Dance of Death*, answers the question of death with the
promise of immortality for the steadfast, faithful archbishop. In *Blood
Meridian*, death itself is the desideratum. One may find explanations located in the will, or the masculine psyche, for the behavior of McCarthy's

killers; Tompkins suggests, for instance, that the western—of which *Blood Meridian* is in some ways a prime example—is not so much about the actual West as about "men's fear of losing their mastery, and hence their identity" (45). Control, then, becomes the issue: "control not only over feelings but over one's physical boundaries" (56). The kid, the Glanton gang, and preeminently the huge, hairless, swollen-tick genius of a killer, Judge Holden, exemplify the macho ideal defined by Octavio Paz as "hermetic being";[13] they are closed systems that maintain "the integrity of the boundary that divides [them] from the world" (56). To shoot, scalp, rape, pierce the bodies of others with arrows, is by this light to foster the illusion that one is omnipotent, immortal. And Americans, according to McCarthy, have excelled in this illusion; warriors and settlers have pushed southward, westward, "half-crazed with the enormity of their own presence in that immense and bloodslaked waste" (177). But **125** *Blood Meridian* goes further, to suggest that, desiring death, the warriors desire not the preservation but the extinction of identity and boundaries. Death itself is absolute, "the very life of the darkness," and to embrace death, to inflict death joyously, carelessly—or to receive death—is to experience the "profound continuity" of the holy.[14] *Blood Meridian* literalizes, in detail, Georges Bataille's definition of the sacred as "our desire to consume, to annihilate, to make a bonfire of our resources, and the joy we find in the burning" (185). Bataille is writing of sex but also of eroticized forms of violence such as Aztec human sacrifice, and what he writes fits precisely with Judge Holden's view of war: "War is the ultimate game because war is at last a forcing of the unity of existence. War is god" (249).

> *Your Majesty, encounters have become my meditation.*
> —Alvar Núñez Cabeza de Vaca

During World War II, an American Quaker named Haniel Long made what he called an "interlinear," or freely interpretive, translation of the long narrative letter called the *Naufragios,* or "Shipwrecks," that Alvar Núñez Cabeza de Vaca sent back from Mexico City to the king of Spain. Cabeza de Vaca was treasurer of the Narváez expedition in 1528, which attempted to conquer Florida with four hundred men, but which, through a series of disasters, ended with the death of all but four. With his three companions, Cabeza de Vaca wandered through northern Mexico until 1536, and in the men's hardship and solitude they discovered that they had healing powers. "Lashed by starvation, scorched and baked by the sun,"[15] they traveled from village to village, praying, laying on hands, healing the throngs of Indians who came forward to meet them. In Long's translation, Cabeza de Vaca writes:

> Our journey westward was but a long series of encounters. Your Majesty, encounters have become my meditation. The moment one accosts a stranger or is accosted by him is above all in this life the moment of drama. The eyes of Indians who crossed my trail have searched me to the very depths to estimate my *power*. It is true the world over. (25)

**126**

These sentences, supposedly written by a conquistador who found to his own amazement that he had parted "little by little with the thoughts that clothe the soul of a European, and most of all . . . [with] the idea that a man attains strength through dirk and dagger" (17), remarkably redefine power in ways I find suggestive for *Death Comes for the Archbishop* and, not *Blood Meridian*, but the second novel in Cormac McCarthy's Border Trilogy, *The Crossing*.

*Death Comes for the Archbishop* shares its historical moment with *Blood Meridian*, in Manifest Destiny and the conquest of the Southwest. But there is a counterstory to conquest; the Zuñi runners inhabit the same world as, for instance, Billy Parham, the twentieth-century protagonist of *The Crossing*. And I suggest that this other world shimmers throughout *Death Comes for the Archbishop*. The novel is about conquest, empire, colonization. The charges that have been brought against Cather for her Francophilic vision—her slanted treatment of Father Martínez, for instance—and for her seemingly automatic assumption that American cultural and political hegemony are desirable are not inaccurate. And yet, whatever one says against the book seems to miss some deeper point. For years, some quality about *Death Comes for the Archbishop* has eluded my efforts to explain it. Latour is never stripped of his European soul, like Long's Cabeza de Vaca; nor, as Latour's revulsion against the Stone Lips cave exemplifies, does he ever move, like Long's Cabeza de Vaca, fully, with spiritual nakedness, into an experience of the Other. But of Latour, as of McCarthy's Billy Parham, in some sense it is true that encounters have become his meditation. His Pecos Indian guide Jacinto notices, for instance, that he does not put on a "false face" when dealing with non-Europeans; he "stood straight and turned to the Governor of Laguna, and his face underwent no change" (94). In fact, as he moves about the landscape, among people or alone, he possesses the quality Jane Tompkins remarks in nature of "being-in-itself," "not fissured by self-consciousness" (57).

But perhaps what I sense in *Death Comes for the Archbishop* has more **127** to do with the narrative than with the character. At one point in *West of Everything,* Tompkins discusses the Western in terms of Christian monasticism and writes:

> The desert landscape is the fullest realization of . . . materiality, the place where language fails and rocks assert themselves. But by the same token it is the place where something else becomes visible, an ineffable thing that cannot be named. . . . The landscape, which on the one hand drives Christianity away, ends by forcing men to see something godlike there. (84–85)

Or, in a sentence Cather quotes from Balzac: *"Dans le désert, il y a tout et il n'y a rien; Dieu, sans les hommes."*[16] *The Crossing* shares with *Death Comes for the Archbishop* the desert, the god-place, and for all the differences between the novels, they share as well a profound meditative overlay in response to the desert, attained partly by the continual interruption of the linear narrative by inset legends, stories. In *Death Comes for the Archbishop* stories spread a wash of grace over what would otherwise seem an inimical landscape; they tell of saints, of miracles, of temporary falterings in the gradual (and, we know in hindsight, successful) spread of the Catholic faith. Latour moves through space and time, or, the *book* moves through space and time, with a serene constancy. It portrays episodes in a calm, luminous, unaccented style—the style, Cather wrote, in which Puvis de Chavannes painted his frescoes of the life of Saint Geneviève.[17] Its inset stories are like turquoises "set in dull silver" (in Louie Marsellus's image from *The Professor's House*)[18] or like rooms that open up off a central corridor to delay the process toward the narrative's "death."[19] Even the ones that, handled differently, would be full of conflict, violent, add to the steady progress of faith and reveal the bishop's life as replete, redeemed.

The use of *cuentos*—stories—in *The Crossing* is somewhat different. This novel of overwhelming desolation tells the tale of a boy named Billy Parham who makes three failed trips to Mexico: the first, to return a wandering pregnant wolf to freedom in the North Mexican mountains; the second, with his younger brother Boyd to find the horses that were stolen from his parents, who were murdered while he was in Mexico; the third, to find the bones of his brother Boyd, who was martyred when he became a guerrilla hero during his second trip to Mexico. On each trip Billy's defeat seems absolute, yet each defeat opens on to a further stage in his pilgrimage into suffering and loneliness. Finally, at the novel's end, alone in the New Mexico desert, he

> looked again at the road which lay as before yet more dark and darkening still where it ran on to the east and where there was no sun and there was no dawn and when he looked again toward the north the light was drawing away faster and that noon in which he'd woke was now become an alien dusk and now an alien dark and the birds that flew had lighted and all had hushed once again in the bracken by the road.[20]

It is easy to forget, but Billy's three trips to Mexico, Billy's three rounds of losses, have been set all along against a backdrop of World War II. Now, it seems, his personal story blends with global apocalypse, for the "alien dark" of this morning, James Lilley has argued, was very likely caused by the first test atom bomb.[21] So deep is McCarthy's darkness in *The Crossing* that the novel reminds one of Edgar's line in *King Lear:* "The worst is not / So long as we can say 'This is the worst.'"[22]

Still, there is a countercurrent to Billy's doomed and largely solitary wanderings. After the death of the wolf, he meets at different times a priest, a prima donna, a blind man, a band of gypsies. All of them tell him parables or stories that instruct him in the endless tale of the living universe. Their stories are offerings; their encounters with Billy become the novel's meditation. Life is a mask, the prima donna tells him. But "it is not a matter of illusion or no illusion," the blind man says, for "the broad dryland barrial and the river and the road and the mountains beyond and the blue sky over them" are merely "entertainments" to keep at bay the "true and ageless world" that moves in "eternal darkness" (283). Narrative, then, becomes the ceaseless unfolding of this tragic "entertainment." Legends preserve the dead, as Boyd and his Mexican lover become the subject of a *corrido,* or ballad, that commemorates their transfiguration. Stories accompany the emptiness; one of the novel's most touching moments, for instance, is of Billy after Boyd has been shot, in flight from his Mexican pursuers. Desperate, out of water, he coaxes his father's horse Niño, "so crusted with white salt rime it shone like some prodigy embarked upon the darkening plain," to keep walking. "When he'd said all he knew to say he told it stories. He told it stories in Spanish that his grandmother had told him as a child and when he'd told all of those that he could remember he sang to it" (274).

Finally, in *The Crossing,* stories gesture continually beyond themselves back into what the blind man calls the "perfect cohesion," "sentient to the core and secret and black beyond men's imagining" (283). There, the murdered wolf runs, "huntress" that "cannot be held"—"[runs] in the mountains, [runs] in the starlight where the grass [is] wet and the sun's coming as yet [has] not undone the rich matrix of creatures passed in the night before her" (127). And the stories of Billy's encounters help him—help us—to know the wolf. In this world of ever-deepening loss, where all men are orphans and God himself does not exist apart from *la matríz* (the matrix) of eternal darkness (283), all stories open into each other, all *encuentros* tell the same *cuento*, and "the tale has no abode or place of being except in the telling only and there it lives and makes its home and therefore we can never be done with the telling. Of the telling there is no end" (143).

## Notes

1. Willa Cather, *My Antonia* (Boston: Houghton Mifflin, 1918), 8.

2. Willa Cather, *Death Comes for the Archbishop* (New York: Random House, 1927), 233. Subsequent references are noted parenthetically in the text.

3. Lawrence Buell, *The Environmental Imagination: Thoreau, Nature Writing, and the Formation of American Culture* (Cambridge, Mass.: Belknap Press of Harvard University Press, 1995).

4. Suellen Campbell, "The Land and Language of Desire: Where Deep Ecology and Post-Structuralism Meet," in *The Ecocriticism Reader: Landmarks in Literary Ecology*, ed. Cheryll Glotfelty and Harold Fromm (Athens: University of Georgia Press, 1996), 128.

5. Paula Gunn Allen, "The Sacred Hoop: A Contemporary Perspective," in *Ecocriticism Reader*, ed. Glotfelty and Fromm, 243.

6. Michael Paul Rogin, *Subversive Genealogy: The Politics and Art of Herman Melville* (New York: Knopf, 1983), 103.

7. Cormac McCarthy, *Blood Meridian: Or the Evening Redness in the West* (New York: Random House, 1985), 4, 3. Subsequent references are noted parenthetically in the text.

8. Joseph Urgo, *Willa Cather and the Myth of American Migration* (Urbana: University of Illinois Press, 1995), 175. Subsequent references are noted parenthetically in the text.

9. Gloria Anzaldúa, *Borderlands/La Frontera: The New Mestiza* (San Francisco: Aunt Lune Books, 1987), 27. Subsequent references are noted parenthetically in the text.

10. John Sepich, *Notes on "Blood Meridian"* (Louisville: Bellarmine College Press, 1993), passim.

11. D. H. Stewart counts ninety-six deaths in the novel. See "Willa Cather's Mortal Comedy," *Queen's Quarterly* (Summer 1966): 247, cited in James Woodress, *Willa Cather: A Literary Life* (Lincoln: University of Nebraska Press, 1987), 403.

12. Jane Tompkins, *West of Everything: The Inner Life of Westerns* (New York: Oxford University Press, 1992), 74–75. Subsequent references are noted parenthetically in the text.

13. Ibid., 56, quoting Peter Schwenger, *Phallic Critiques* (London: Routledge & Kegan Paul, 1984), 43.

14. Georges Bataille, *Erotism: Death and Sensuality,* trans. Mary Dalwood (San Francisco: City Lights Books, 1986), 15; first published as *L'Erotisme* (Paris: Les Editions de Minuit, 1957). Subsequent references are noted parenthetically in the text.

15. Haniel Long, *The Power Within Us: Cabeza de Vaca's Relation of His Journey from Florida to the Pacific, 1528–1536* (New York: Duell, Sloan and Pearce, 1944), 25. Subsequent references are noted parenthetically in the text.

16. In Phyllis C. Robinson, *Willa: The Life of Willa Cather* (Garden City, N.Y.: Doubleday, 1983), 177.

17. Willa Cather, *Willa Cather on Writing* (New York: Random House, 1949), 9. Clinton Keeler discusses the influence of the Puvis de Chavannes frescoes on *Death Comes for the Archbishop* in "Narrative Without Accent: Willa Cather and Puvis de Chavannes," *American Quarterly* 17 (Spring 1965): 119–26; rpt. in *Critical Essays on Willa Cather,* ed. John J. Murphy (Boston: G. K. Hall, 1984). See also Woodress, *Willa Cather,* 399.

18. Willa Cather, *The Professor's House* (New York: Random House, 1925), epigraph.

19. The concept of narrative "death" is developed by Peter Brooks according to a Freudian theoretical model of eros in struggle with thanatos, whereby "desire is the wish for the end, for fulfillment"—for the death, as it were, of the narrative—"but fulfillment must be delayed so that we can understand it in relation to origin and to desire itself." See *Reading for the Plot: Design and Intention in Narrative* (Cambridge, Mass.: Harvard University Press, 1984), 111.

20. Cormac McCarthy, *The Crossing* (New York: Random House, 1994), 425. Subsequent references are noted parenthetically in the text.

21. James Lilley, "Borders and Bodies: The Dynamics of Cormac McCarthy's Environmental Imagination," unpublished essay.

22. *King Lear* (IV.i.27–28). I quote from *The Riverside Shakespeare,* ed. G. Blakemore Evans et al. (Boston: Houghton Mifflin, 1974).

*Chapter 9*   **NOEL POLK**

# Welty and Faulkner and the Southern Literary Tradition

T he eye of William Faulkner is a defining eye. Generations of post-Faulkner Southern writers and readers have adopted his vision and so seen "the South" through his experience rather than through their own, or struggled against that vision, as a barrier to be gone through or over or around. In either case, Faulkner's vision has defined what can be seen, so that Southern writers following Faulkner are indeed in a double bind. But as large and encompassing as Faulkner's vision is, it is, finally, only a single vision, and he would have been less likely than anyone else to assume that his was the only one.

Discussions of the relationships between William Faulkner and Southern writers following him have been largely hamstrung because they are normally driven, willy-nilly, by questions of Faulkner's influence, questions with which interviewers have plagued writers who have had to operate in Faulkner's wake if not always in his shadow. Because the questions assume that the subsequent generations are both junior and inferior, these writers have spent far too much of their energy escaping and denying—*dealing with*—Faulkner's legacy, even if only in being conscious of reviewers' inevitable for-better-or-worse comparisons of their work with the tradition of "Southern" letters that Faulkner so forcefully defined.

Their denials, of course, are the most compelling evidence of how completely inescapable he and his work are. The interviews and the criticism would suggest that as a generation they engage in a collective fretting, wailing, like Quentin Compson at the end of *Absalom, Absalom!:* "I dont hate him! I dont! I dont! I dont hate him!" On the other hand, it may be that what they are really saying is not *I dont hate him* but rather, *I hate that question. I hate it. Why do professors keep asking me that question?* It must be difficult enough for writers to grapple honestly with Faulkner's Founding Presence in the tradition, without having to respond to interviewers' presumptive questions about an influence they may not completely understand, or need to care about, having books to write and better things to do.

In point of fact, then, probably more critics than writers have been overwhelmed by Faulkner, more critics than writers have felt that Faulkner alone has defined the terms by which we can talk about the South. Thus writers like Walker Percy and Barry Hannah, who deal with a more urban world than Faulkner does, a world more directly a part of their own experiences than Faulkner's, have occasionally had a hard time with many traditional critics, who believe that they therefore represent a decline in "Southern literature," whatever that is. As Thomas L. McHaney has suggested, the old guard of Southern critics want to penalize southern writers who have indoor plumbing and give extra credit to them if they write about people who do not.[1] To my knowledge, Hannah has not addressed himself seriously to the problem (although he has done a bit of Welty-bashing, perhaps his own version of escaping "the influence"), but Percy, with more than a little wit, spent more time than he should have actually denying that he is a Southern writer, and Richard Ford has written that all writers, even Southerners, should be left alone to create their own categories of expectation.

But I seem already on the verge of defending Eudora Welty against some accusation or other.[2] This defensive posture seems inevitable under any circumstance that forces us to consider *Faulkner and* whoever, just as we Faulknerians somehow always seem to wind up defending him against charges of subordinance such as govern discussions of James Joyce and Faulkner or Shakespeare and Faulkner—which discussions are

**133**

also nearly always driven by questions of influence or borrowing. It is as though critics must or do always operate chronologically, following T. S. Eliot's "Tradition and the Individual Talent" and, more recently, Harold Bloom's *Anxiety of Influence*, without recognizing that writers do not necessarily operate chronologically and that what *they* derive from their predecessors may not be anything that they can or need to articulate or that critics can possibly understand. And since Bloom deals exclusively with male writers and their oedipal struggles with their predecessors, it is certainly worth noting that women writers stand in an entirely different relationship to the "tradition," and it would be surprising indeed if they dealt with it in the same way male writers do; we have fostered a good deal of misunderstanding of women writers, especially Southern women, by assuming that they do.

**134**      Eudora Welty, quite simply, has mostly had none of this question: she has not even generally entertained the question of Faulkner's influence on her as worth her time. "It was like living near a mountain," she says, with characteristic and modest acknowledgment of The Presence in north Mississippi. Unspoken in her image, and perhaps even unthought, is the simple fact that what most often lives near a mountain is another mountain.

It is fairly easy to trace the points at which Welty's and Faulkner's lives intersected. It was not often, even though they lived barely 150 miles apart. Faulkner wrote her from Hollywood in 1943: "Dear Welty," he wrote, "You are doing fine. You are doing all right." He then named *The Robber Bridegroom* and the "collection called GREEN something" and "The Gilded Six Bits"—a story by Zora Neale Hurston, which he had mistakenly thought was one of Welty's, perhaps because Zora and Eudora rhyme. He told her that he thought of Djuna Barnes when he read *The Robber Bridegroom* but expected her to pass that. He asked about her background, then confessed that he had not read Green something yet but "expect nothing from it because I expect from you. You are doing very fine. Is there any way I can help you? How old are you?"[3]

According to Welty, they met occasionally at Faulkner's home in Oxford, ate dinner, sang hymns, and went sailing, but never discussed writing or literature. She reviewed *Intruder in the Dust* in 1949[4] and responded to Edmund Wilson's *New Yorker* attack on *Intruder* with a savagely funny indictment of Wilson's condescending presumption that Faulkner's Southern *material*, rather than his intellect or even his hard work, was responsible for the quality of his work and that Faulkner would have been a better writer if he had spent more time in such literary centers as New York talking to such writers as Edmund Wilson about literature.[5] Welty's response to this pomposity was, I think, the germ of her thoughts about the relationship between a writer's geographical place and the quality of the writing, thoughts that resulted in her well-known (and much misunderstood and much abused) essay of six years later called "Place in Fiction."[6] She reviewed Joseph Blotner's edition of Faulkner's letters in 1977[7] and used examples from his work as illustrations in several essays, among them "Place in Fiction," "Some Notes on Time in Fiction,"[8] and *Short Stories*. Faulkner mentioned Welty only once more, in **135** the late 1950s, during his time at the University of Virginia where, when asked about Welty, he again mentioned *The Robber Bridegroom*. They met a couple of months before his death in New York, at a ceremony during which Welty presented him with the Gold Medal for Fiction of the American Institute of Arts and Letters. She wrote an elegant obituary for the Associated Press upon his death in July 1962.

So far as I can determine, this is the sum total of their public interaction. Privately, of course, we have no way of knowing what, if anything, they meant to each other. There is no evidence that Faulkner borrowed anything from Welty, and, for all of her manifest reverence for his work, for all that she claimed to have learned from him, there is no more evidence that she ever borrowed a single line or character or scene from him or ever crossed the state line of his Mississippi except as a grateful reader. Perhaps she made some conscious effort to honor the claim he had staked and simply avoided his territory. More likely, she saw a different landscape than the one he saw and so had no need to mine his. But her work does respond to his in significant ways that suggest that in her manifest reverence she was by no means unaware of his sources in a problematic tradition or uncritical of the implications of his accomplishment for those standing in a different relation to that tradition.

It is no credit to the scholarly world that Welty and Faulkner have been lumped together by traditionalist critics who have wanted to see them as somehow both empowered and limited by their "place" in Mississippi, who have argued that their literary strengths lie directly in their roots in the South (instead of in their brains), and who therefore, for example, have found it necessary (or convenient) to dismiss the relatively few works that they had the temerity to set outside Mississippi, as though they had committed gratuitous acts of literary suicide. Welty, of course, has suffered most in traditionalist readings of her work. Even sympathetic and admiring critics have seen her fiction as a sort of genteel, domestic, nonaggressive, *female* version of Faulkner and, to paraphrase her comment about Faulkner, we have generally asked her to stand on a lower step when posing for the group photograph.[9]

    Faulkner's work self-consciously addresses epic issues and deals with them on an epic scale, in an epic landscape: his language strains at its own outermost limits to raise every event, every gesture, to its highest, most intense pitch of significance. The universe is his world; he moves fluidly and freely within it, and he strides with the certainty of a colossus to get where he wants to go. His novels deliberately engage the "great" themes of Western literature, and his tragedies and comedies are rich in their analyses of culture and of human life in the twentieth century. The problems with this reading of Faulkner (as of other canonical male writers), as we have finally begun to learn from feminist critics, are the operating assumptions behind traditionalist views, which hold as given that Faulkner's historically canonized themes and epic struggles are larger, more cosmic, more significantly responsive to crises in Western culture and so are therefore more important than the seemingly tamer, less grandiose, more domestic work of Welty—and other women writers, of course.

    Driven by these assumptions of what constitutes "great" literature, traditionalist critics have paid the wrong kind of attention to the surface geniality—the face of the familiar—of much of Welty's fiction and have missed how profoundly, how troublingly, she has opened up the atom of the domestic and found there another universe, her own, an infinity of space that affords her an absolutely original engagement with the world and, more particularly, with that Western and Southern literary tradition

**136**

that both defined and delimited her, though hardly in the ways we have assumed.[10] She slices away at the exteriors of the familiar, a familiar that is Southern only incidentally, and takes us into the hardest to reach nooks and crannies of human life. She dissects our comfortable assumptions about family, about community, about ourselves, and in doing so she offers us a more comprehensive, a more intensely local, understanding of those traditionally cosmic concerns than Faulkner does, precisely because she demonstrates how these "cosmic" concerns work on us, individually, in the most private, the least dramatic, least epical, places of our lives.

Welty thus offers alternative visions of our relationship with the cosmos, equally powerful visions that suggest other, equally potent options for responding to our worlds, options that may threaten us in ways that Faulkner's traditional vision does not. His world is tragic; things fall apart: we live, we suffer, we die. But in Faulkner we usually know who the enemy is, what the stakes are, we know that we must struggle, and we know how to struggle. In spite of her vision of the universe's wholeness, however, Welty's world is considerably harder to negotiate than Faulkner's, precisely because she knows that the enemy is not so easily recognizable, that the battleground is more nearly the minefield of our own backyards than the "universe." For her, and for her readers, the enemy is terrifyingly close; it resides permanently in and is inextricable from those structures of family and community that traditional readings of Southern literature always invoke as the enduring source of value in Southern life.

One of Faulkner's most touching pieces is the quasi-autobiographical "Mississippi," which he published in 1953 at a time when he had just begun an overtly political engagement with his native state, writing letters to editors and essays and giving speeches in which he argued against the racial status quo.[11] "Mississippi" is an eloquent and moving record of his attempts to grapple with the problems and pressures his native land had caused for him and of his reconciliation with past and present Mississippi.

The protagonist of "Mississippi" is Faulkner the citizen, not Faulkner the artist. He makes this distinction clear throughout by referring to the citizen in the third person—"he," "the boy," "the young man," "the man," "the middleaged," "the gray-haired"—and by refusing to speak of his career as a writer, although we are never very far from that career: "Mississippi"'s narrative moves freely, fluidly, back and forth between Faulkner's two Mississippis, as if to demonstrate just how thin the line separating them is.

"Mississippi"'s opening pages outline the state's history from its beginnings in "the alluvial swamps" (11), bring it up through the prehistoric Indian inhabitants, the European settlers, the frontier, the cotton economy, the Civil War, Emancipation, Reconstruction, and right on up to the end of the nineteenth century, when "the boy" is born into that powerful flood of specifically Southern history. Though he will be a child of the twentieth century, the forces shaping his life as a Mississippian are very much those of the nineteenth: the boy hears about the Civil War even before he hears about Santa Claus at Christmas, and the first character he speaks of from his childhood is Mammy Callie, the family nurse, a former slave who refused to leave the Faulkners after Emancipation and who was to survive into Faulkner's forty-third year, a constant reminder that the Civil War and Reconstruction in the South are not mere historical circumstances but ever-present, daily realities. She plays a little game with the family, constantly reminding them that they "owe" her $89 in back wages, wages—the dollars, at any rate—that have been offered over and over again and which she has refused to accept (16). This "debt" becomes Faulkner's gentle, unforced metaphor for all that white Mississippi owes to its black citizens, that it will never repay partly because Mammy Callie—the Negro—does not really want the debt wiped out and partly because what is owed cannot really be repaid. Along with the chief protagonist, Mammy Callie is "Mississippi"'s most important character. Her life runs through the essay as a moving counterpoint to the boy's own maturation.

She sees the child into his life; "Mississippi" reaches its elegiac end as "the middleaging" sees her out of hers, delivering her funeral oration and "hoping that when his turn came there would be someone in the world to owe him the sermon which all owed to her who had been, as he had

138

been from infancy, within the scope and range of that fidelity and that devotion and that rectitude" (42). Her death is the thematic climax of "Mississippi," and in her life and death are encapsulated all that Faulkner's citizen protagonist has learned in his progression from infancy to middle age about his native state: how, that is, one can be so completely a victim—of color, of law, of economics—as Mammy Callie had been and still find room to love even that which had victimized her; and how it might be possible for him, the middle-aging, both to hate the people and the system that had victimized Mammy Callie and to follow her example in being able to find something to love, even in her oppressors.

"Mississippi" moves to closure as "the man" returns from travel to find himself "Home again, his native land; he was born of it and his bones will sleep in it" (36). His first articulation of an emotional reconciliation with Mississippi recognizes that love and hate are not mutually exclusive: **139** "loving it even while hating some of it" (36). He hates the greed, he writes, the waste of the lumbermen and the land speculators who changed the face of the landscape by cutting down the big trees for timber, moving the Big Woods farther and farther away from the areas he hunted in as a child. "But most of all," he writes,

> he hated the intolerance and injustice: the lynching of Negroes not for the crimes they committed but because their skins were black . . . ; the inequality: the poor schools they had then when they had any, the hovels they had to live in unless they wanted to live outdoors: who could worship the white man's God but not in the white man's church; pay taxes in the white man's courthouse but couldn't vote in it or for it; working by the white man's clock but having to take his pay by the white man's counting . . . ; the bigotry which could send to Washington some of the senators and congressmen we sent there and which could erect in a town no bigger than Jefferson five separate denominations of churches but set aside not one square foot of ground where children could play and old people could sit and watch them. (37–38)

"Mississippi" concludes with Mammy Callie's death, the gathering of her children, her laying out, and the middle-aging's funeral sermon, all of which build to the essay's final paragraph, Faulkner's second, more complex articulation of the relationship between love and hate: "Loving all of it even while he had to hate some of it because he knows now that you dont love because: you love despite; not for the virtues, but despite the faults" (42–43).

For Faulkner, as I say, the struggle is always epic, a heroic confrontation between contending forces—love and hate; justice and injustice; life and death—that are eternally antagonistic to each other and to human peace: one lives only under the terms of existential combat. It is an intensely moral struggle, with Faulkner, humanity—*man* he would say—caught in the middle of an irresolvable universal conflict whose antagonisms are permanently fixed in the nature of things. In Faulkner the best we can hope is to turn the tension itself into part of our weaponry, to counter force not with reason but with superior force: you don't love *because,* you love *despite;* you choose what you will struggle for and against, and you wrestle to the ground those opposing forces that would have you doubt the meaning or validity of your choices. For Faulkner, then, it is a matter of will, of main strength, a test of himself against the cosmos.

There is in all this, of course, a tragic heroism, attractive and indeed essential to those of us raised in his tradition. But the Pyrrhic irony of Faulkner's victory—*our* victory, too, when we manage it—is that to assert victory is simultaneously to admit defeat: to win he must submit to the *ought,* the *should,* the moral imperatives that require him to love despite when he can't find a sufficient because, imperatives that derive from the value systems of the cultural tradition of which he is so vital a part. The victory thus requires him to suppress his own powerful emotions of despair and frustration in favor of the communal mandate that love is better than hate, reconciliation better than alienation.

Put so baldly, of course, these sentiments are hard to argue with. Who wouldn't prefer the comforts of love and community to wandering alone in the existential wasteland of the twentieth century? At the same time, their baldness permits us to see them also as platitudes, which like all platitudes operate in the service of a cultural status quo, offering themselves up as Truth that ratifies and ensures a community's cohesion and stability. But such platitudes, uncritically enforced, take communities one step beyond stability and into rigidity. Faulkner's powerful conclusions in "Mississippi," of course, beg numerous questions that his fiction does not; indeed, most of his fiction offers very precise analyses of the dangers of cultural stasis. But even the fiction, finally, in its assumptions, or perhaps assertions, of its own universality, also begs many of the same questions about the hierarchical structures of community and about their profoundly different effects on men and women. In "Mississippi" and elsewhere, Faulkner takes for granted his own capacity—indeed, his need, often articulated as an artistic credo: life is motion, stasis is death—always to keep in motion, to avoid the rigidity that his platitudes here clearly can lead to. As a male, Faulkner bears a different relationship to the tradition that valorizes "love" and "reconciliation," that prefers its own definitions of "justice" and "injustice," "family" and "community," than women do. As a man, like Welty's King MacLain, Faulkner can choose what he wants to love and be reconciled with. Women traditionally do not have that freedom: to them falls the dailiness of love and reconciliation, of cohesion, their practice rather than their rhetorizing. Thus it seems not only fair but necessary to ask just *how* and *why* love is better than hate, reconciliation better than alienation: for whom are they better?

These are, I think, important questions in Welty's *The Golden Apples* and central to that collection's magnificent final story, "The Wanderers," which, like "Mississippi," also involves a homecoming, a confrontation with these same contending emotions of love and hate, the same challenge of reconciliation. Her responses to them are quite different from Faulkner's. Virgie Rainey, the chief character of "The Wanderers," is "over 40" years old. Like King MacLain, the heroic and fascinating wanderer of the town's romanticizing imagination, she too has been away from Morgana, for her own reasons and we do not know where, and has some time before now come home. She is a subdued version of her "June Recital" self, the wild and free spirit who as an adolescent rejected the tyranny of Miss Eckhart's metronome; she is obliged now in her middle age to care for a senile and problematic mother, who forces her to submit to the deadening metronomic regularity of domestic life in Morgana,

141

of which Miss Eckhart's hated metronome is the collection's metaphor.

Welty's staging of the ritualized activities of Virgie's mother's funeral—the coming and going, the visits, the laying out of the body, the gestures of sympathy, Virgie's necessary (and unwelcome) commingling with all these figures from her life (none of whom, she notes, except Snowdie MacLain, has ever been to visit her or her mother)—is Welty's unrelentingly unsentimental and often savagely funny analysis of such communal rituals. The story's spine is Virgie's growing capacity to admit to herself just how and why she is different from, and also just how little she cares for or needs, any of these folks whom Faulkner's tradition would ask her to love despite; how little she cares for this "community," nominally and traditionally the center of value in Southern life. In fact, Virgie discovers a wonderfully liberating and purifying capacity to hate, to be angry, which becomes her salvation precisely because it frees her from the need to love or even tolerate any of them, her own mother included, much less to continue to live among them.

142

Several times throughout the day of the funeral she deliberately shuns all contact—"Don't touch me," she repeats to Cassie and others, who touch her in embrace or pull her in one direction or another and who ignore her demands to be left alone. Virgie's efforts to be physically separate from them reaches a moment of high comedy in one of the closing scenes in which Cassie—who wants desperately to force Virgie to feel about her mother as she, Cassie, is obligated to feel about her own mother, a suicide—chases Virgie out of town in her car, pulls up beside her, and drives side by side out of town with her; they shout at each other through the open windows, Cassie forcing a conversation that Virgie clearly doesn't want to have; Cassie insists that Virgie drive by her yard to see how she has spelled out her own mother's name in 232 narcissus bulbs, to ensure her return every spring.

Most of all Virgie wants to be free of her mother. One of the story's most affecting scenes culminates in the moment of Katie's death, as Virgie fans her: "The clock jangled faintly as cymbals struck under water, but did not strike; it couldn't." There is no Faulknerian dingdong of Time and Doom here but rather a liberating pulse of time now become accommodating and friendly. The clock jangles "faintly," not in alarm but as a sign of some impending revelation, something just about to be understood; the "cymbals struck under water" (431)[12] likewise suggest some stirring impulse of fanfare, of celebration, of simple unadmittable delight in her freedom that she is not, at this moment, prepared to let become conscious but which will provide the specific energy for her reactions through the rest of the story. She realizes, at the moment of her mother's death, that she herself is "not much afraid of death, either of its delay or its surprise" (431), and she feels "a torrent of riches . . . flow over the room, submerging it, loading it with what was over-sweet" (432). Not her years of self-sacrifice but her mother's long overdue death offers her release from the prison of home and family and community that her self-sacrifice has placed her in.

She endures the opening skirmishes with the visitors who come when **143** they hear that Katie is dead. When in the evening they leave, they seem in their parting "to drag some mythical gates and barriers away from her view" (439) making it possible for her to see what she has never been able to see: the world "shimmers" in the "lighted distance" when she sees the "little last crescent of hills before the country of the river, and the fields" (439). In the face of human death, the cotton fields still "look busy on Sunday; even while they are not being picked they push out their bloom the same" (439). She sees, for the first time, a landscape artificially divided into families and property and seasons and even meteorological conditions: "the frail screens of standing trees still measured, broke, divided—Stark from Loomis from Spights from Holifield, and the summer from the rain" (439). Welty punctuates Virgie's meditations on these divisions with the appearance of Old Plez's ancient automobile, which appears to Virgie "cracked like some put-together puzzle of the globe of the world. Its cracks didn't meet from one side across to the other, and it was all held together with straightened-out baling wire, for today" (439). Like Plez's car, Morgana is a ramshackle vehicle, held together by no more force than the used baling wire of tradition.

Her mother having gone to the underworld, this Virgie/Virgo/Persephone releases herself to the upper world, not in the spring for the plowing and the harvest but in the fall—September, the month of Virgo—the time of harvest. She has reached her own fullness: at more than forty Virgie is at least premenopausal, and so free, or nearly, not just of her own history (now that her mother is dead) but even of the metronomic cycles of her own body that have bound her to time, to the rhythms of the earth, even to the natural rhythms of life and death. In a quite extraordinary passage, Virgie goes down to the river for a swim:

> It was bright as mid-afternoon in the openness of the water, quiet and peaceful. She took off her clothes and let herself into the river.
> She saw her waist disappear into reflectionless water; it was like walking into sky, some impurity of skies. All was one warmth, air, water, and her own body. All seemed one weight, one matter—until as she put down her head and closed her eyes and the light slipped under her lids, she felt this matter a translucent one, the river, herself, the sky all vessels which the sun filled. She began to swim in the river, forcing it gently, as she would wish for gentleness to her body. Her breasts around which she felt the water curving were as sensitive at that moment as the tips of wings must feel to birds, or antennae to insects. She felt the sand, grains intricate as little cogged wheels, minute shells of old seas, and the many dark ribbons of grass and mud touch her and leave her, like suggestions and withdrawals of some bondage that might have been dear, now dismembering and losing itself. She moved but like a cloud in skies, aware but only of the nebulous edges of her feeling and the vanishing opacity of her will, the carelessness for the water of the river through which her body had already passed as well as for what was ahead. The bank was all one, where out of the faded September world the little ripening plums started. Memory dappled her like no more than a paler light, which in slight agitations came through leaves, not darkening her for more than an instant. The iron taste of the old river was sweet to her, though. If she opened her eyes she looked at

blue-bottles, the skating waterbugs. If she trembled it was at the smoothness of a fish or snake that crossed her knees.

In the middle of the river, whose downstream or upstream could not be told by a current, she lay on her stretched arm, not breathing, floating. Virgie had reached the point where in the next moment she might turn into something without feeling it shock her. She hung suspended in the Big Black River as she would know to hang suspended in felicity. Far to the west, a cloud running fingerlike over the sun made her splash the water. She stood, walked along the soft mud of the bottom and pulled herself out of the water by a willow branch, which like warm rain brushed her back with its leaves.

At a distance, two little boys lying naked in the red light on the sandbar looked at her as she disappeared into the leaves. **145** (439–40)

This is a remarkably Emersonian passage, and its resonances with Faulkner's "The Bear" seem also unmistakable and deliberate. But Virgie is no transparent eyeball, she is no Isaac McCaslin bemoaning the loss of the Big Woods. Far from contending with it or from seeing herself as in any way separate from it or even transparent in it, Virgie *becomes* the universe, the constellation Virgo; she melds with it, absorbs it, assumes her position in the larger, the truly "universal," scheme of things as unselfconsciously and magisterially as Botticelli's Venus.

This scene occurs early, hard on the heels of her mother's death. From this point Virgie gradually divests herself of all the impedimenta of her containment in Morgana—her childhood friends, the remnants of her father's family, who come only to funerals; her parents' generation, who have gossiped her into running away; the men she's worked for, slept with, including her sailor lover Kewpie Moffatt (whom she misremembers, with a puckish smile, as Bucky); Miss Eckhart and a countrywoman's dead baby, both of whom she remembers as she walks through the cemetery: and both of whom, she realizes and admits, she hates.

But free now to hate, she discovers that in fact she doesn't hate Miss Eckhart, and she understands that

> she has never doubted that all the opposites on earth were
> close together, love close to hate, living to dying; but of them
> all, hope and despair were the closest blood—unrecognizable
> one from the other sometimes, making moments double upon
> themselves, and in the doubling double again, amending but
> never taking back. (452–53)

Almost simultaneously with this revelation, near the end of the story, Virgie sits majestically alone, contemplating all her possibilities. The earth and sky gather around her, stopping their motion, in salute and approbation:

> It was ripe afternoon, and all about her was that light in which
> the earth seems to come into its own, as if there would be no
> more days, only this day—when fields glow like deep pools
> and the expanding trees at their edges seem almost to open,
> like lilies, golden or dark. She had always loved that time of
> day, but now, alone, untouched now, she felt like dancing;
> knowing herself not really, in her essence, yet hurt; and thus
> happy. The chorus of crickets was as unprogressing and out of
> time as the twinkling of a star. (453)

This is a paradigmatic moment in Welty, one she will repeat, with variations, in the stories of *The Bride of the Innisfallen:* a moment in which a lone woman comes to herself in a dark wood but responds to it not as a moment of fear and perplexity, but rather savors it as a moment of epiphany, in which she discovers that she can be happy alone and stops to luxuriate in her freedom.

In "Mississippi" Faulkner resolves his conflicts with his home, his place, by overcoming his hatred not with love so much as with the *will to love*, so that the exercise of love is an act of main strength that must subdue hate, suppress it as something inimical to love. Virgie, by contrast, overcomes the cultural mandate to love her family and friends by giving herself permission to hate them. She discovers that hatred is purgative and liberating in ways that love can never be: hate does not require the suppression of what you love, but love often tyrannically demands the suppression of the things you hate. The freedom to hate can bring us closer to the things we love because in the free exercise of both emotions we can come closer to our own true terribly complex selves: as Virgie comes to understand, hate and love, hope and despair, are not antagonists at all, as in Faulkner's vision, but closely connected, intimate, and essential to our human wholeness.

This is not a Eudora Welty that we are accustomed to or prepared to accept. We have preferred to think of her as a gentle purveyor of the domestic, the odd, the grotesque. We have been comfortable reading her through the critical language of Southern literary studies that developed at about the time Welty began her publishing career. That language has never been large enough to contain either Faulkner or Welty, but it has worked most perniciously to keep us from understanding Welty. By reading her through such so-called Southern filters as place, humor, race, history, and the grotesque, our critical vocabulary, our cultural assumptions, have protected us from the parts of Welty's work that might unsettle and threaten us since they are actually subversive of those so-called values of family and community—place—that are so much a part of what we have been taught to think of as central to "Southern" literature.

But we can no longer ignore what is so manifestly *there* in Welty's work. In *The Golden Apples* she rewrites Southern literature, or at least provides us an opportunity to erase it and start over. The "community" of Morgana is a community only in the sense that a group of people live more or less together geographically. Mrs. Stark knows that one old woman owes another old woman a decent and respectable funeral, but nothing in the book suggests that anybody in this "community" feels any obligation to the living, to themselves or any other. Morgana, like the Southern communities of our agrarian traditions, worships the metronomic rhythms of night and day, of lunar and menstrual cycles and seasonal change. Instead of offering change and renewal, however, the natural rhythms of *The Golden Apples* become other forms of communal limitation, which Virgie and King MacLain have resisted but to which the community has prostrated itself because it cannot see beyond the next tick of the clock, the next five P.M. when the cows need calling and

147

milking, the next spring when we must plant. As a "community," then, Morgana constantly turns inward, using its rituals of life, death, and June recitals, not to regenerate itself but merely to replicate. Morgana is thus trapped in the deadening circularity of cycles: it worships its seasons, its rituals, its monuments, its cemeteries: finally, it worships death. Perhaps death is the only way out of the cycle: suicide is not unknown in Morgana.

Through no particular act of her own, Virgie no longer has to submit to these rhythms. Free of her past, she no longer has to replicate her life from one day to the next; she can now regenerate a free and independent self, one yet to be discovered, or perhaps one that can be *re*covered from her "June Recital" adolescence. Looking outward, she exfoliates, en-larges, and *becomes* the universe with which Faulkner so constantly and epically contends and to which the people of Morgana have long since surrendered. At the story's close, true to her name, Virgie has brought rain to the wasteland and she sits under a tree. The French origins of her name suggest that she has become Virgie *reine*, Virgie the Queen, the Virgin Queen, Aphrodite and Virgo, sitting on a stile throne with her back to the MacLain courthouse—the house of the court, the royal palace of the king. As Danièle Pitavy-Souques has suggested, it could specifically be the Yoknapatawpha County courthouse to which Virgie and Welty have turned their backs.[13] It is certainly the symbolic counting house of the political landscape of the Southern literary tradition that Faulkner's courthouse so powerfully symbolizes. Her back squarely turned to that courthouse and that tradition, Virgie looks not inward but outward, facing the rich, lubricious, and delicious landscape of her own future: the landscape of possibility.

This, too, is a paradigmatic moment in Welty, a repetition of the ear-lier one when the universe stopped to acknowledge her freedom. It is a striking moment and difficult to understand because we are not accus-tomed to seeing women happy *and* alone, happy *because* alone. Likewise, and perhaps even more important, traditional readings of "Southern" lit-erature teach us to believe that change is loss, that loss is a bad thing, that what we lose is always more valuable than what we gain: all this because change always involves a direct assault on the "old verities"—the *old* ver-ities, verities *because* old, and always inextricable from our communal

148

memories of a past that was somehow better, more stable, than the present. We have thus too easily accepted a "sense of place" as a mantra of Southern literary study and have been reluctant to understand how often history, our sense of the past, of place, keeps the present in a virtual chokehold. I hasten to point out that though many of Faulkner's characters and critics make the mistake of idealizing the past so strongly as to resist change, Faulkner himself never does. He constantly argues that the capacity to cope with change is the test of maturity in an individual; but even these terms—*cope* and *test*—testify to the intensity of the moral struggle that change entails for a people whose individual and communal lives, their places in time and space, are invested in the values of the past, those "old" verities.

In this struggle, Morgana is undoubtedly a Faulknerian, a Southern, community. This is precisely the community that Virgie, at the end of **149** "The Wanderers," is poised to reject. She sees change not as loss but as opportunity, as possibility; if she chooses, she can now step aside from history, as so many of Faulkner's characters want desperately to do but cannot. Virgie refuses to be imprisoned in the past, and she faces a future limited only by the choices she is now, as never before, capable of making. She is willing to discover new verities, new configurations of social organization, that could give new and vital meaning to her life.

We are prepared to be thrilled and moved by the traditional visions of the William Faulkners. We are not so prepared to be discomfited and challenged by "the wildness of the world behind the woman's view." But that view, especially Eudora Welty's, can give us a fix on the most intimate and frightening parts of our lives that the Faulkners, with all their clashing and clanging and self-conscious commitment to Cosmic Significance, never have. Faulkner of course saw what he saw, as Shakespeare did, and we are immeasurably the richer for it. But he didn't see it all, nobody can, and like Shakespeare he saw what his tradition allowed him to see.

Eudora Welty's eye, too, is a defining eye, but it is also a subversive eye that looks at things other eyes don't know to look at or, worse, avoid. But hers too can be an enlarging and enriching vision if we have the courage to see what she is showing us instead of what we want to see.

# Notes

1. Thomas L. McHaney, Review of Walter Sullivan, *A Requiem for the Renaissance. Mississippi Quarterly* 30 (1976–77): 185–88.

2. The portions of this essay on Welty are adapted from my "The Landscape of Illusion in Eudora Welty's 'The Wanderers,'" in *Southern Landscape*, ed. Tony Badger, Walter Edgar, and Jan Nordby Gretland (Tübingen: Stauffenburg-Verlag, 1996), 236–42.

3. Joan St. C. Crane, "William Faulkner to Eudora Welty: A Letter," *Mississippi Quarterly* 42 (1989): 223–28.

4. Eudora Welty, *The Eye of the Story* (New York: Random House, 1979), 207–11.

5. Eudora Welty, "Department of Amplification," *New Yorker* 24 (January 1, 1949): 41–42.

6. Welty, *Eye of the Story*, 116–33.

7. Ibid., 212–20.

8. Ibid., 163–73.

9. Welty, "Department of Amplification," 41–42.

10. See, for example, Rebecca Mark, *The Dragon's Blood: Feminist Intertextuality in Eudora Welty's "The Golden Apples"* (Jackson: University Press of Mississippi, 1994).

11. All references to "Mississippi" are to the edition by James B. Meriwether in *Essays, Speeches, and Public Letters by William Faulkner* (New York: Random House, 1965); page numbers are noted parenthetically in the text.

12. All references to "The Wanderers" are to Welty's *Collected Stories* (New York: Harcourt Brace Jovanovich, 1980) and are noted parenthetically in the text.

13. Danièle Pitavy-Souques, *La Mort de Méduse* (Lyon: Presses Universitaires de Lyon, 1992), 47.

# Pragmatic Humanism in
# *The Ambassadors* and *Absalom, Absalom!*

## *A Philosophical Link between*
## *James and Faulkner*

James and Faulkner? How does one compare the creators of     **151**
Lambert Strether and Ike Snopes? It is hard to imagine Henry
James and William Faulkner even speaking to each other had
they ever met, and neither would have been likely to
acknowledge similarity, let alone a shared approach.

—Jeanne Campbell Reesman, *American Designs: The Later Novels of
James and Faulkner*

**S**ometimes the best approach to a difficult subject is an enigmatic
prefatory statement that defines and titillates as well as challenges. Thus I was pleased to discover that the almost perfect
preface I was wracking my brain to write had already been written—by Jeanne Campbell Reesman, whom I quote in the epigraph. Reesman to my delight had put her finger precisely on the
spot of paradox: Henry James and William Faulkner—"arguably
America's two greatest novelists"[1]—who between them have attracted more criticism than any other two literary figures in the
United States, have frequently been viewed as polar opposites,
with little in common but a propensity for exasperating and ex-
acerbating the uninitiated with their strikingly different kinds of
complexity and profundity in language, style, technique, and
philosophy. Yet the two share convictions about the role of man

in a pluralistic universe; of the innumerable treatises on James and on Faulkner, separately, it is little short of amazing that Reesman's ground-breaking *American Designs* is the only book to link the two in an affirmative philosophy at odds with naturalism, the prevailing mode when both were writing. And even Reesman, who finds in both James and Faulkner the theme that "the problem of knowledge" constitutes the most serious "moral problem in American thought and culture,"[2] does not touch upon what I believe to be an even more significant attitude[3] held by both authors—pragmatic humanism as articulated and nurtured by William James, philosopher and older brother to Henry James. This brief essay is limited to one important aspect of humanism in *The Ambassadors* and *Absalom, Absalom!*, each acknowledged as a literary masterpiece reflecting its author's main ideas; but if my contention that humanistic philosophy pervades the fiction of both writers is correct, a thorough, comprehensive study of humanism in James and Faulkner is needed to fill a cultural gap in American literary scholarship.[4]

**152**

Humanism, it must be recognized, has different meanings in different times and places; before humanism in Henry James and Faulkner can be considered, the word as used in this article must be precisely defined. When defined broadly, humanism is any attitude that exalts the human element, as opposed to the supernatural, divine elements, over the grosser, animal element. Dating back to ancient Greece and Rome, humanism took on added significance in the Renaissance, when humanists agreed with the ancients in asserting the dignity of mankind and the importance of the present life, as against those medieval philosophers who considered the present life primarily as a preparation for the future life. In the history of epistemology it has been alternately revered and reviled. For the purposes of this essay, the main point is that, while Henry James and Faulkner take much from early forms of humanism, they much more specifically embrace the twentieth-century concept of humanism as promulgated in William James's seminal book *Pragmatism* (1907).

In *Pragmatism* (which he subtitles *"A New Name for Some Old Ways of Thinking"*) William James in effect discards the word *humanism* and substitutes for it *pragmatism*, because (as he puts it) "the name of pragmatism seems fairly to be in the ascendant." But William James makes clear that he had replaced the word, not the philosophy. His position is still "the humanist position,"[5] and his book both an energetic defense and a careful exegesis of the philosophy. "I am all aflame with it," he writes, "as displacing all rationalistic systems"; he further calls it "the only philosophy with *no* humbug in it."[6] Central to William James's pragmatism are two ideas. First, nothing in a pluralistic universe still in an evolutionary process is rigid and predetermined. There are no absolutes: no absolute rights, no absolute wrongs, no absolute principles. Even the most hallowed of moral and religious principles are assumptions of truth that are validated only by testing, experience, and results. "How can principles and general views ever be anything but abstract outlines?" William James asks.[7] Second, man with his freedom of will, his inquiring mind, and his conscience has the intellectual, moral, and aesthetic power "to change the character of future reality."[8] With the whole outcome of the universe as yet undecided, human decisions carry cosmic importance. Human consciousness gives man adaptability, power, and responsibility in a "world [that] stands really malleable, waiting to receive its final touches at our hands."[9] Both Henry James and Faulkner, believing as William James did in the dignity of man, hold man to have freedom of choice and thus responsibility for his actions; neither author is absolutist in belief, each like William James eschewing dogmatism and rigidity, and advocating openness and adaptability. Both have high moral and ethical standards in their fiction, standards that differ from the conventional in that they are more enlightened and less rigid. Principles offer guidelines for the conduct of the individual; but people "on whom nothing is lost"[10] (Henry James's term) have an obligation, a responsibility, to forsake even hallowed principles if thorough and judicious search invalidates the principle in the specific circumstances at hand. The pragmatic humanist asks: Does adherence to principle provide a beneficial result, one that is fair, compassionate, and altruistic? The final test of principle in a unique situation is its effect: "the proof of the pudding is in the eating"[11]—experience, not theory, is the ultimate determiner. But, because the knowledge gained by experience is ex post facto, the individual on whom nothing is lost must look behind every issue, become aware of its complexities and subtle ambiguities, before a decision that is wise, equitable, and

153

beneficial to the most deserving can be made. To a William James humanist, justice to humanity has precedence over adherence to principle. With strikingly different approaches,[12] Henry James in *The Ambassadors* and William Faulkner in *Absalom, Absalom!* both illustrate that the achievement of fairness and equity in human affairs sometimes requires the rejection of principle. *The Ambassadors* seems by design the almost perfect embodiment of William James's version of pragmatic humanism, whereas the humanistic theme of *Absalom, Absalom!*, though present, is obscured in the violence and tragedy of the narrative. Although other characters could have been chosen for study, the actions and decisions of a single character in each novel—Lambert Strether in *The Ambassadors* and Thomas Sutpen in *Absalom, Absalom!*—serve to illustrate, in contradictory fashion, the humanistic concept of William James: when humanity seems at odds with principle, it is the person, not the principle, that should be protected.

First, then, let us consider *The Ambassadors*. Lambert Strether was carefully selected by Henry James to serve as the novel's single vessel of consciousness through whose voice, eyes, ears, perceptions, and senses all action is gradually revealed. Projected from the beginning to be the very embodiment of the New England conscience,[13] Strether is a middle-aged, high-minded magazine editor, engaged to the wealthy widow patron of his magazine. His fiancée, Mrs. Newsome, has commissioned him for a special pilgrimage to Paris: his mission is to bring safely home to Woollett, Massachusetts, the widow's son presumed to be in an immoral relationship with a Parisian woman. Still naive and unsophisticated at fifty-five—a widower who has lost his wife and only child—Strether has had his creativity and imagination stifled in a dull, conventional existence without passion or expectation. Like many of James's male protagonists, Strether has been the passive observer, rather than the active participant in life. His youthful years, he feels, were wasted; "it's as if the train had fairly waited at the station for me," he confesses, "without my having had the gumption to know it was there."[14] His early impressions of Paris, of Chad Newsome, and of Chad's circle of friends awaken in Strether the sense that life is a many-splendored thing; to have missed it is to have missed everything. "Live all you can; it's a mistake not to," he says to Little Bilham. "It doesn't so much matter what you do in particular, so long as you have your life. If you haven't had your life, what have you had?" (153). Strether's perception of the intellectual and aesthetic advantages of Paris—his recognition of the dullness of his past, unimaginative existence and his awareness of the excitement and adventure he has missed—all cause him to feel that he, as well as Chad, is being tried by Woollett's standards. He sees that, if he is honest with himself, he cannot follow Woollett's conventional interpretation of Chad's life in Paris, for he now perceives its richness and depth. The gradual evolution of his insight and understanding lead inevitably to the conclusion that he must disobey the mandate from Mrs. Newsome which had sent him to Paris. Rather than bring his fiancée's prodigal son home to take over the family business, Strether now knows he must persuade Chad to remain in Paris with Mme. de Vionnet—the sensitive and intelligent woman of culture who has taught the dissolute young American how to find himself, how to live graciously and handsomely in an engaging social and aesthetic environment.

Since the novel turns on this momentous decision by Strether to recommend as a demonstration of gratitude and good faith the continuance of what Woollett could see only as an adulterous relationship, it is crucial that James make plausible the radical change in his protagonist's position. When Strether accepted his mission as ambassador, he was fully dedicated to the Woollett view that any liaison by Chad with a woman in Paris, outside of marriage, was necessarily depraved. Believing at first that the "virtuous attachment" (128) between Chad and Mme. De Vionnet was purely platonic, Strether is taken aback when he perceives for himself that the relationship is also sexual. In the dramatic scene memorable for its striking imagery (chapter 31), Strether through his own awakened awareness and powers of perception discovers "their eminent 'lie,' Chad's and hers" (403). Yet in the light of all circumstances Strether decides in the end that consideration for the "sublime" person who had "saved" what had been a boorish Chad had moral precedence over longstanding ecclesiastical principle. Close to becoming the Jamesian person upon whom nothing is lost, Strether has so grown intellectually, ethically, and spiritually that, even in opposition to traditional morality, he now

155

can see and appreciate the value of a human relationship he once considered sordid. Strether has learned not to accept a situation at surface value, but to look behind it for all its hidden complexities and ambiguities—to regard it as a complicated situation in which all factors must be carefully weighed before the best remedy can be deduced.

This change in Strether's point of view reflects James's position that every moral dilemma is unique, that each calls for a creative resolution independent of precedent or rule. Strether's penchant for close observation and pragmatic decision-making stand in sharp contrast to the unbending despotic sanctity of Sarah Pocock, who has been sent to Paris to replace him as her mother's emissary. Strether's observations about Mme. de Vionnet and her effect on Chad reveal the openness of his own search for truth:

**156**

> I think tremendously well of her, at the same time that I seem to feel her "life" to be really none of my business. It's my business, that is, only so far as Chad's own life is affected by it; and what has happened, don't you see? is that Chad's has been affected so beautifully. The proof of the pudding's in the eating. (351)

But for Sarah Pocock there can be no extenuating circumstances for a relationship—or for a woman—she has predetermined to be immoral. When Strether in amazement queries Pocock, "You don't, on your honour, appreciate Chad's fortunate development?," her brittle response reveals her closed mind: "Fortunate? I call it hideous" (351–52). And with reference to Mme. de Vionnet, she asks Strether with righteous indignation and in blind rage: "Do you consider her even an apology for a decent woman?" (349). To Sarah Pocock, Strether's favorable assessment of Chad's mistress is highly offensive: "What is your conduct but an outrage to women like us?" she austerely inquires. That "there can be a doubt" in Strether's mind as to "his duty" in choosing between "such another" (347) as Mme. De Vionnet and "decent" Woollett women like herself and her mother is incomprehensible to Pocock, for she and her mother have always adhered to the principle by which they judge Marie de Vionnet. They stand on principles they believe in; they mean well, but in their inability or refusal to take in particular details that render their principles inapplicable, they sacrifice humanity to an absolute standard.

Strether's progress from bigotry to humanistic enlightenment is Henry James's ultimate illustration of what he means by the full life—a life that is intellectually, morally, and aesthetically perceptive, attainable by intelligent and conscientious human beings who seek to become persons upon whom nothing is lost. Lambert Strether, somewhat like Huckleberry Finn in a completely different environment, discovers that the boundaries of conscience, so-called, dissolve before a wider Weltanschauung that rests on the fine discrimination between what is worth saving and losing in any particular life. Humanism is the figure in the carpet of *The Ambassadors*, as I believe it to be in much of James's fiction, **157** including all of his later novels.

The humanism of Faulkner, I hold, is just as strong as James's; but because it is less conspicuous—because it is almost concealed in the complexity of his discourse—the case for it is more difficult to make. As we have seen, humanism is at the core of *The Ambassadors;* James's embracing of it positively and affirmatively contributes to the book's central theme, gradually yet dramatically and fully revealed in the thought processes of the novel's single vessel of consciousness. In contrast, *Absalom, Absalom!* demonstrates humanism—powerfully and tellingly, it is true—by underscoring its *need* (and illustrating the dire consequences of its absence) rather than by showing the positive human effects of its presence. In *The Ambassadors* pragmatic humanism and Lambert Strether are synonymous: the unfolding of the consciousness of the protagonist lays open the philosophical basis of the novel. The humanism of *Absalom, Absalom!* is manifested not dramatically, but expositorily; the reader sees Thomas Sutpen only from the outside, through the eyes of unreliable narrators (Rosa, Mr. Compson, Quentin, and Shreve) and against a background of violence that casts a negative shadow on all actions in the novel. Rather than revealing, as does *The Ambassadors,* the positive result of placing humanity above principle, *Absalom, Absalom!*

focuses on the negative consequences of sacrificing humanity to an absolute principle. Whereas Lambert Strether in his ultimate wisdom decides that human sincerity, intelligence, love, and need outweigh unequivocal adherence to conventional morality, Thomas Sutpen is portrayed by those analyzing him as a militant absolutist who places so high a premium upon being a follower of principle that he totally disregards the dignities—even the right to live—of human beings. Like Hawthorne's Richard Digby, he is the man of principle etched in stone.[15] He is more like Sarah Pocock than like Lambert Strether; but his lack of humanity is Faulkner's point, just as Strether's *attainment* of a mature understanding of humanity is James's. In *Absalom, Absalom!*, Sutpen is seen as a zealous follower of a rigid, idealistic creed to whose bigotry and other shortcomings he is totally blind.

**158**      But Faulkner's portrayal of Thomas Sutpen is not without sympathy for him or his cause. In *Sutpen's Design* Dirk Kuyk, Jr. makes a persuasive case that readers and critics have misunderstood and misread Sutpen, pointing as evidence to a remark by Faulkner himself: "The odd man [Sutpen] was himself a little too big for people no greater in stature than Quentin and Miss Rosa and Mr. Compson to see all at once. It would have taken perhaps a wiser or more tolerant or more sensitive or more thoughtful person to see him as he was."[16]

The critic who perhaps comes closest to fathoming what Faulkner meant in terming Sutpen "a little too big" for people lacking in wisdom, tolerance, sensitivity, and thoughtfulness "to see" is Olga Vickery: she finds Sutpen "a mirror image of the South" who "becomes the staunchest defender of [its] idols" and conducts "his life strictly in terms of its ethical code."[17] Vickery emphasizes the "rigid attitude" of Sutpen, who "never deviates" from "the letter of . . . law" that he sees as "the code of the South."[18] Though Faulkner scholars widely disagree on precisely what motivates Sutpen and why,[19] there is general agreement that a combination of innocence and ambition cause him as a young man to leave his native western Virginia with an obsessive hunger to become a part of the noblesse oblige aristocracy of the genteel white planter of the Old South. A few biographical details about Sutpen from the text itself (and some added commentary) will buttress this statement.

The experience that shocked and stunned young Sutpen elicits the reader's sympathy: his being turned away by what Quentin terms a "monkey-nigger"[20] from the front door of a plantation house and being ordered to use the back door only. Until that moment the youthful mountaineer—unacquainted with slavery and the plantation system—knew neither racial prejudice nor social principle. Confronted, however, with a situation that nothing in his background had prepared him for, Sutpen reacts intelligently: he registers no resentment toward the black butler because he recognizes that the slave's authority came from his master, the owner of the plantation. To make sure that he profits (rather than suffers) from his rebuke, Sutpen vows that he too will become a man of authority and influence, and he focuses on learning, and following to the letter, the rigid code of the Southern aristocracy to which he **159** craved to belong. In his view, the fulfillment of this vow requires the adoption of the set of rigid principles that he sees as defining the *Southern gentleman,* and he decides to adopt it. To Sutpen it is a positive decision unmixed with malice or desire for revenge: he cherishes the noblesse oblige life of the planter of the Old South, and he perceives that the only path to its attainment lies in joining the planter who had rebuked him in adherence to inflexible social principles based on class, race, and land ownership. Although this adherence to principle brings him, temporarily, the social status that he sought, it eventually costs him not only that status, but all of his loved ones, the fruits of his considerable labors, and even his life. From Faulkner's point of view, it may be even more significant that adherence to principle deprives Sutpen of an important part of his intellectual and spiritual *self:* the freedom to make life decisions based on particular circumstances rather than on pre-determined, generalized philosophical guidelines.

Though his well-planned success came quickly, it did not come easily. Knowing that he needed "money in considerable quantities" to carry out his design, Sutpen left Virginia for the West Indies, where it was reported that "poor men . . . became rich" (200). First working as an overseer, he helped put down a rebellion of slaves and at twenty married the daughter of the master of the plantation. Subsequently he rapidly accumulated wealth and became the father of a son—seemingly well on his way to fulfillment of his ambition. Yet Sutpen repudiated both his young wife and his son—presumably because of his discovery that (in Faulkner's words, in the "Chronology") "his wife has Negro blood" (312)—taboo of course in the Southern code of honor. Leaving wife and son, the plantation, and all other resources except for twenty slaves and a sum of money, Sutpen found his way to Jefferson, Mississippi, the site he chose for furthering his life's design. Purchasing from the Chickasaw Indians a piece of fertile bottom-land encompassing one hundred square miles, Sutpen—with the assistance of his slaves and a mysterious French architect—built the region's most substantial mansion. He married Ellen Coldfield, daughter of the respected merchant who had aided him in establishing his magnificent gentleman's estate, and in time she bore her husband two children, a boy and a girl. Again—this time in the American South, the place where in his vision he attained hegemony—Sutpen seemed to have consummated his dream.

**160**

Yet such consummation, if real, was not to last. His son Henry Sutpen went off to college and befriended an older classmate from New Orleans named Charles Bon; and, in the course of events, brought Bon home for Christmas at Sutpen's Hundred. Sutpen seemed suspicious of Bon from the very beginning, and began to investigate his background. When Bon became engaged to Sutpen's daughter, Judith, Sutpen forbade the marriage without making public his reason. When Henry objected, Sutpen revealed to his son some information about Bon that the investigation in New Orleans had turned up, although the precise nature of the revelation is speculative. But whatever its nature, Henry sided with Bon against his father, and the two young men left Sutpen's Hundred together.

Faulkner leaves ambiguous the reasons why Sutpen opposed the marriage, and again critical debate has resulted.[21] Resolution of the controversy is unnecessary for our purposes here. Whether Sutpen's opposition is based on his discovery that Bon is the son he left behind in Haiti (and therefore of mixed blood), or that Bon has an octoroon mistress in New Orleans who bore him an illegitimate son, or that Bon as Sutpen's first-born son (not known to be black) would raise questions about Henry's right to inherit Sutpen's Hundred—any or all or any combination of the above (whether involving incest, miscegenation, challenge to primogeniture, or impugning of family honor)—would be heresy under the code of the Old South which Sutpen rigorously upheld. The point is that Sutpen, unlike Lambert Strether, put principle as he knew it above humanity—without regard for compassion, human dignity, or justness. The simmering animosity that erupted into violence after the Civil War— Henry's murder of Bon, the killing of Sutpen by Wash Jones—reinforces the disastrous consequence of inflexible adherence to a code as antiquated as the Old South of which it was a reflection. During the Civil War, Sutpen was the model Southern gentleman of honor—upholding noblesse oblige in his responsible stewardship and courage in aiding and defending those in his community less fortunate or less gifted than he. His intentions, like those of Sarah Pocock, were good; but unquestioning "keep-off-the-grass morality"[22]—lacking in intelligence, magnanimity, and concern for fairness—only intensified the threat of bigotry to humanity. Thomas Sutpen is a prime example of how the man of principle per se can be destructive of human rights and dignity.

**161**

Both Henry James and William Faulkner reject the naturalistic view that man is devoid of free will and therefore blameless for his actions. Both writers enfold the pragmatic humanism advocated by William James: "On the pragmatist side," William James wrote, "we have only one edition of the universe, unfinished, growing in all sorts of places, especially in the places where thinking beings are at work."[23] The Jamesian pragmatist "believes that the world can be bettered, here and there, bit by bit, in patches—and this by the moral and intellectual actions of individual human beings."[24] Henry James and William Faulkner demonstrate in *The Ambassadors* and *Absalom, Absalom!*, respectively, their own belief that human initiative can change the world—the ultimate in humanism. But if the experience is to be beneficent like Lambert Strether's (rather than destructive like Thomas Sutpen's), the favorable result is brought about by man's creative ability to distinguish what in life is truly important, what is worth saving and what best can be given up, not in robot-like reliance on ecclesiastical, moral, or social creed, without regard to fairness, justice, or compassion. That James and Faulkner embrace the humanistic philosophy has been revealed through a close reading of the texts of *The Ambassadors* and *Absalom, Absalom!* But if the question arises as to whether too much has been read into the texts—that is, too much significance attached to passages the authors themselves did not intend to be significant—there is evidence outside the texts themselves that both James and Faulkner were aware of the philosophical import of their work and that they had no reluctance—perhaps even had a preference—in being identified with it. That the humanistic philosophy exists in the oeuvre of these two masters of American literature is acknowledged by their own explanatory words.

In 1907 Henry James wrote to his brother William some months after having immersed himself in *Pragmatism:*

**162**

> Why the devil I didn't write to you after reading your Pragmatism—how I kept from it—I can't now explain save by the very fact of the spell itself (of interest and enthrallment) that the book cast upon me; I simply sank down, under it, into such depths of submission and assimilation that any reaction, very nearly, even that of acknowledgment, would have almost the taint of dissent or escape. Then I was lost in the wonder to the extent to which all my life I have (like M. Jourdain) unconsciously pragmatised. You are immensely and universally *right.*[25]

Later, after reading William James's *A Pluralistic Universe,* Henry James again professed:

> It may sustain and inspire you a little to know that I am with you, all along the line—and can conceive of no philosophy that is not yours! As an artist and a 'creator' I can catch on, hold on, to pragmatism and can work in the light of it and apply it.[26]

In August, 1955, in Nagano, Japan, William Faulkner responded to a question about how he would classify himself:

Q: They say you are not so interested in what is called "literary classification." You have been called a lot of things, such as naturalist, traditionalist, Symbolist, etc. I wonder what school you feel you belong to.

F: I would say, and hope, the only school I belong to, that I want to belong to, is the humanist school.[27]

No less than the differences in style between *The Ambassadors* and *Absalom, Absalom!*, the differences in the language of these quotations underscore the commonly held perception of Henry James and William Faulkner as writers perhaps as different from each other as any other pair in the American canon. More surprisingly—and more significantly—the quotations also establish outside of the novels a philosophical common- **163** ality made plain within them: subscription to the pragmatic humanism, espoused by William James, that values intellectual flexibility more highly than adherence to hidebound principle.

# Notes

1. Jeanne Campbell Reesman, *American Designs: The Late Novels of James and Faulkner* (Philadelphia: University of Pennsylvania Press, 1991), ix (preface).
2. Ibid.
3. I choose the word *attitude* deliberately to reflect William James's emphasis; he wrote in 1907: "an *attitude* [emphasis added] of orientation, is what the pragmatic method means. *The attitude of looking away from first things, principles, 'categories,' supposed necessities: and of looking towards last things, fruits, consequences, facts.*" Earlier in the same chapter, entitled "What Pragmatism Means," William James had stated succinctly: "It has no dogmas, and no doctrines save its method." See William James, *Pragmatism* (orig. pub. 1907), ed. Bruce Kuklick (Indianapolis: Hackett, 1981), 29, hereafter cited as WJ. Neither in his monumental five-volume biography nor in the more recent one-volume abridgement, *Henry James, a Life* (Cambridge, Mass.: Harper & Row, 1985), does Leon Edel make the relationship between William and Henry James an association of philosophical (rather than personal or psychological) significance. Other recent books on James that pay little more than scant attention to Henry James's adoption of his older brother's pragmatic humanism include

Millicent Bell, *Meaning in Henry James* (Cambridge, Mass.: Harvard University Press, 1991), 305–06; and Ross Posnock, *The Trial of Curiosity: Henry James, William James, and the Challenge of Modernity* (New York: Oxford University Press, 1991), 92–93. R. W. B. Lewis, *The Jameses: A Family Narrative* (New York: Farrar, Strauss, and Giroux, 1991), 556–64, devotes a section to "Pragmatism" and William James's joyful enthusiasm for it, as well as Henry James's more moderate acceptance. Richard A. Hocks, *Henry James and Pragmatistic Thought: A Study in the Relationship between the Philosophy of William James and the Literary Art of Henry James* (Chapel Hill: University of North Carolina Press, 1974), 15–37, 152–81, is the only published book that relates directly to the liaison between philosophy and literature—i.e., between William and Henry James—in the fiction of the novelist; Hocks's study is judicious and provocative, but the most thorough analysis of the humanistic basis for Henry James's late-phase novels is Ruth Taylor Todasco, "The Humanism of Henry James: A Study of the Relation between Theme and Imagery in the Later Novels" (Ph.D. dissertation, Texas Technological College, 1963), an excellent monograph that influenced my own ideas about James and humanism. The book of the most value to students of Henry and William James and their symbiotic philosophical/literary relationship is the incomparable pioneering work of F. O. Matthiesen, *The James Family, including Selections from the Writings of Henry James, Senior, William, Henry, and Alice James* (New York: Knopf, 1947), 112, 211, 24–42, 342, 343, passim.

4. A further tie of both authors to William James which would be worth pursuing is the use each makes of William James's doctrines of "stream of consciousness" and the social formation of the self, topics not treated in this essay. For an excellent article dealing primarily with William James's influence on his brother's technique, see J. N. Sharma, "Humanism as Vision and Technique in *The Ambassadors*," in *The Magic Circle of Henry James*, ed. Amritjit Singh and K. Ayyappa Paniker (New York: Envoy Press, 1989), 146–59.

5. WJ, 33, 110. William James recognized that the "severe attack" on F. C. S. Schiller (after the publication of Schiller's book *Humanism* in 1904) had a pernicious effect on the reputation of philosophers who embraced humanism as well as on the philosophy itself. But William James also acknowledged the negative connotation given to "the name 'pragmatism,'" with its suggestions of action" and concluded that it "has been an unfortunate choice, I have to admit" (Matthiessen, *James Family*, 240). But in a letter to Schiller, James professed that reading the former had enabled him to grasp "the full import for life and regeneration, the great perspective of the programme, and the renovating characters for *all things* of Humanism" (*The Letters of William James, Edited by His Son Henry James*, 2 vols. [Boston: Atlantic Monthly Press, 1920], 2: 245).

6. Matthiessen, *James Family*, 240.

7. WJ, 19.

8. William James, *The Meaning of Truth: A Sequel to "Pragmatism"* (New York: Longmans, Green, 1909), 94.

9. WJ, 115.

10. Henry James, "The Art of Fiction," in *Partial Portraits of Henry James*, intro. Leon Edel (Ann Arbor: University of Michigan Press, 1970), 390.

11. Pithy statement made by Strether in his defense of Mme. De Vionnet to Sarah Pocock, quoted below.

12. The most conspicuous difference is in the narrative techniques of the two authors: James's emphasis is on the revelation of the inner consciousness of his protagonist, whose words, thoughts, and actions illustrate humanism in its finest form; Faulkner, on the other hand, remains outside of his central figure, whose obsessive character and destructive actions are seen only through the eyes of unreliable and unsympathetic narrators.

13. Henry James, "Project of Novel," in *The Notebooks of Henry James*, ed. F. O. Matthiessen and Kenneth B. Murdock (New York: Oxford University Press, 1947), 374.

14. Henry James, *The Ambassadors*, ed. Christopher Butler (Oxford: Oxford University Press, 1985), 153; all future references to *The Ambassadors* are to this edition, with page numbers given within parentheses in the text.

15. Hawthorne, also a humanist, shared William James's skepticism about individuals with rigid, inflexible views. In contrast to paying homage to "men of principles," William James uses the term almost in derision. See WJ, 117.

16. Dirk Kuyk, Jr., *Sutpen's Design: Interpreting Faulkner's "Absalom, Absalom!"* (Charlottesville: University Press of Virginia, 1990), 4. The quotation cited is from Frederick L. Gwynn and Joseph Blotner, eds., *Faulkner in the University: Class Conferences at the University of Virginia, 1957–1958* (Charlottesville: University Press of Virginia, 1959), 274.

17. Olga W. Vickery, *The Novels of William Faulkner*, rev. ed. (Baton Rouge: Louisiana State University Press, 1964), 93, 94. Vickery does not consider Sutpen's actions in the context of pragmatic humanism, but she does acknowledge that his unwavering commitment to an absolute standard violates human rights and dignity, his own included. The interpretation of *Absalom, Absalom!* by Vickery is skillfully done, even without her recognition of the significance of its philosophical vein. A book by Joseph Gold emphasizes the "generally humanistic attitude" of Faulkner's work after 1948, but overlooks the strong current of pragmatic humanism in the major novels. See Gold, *William Faulkner: A Study in Humanism from Metaphor to Discourse* (Norman: University of Oklahoma Press, 1966), 8. It is surprising that Gold omits *Absalom, Absalom!* from his detailed discussions of humanism in Faulkner (including "The Bear" and the six novels that followed it), because he sees "the absence of human values" in Sutpen: "The horror of Sutpen lies not in his being the 'demon' into which Rosa oversimplifies him, but in his total unawareness of good and evil, in his want of humanity"(34). As the only scholar to write a book that associates Faulkner with humanism, Gold sees Faulkner's Nobel Prize acceptance speech as the beginning of his fully embracing humanistic thought. The Nobel Prize speech is more properly

viewed as a culmination and synthesis of what had gone before, rather than as the beginning of something new or different.

18. Vickery, *Novels of William Faulkner*, 94.

19. See Kuyk, *Sutpen's Design*, 9–15; Noel Polk, *Children of the Dark House: Text and Context in Faulkner* (Jackson: University Press of Mississippi, 1996), 137–43; Donald M. Kartinganer, *The Fragile Thread: The Meaning and Form in Faulkner's Novels* (Amherst: University of Massachusetts Press, 1979), 88; Michael Millgate, *The Achievement of William Faulkner* (1966; rpt. Athens: University of Georgia Press, 1989), 158–59; David Minter, *William Faulkner: His Life and Work* (Baltimore: Johns Hopkins University Press, 1980), 154; John T. Irwin, *Doubling and Incest/Repetition and Revenge: A Speculative Reading of Faulkner* (Baltimore: Johns Hopkins University Press, 1975), 98; Estella Schoenberg, *Old Tales and Talking: Quentin Compson in William Faulkner's "Absalom Absalom!" and Related Works* (Jackson: University Press of Mississippi, 1977), 81–82; Elizabeth M. Kerr, *William Faulkner's Gothic Domain* (Port Washington, N.Y.: Kennikat, 1979), 38; Cleanth Brooks, *William Faulkner: Toward Yoknapatawpha and Beyond* (New Haven: Yale University Press, 1978), 293; Donald Paul Regan, *William Faulkner's "Absalom, Absalom!": A Critical Study* (Ann Arbor: UMI Research Press, 1987), 112; Ilse Dusoir Lind, "The Design and Meaning of *Absalom, Absalom!*," in *William Faulkner: Three Decades of Criticism*, ed. Frederick J. Hoffman and Olga W. Vickery (New York: Harcourt Brace Jovanovich, 1963), 298; Doreen Fowler, *Faulkner's Changing Vision: From Outrage to Affirmation* (Ann Arbor: UMI Research Press, 1983), 41–42.

20. William Faulkner, *Absalom, Absalom!* in *William Faulkner: Novels 1936–1940*, eds. Joseph Blotner and Noel Polk (New York: Library of America, 1990), 190; Hereafter, all citations to *Absalom, Absalom!* are to this edition, with page numbers given within parentheses in the text.

21. Schoenberg, *Old Tales and Talking*, 75, 80–81, 135; Hyatt Waggoner, *William Faulkner: From Jefferson County to the World* (Lexington: University of Kentucky Press, 1959), 166; Lind, "Design and Meaning of *Absalom, Absalom!*," 288; Vickery, *Novels of William Faulkner*, 96; Brooks, *William Faulkner*, 298; Irwin, *Doubling and Incest*, 116–17; Kerr, *William Faulkner's Gothic Domain*, 39; Gerald Langford, *Faulkner's Revision of Absalom, Absalom!: A Collation of the Book and the Manuscript* (Austin: University of Texas Press, 1971), 9.

22. The term is used by Edith Wharton in her short story, "Souls Belated": "the same fenced-in view of life, the same keep-off-the-grass morality" (*Scribbling Women: Short Stories by 19th-Century American Women*, ed. Elaine Showalter [New Brunswick: Rutgers University Press, 1997], 408). James has Strether, with Mrs. Newsome in view, refer to "the whole moral and intellectual being or block, that Sarah brought me over to take or leave" (323). Of Sarah Pocock, Strether says: "She hangs together with a perfection of her own that does suggest a kind of wrong in *any* change in her composition" (ibid.).

23. WJ, 116; Lewis, *The Jameses*, 563.

24. Matthiessen, *James Family,* 343.

25. Ibid., 344. For a fuller explanation of the quoted passage, see Richard A. Hocks, *Henry James,* 15–18.

26. Matthiessen, *James Family,* 344.

27. Robert A. Jelliffe, ed. *Faulkner at Nagano* (Tokyo: Kenkyusha, Ltd., 1956), 95.

# Revolution Has Not Yet Entered Their Souls

## *The Jilting of Katherine Anne Porter*

**K**atherine Anne Porter's troubled relationship with Mexico began as a love affair with the entire culture. She states in her book of essays, *The Days Before,* that she had been in love with Mexico since hearing her father's fantastic stories of the strange and beautiful landscape, stories that prepared her to appreciate the country's starkness.[1] A growing awareness over the years of the complex social/revolutionary/traditional corruption in Mexico, however, gave Porter an unexpected, and certainly undesired, new viewpoint of Mexico's inner and outer landscapes, a transition of attitude that is marked in the two versions of her short story "Hacienda."

At first, Porter was enthralled by the romance of revolution. She came to Mexico when hopes for a revolution ran high, and President Alvaro Obregón had recently been inaugurated. Describing her reaction in a 1963 interview with Barbara Thompson, Porter stated, "I ran smack into the Obregón Revolution, and had, in the midst of it, the most marvelous, natural, spontaneous experience of my life."[2] Early in Porter's Mexico experience, in one of her essays called "The Mexican Trinity: Report from Mexico City, July 1921," she defends and idealizes the Mexican people, saying that "the passion for individual expression without hypocrisy is the true genius of the Mexican race" (241).

Moreover, Porter seemed convinced that, once the revolution concluded successfully, the plight of Mexico's poor would be alleviated quickly because the campesinos would be willing to enter the industrial age. She expresses her conviction in "Leaving the Petate," another essay in the collection. The Mexican *indios*, or Indians, as she calls them, would immediately give up their traditional primitive existence and improve their lot in life if given the opportunity (243). The only drawback, Porter continued, was that "the revolution has not yet entered the souls of the Mexican people" (253). Her "keen sympathy with such aspirations," as Janis Stout calls it, would in a very short time turn to equally keen disillusionment when Porter realized that the ideals and principles of the revolution were doing nothing to help the poor and oppressed in Mexico.[3] These two sides of Porter's textual portrait of Mexico—enthusiasm and disappointment—are embedded in the two "Hacienda" stories.

**169**

The first version of "Hacienda," which will be referred to as H-1, was thought to be a documentary or creative nonfiction essay when it was first published in *Virginia Quarterly Review* in October 1932. The story is taken directly from notes that Porter wrote during her trip to Hacienda Tetlapajac in July 1931 to observe the filming of *Que Viva Mexico* by Russian director Sergei Eisenstein. The adventurous tone of the story was not to last, and the second version of "Hacienda" monumentally revises the author's tone and the narrator's voice. Joan Givner, in her book *Katherine Anne Porter: A Life*, says that although the story "was one of [Porter's] most substantial," it took Porter many drafts and three years to get the story into its final form because of her deep sense of despair at the end of her last stay in Mexico.[4] For several months after leaving Mexico, Porter felt as if she were convalescing from a nightmare (242). Porter explained in a 1965 interview that, by the time she had started revising "Hacienda," she had begun "to separate the villains from the heroes."[5]

In accordance with the story's journalistic reality, H-1's characters are understood to have represented the real people at Hacienda Tetlapajac, and most of the characters are designated either by the first letter of their names or by their occupation. Darlene Unrue notes, however, that when Porter published the second, very expanded version (referred to here as H-2), she included a disclaimer, saying that *all* the characters and events

in the story are fictional,[6] obviously an attempt to obliterate links between the real hacienda occupants and the jaded characters in her more
controversial version of "Hacienda."

The characters who are given complete names in H-1 are Justino and
Vicente. Their story is pivotal in this first version, combined with lengthy
descriptions of the Indians' plight against what Porter calls "the great triumvirate" of Church, Land, and Oil (or the priests, the Spanish *hacendados*, and foreign investors).[7] Justino's story, like that of the oppressed
and victimized Indian, relates to three socialist issues that correspond to
Porter's triumvirate: the moral issue of accidental murder (which in H-2
appears to have been premeditated murder), the inherited "rights" of the
Spanish don over his Indian peon, and the influence of the money-grab-
bing government officials who hold Justino prisoner. Perhaps Porter
makes a distinction with the names of Justino and Vicente in H-1 because she wished to emphasize or authenticate their story or perhaps because she perceived no possible litigious retaliation from using Indians'
names. In the second "Hacienda," however, the bitingly ironic tone she
would take undoubtedly motivated her to alter characters' names, to
name but to veil the name, so that no connection to living persons could
be proven.

H-2 was published in book form by Porter in 1934. Like H-1, it is
written in first person (the only other of Porter's short stories to be in first
person is "Holiday"). Darlene Unrue believes that Porter's uncharacter-
istic use of present tense in H-1 was due to her desire to incorporate the
story into a particular book; she had been planning a collection of her
Mexican writings tentatively titled "The Historical Present."[8] Another
reason for first person could be that she initially recorded her visit to
Hacienda Tetlapajac in a journalistic fashion, using first person and present tense. And according to reports of her depression and inability to
write well in the year that immediately followed, she may have not been
inclined to make major revisions in the manuscript prior to its first publication.[9]

While H-1 is written in a mixture of present and past tense, H-2 is in
the past. Past tense makes the story seem less like a journal entry by distancing the narrator from the action, pulling the reader back to scrutinize

the events with the narrator from a more objective locus. Considering Porter's negative feelings about Mexico when she revised "Hacienda," the past may have been the only viable tense for her to use at the time. The viewpoint in H-2 also projects a greater omniscience on the part of the narrator. Because of the more complex character sketches Porter creates in H-2, the viewpoint plumbs deeper into the characters' psyches to reveal thoughts that a first-person narrator would not know. This device further separates the narrator from the microcosm of the hacienda's world. The narrator becomes subordinate to the observations of a disillusioned author, an author who is divorcing herself from the story's macrocosm of Mexico.

A significant formal difference between the two versions is that H-2 has a long introduction before the versions begin to coincide on page 4 of H-2. This longer beginning introduces the nameless female narrator, Kennerly, and Andreyev, while it also sets up the premise of their train trip. A 1965 interview with Hank Lopez illustrates that Porter's description of a train trip in Mexico in 1920, complete with two men who were also Americans, may have been the source of her material for the introduction's train ride.[10] However, Unrue suggests Porter's inspiration for H-2's introduction came from letters she was writing to Ernestine Evans in 1930 regarding her general travels in Mexico on "walloping little tubs."[11] Although Porter is often difficult to pin down in terms of the process of her writing, the interview with Lopez delivers much stronger support for the introduction's inspiration. Since the train trip Porter speaks of in H-2's introduction occurred during her first visit to Mexico in 1920 while she was still impressionable and idealistic about the country, the more powerful images for Porter's introduction likely come from this experience rather than from nonspecific travels. The letters to Evans may have sparked her memory again, but the details for the introduction seem to have come from a very specific event.

From the outset of the second "Hacienda," Porter builds a mood of resignation and corruption using a sense of degraded character that prevails in all the participants, Mexican and white. For example, K— in H-1 has become Kennerly in H-2, and like most of the characters, Kennerly undergoes a transformation that reflects not merely the author's development of character but also Porter's acquired bitterness about Mexico. No longer just another nervous traveler, Kennerly receives double doses of Porter's irony in H-2. He worries more about failure and his brother-in-law's reaction, he worries about putting up a good front, he imagines he will write a book. A significant change in his character description is evident at the end of the fourth page of text. In H-1, Kennerly is given some backbone, at least in the narrator's view, when the narrator describes him as having everything "against him, but he will win! His loud voice and commanding stride must advertise to the world that here walks a man nothing can stop."[12] In the revised H-2, the playful jabbing is gone. Kennerly becomes pitiful and hopeless about the film, "slamming himself into a fight in which there are no rules and no referee and the antagonist is everywhere."[13] His fears are exemplified, in a passage that Porter added near the end of H-2, when he says in a trembling voice, "My God! I've got to worry and somebody has got to think of the future around here!" (170). Yet this "fight," for both Kennerly and Mexico, produces nothing that can defeat the invulnerable political antagonist about which Porter herself finally despaired. The story's film and its larger scope, which includes the Mexican revolution, cannot be finished in this impotent world that she has described.

Other important characters that become negatively transformed in H-2 are Don Genaro and Doña Julia, as well as the third member of their love triangle, Lolita. Julia becomes more of a childlike pet in H-2, whereas she was previously known in H-1 only as Don J——'s wife and only marginally described as "a figure from a Hollywood comedy" (562). In H-2 she is "an exotic speaking doll" (152), a little girl-woman who says, "I love sitting up all night. I never go to bed if I can possibly sit up" (161). Her bedroom is full of dolls and white wigs, the articles of imitation motherhood and of dress-up. She is full of self-concerns and indulgences rather than the flat, passive character she was in H-1.

With his power dissipated in the transition into H-2, the landowner Genaro, whose name derives from the Spanish *genero* meaning "class," becomes impotent. In the first version we meet him as he storms in the door "in a fury. This fury is part of his role" (562). His toughness in attitude is a part of his inherited authority. By version H-2, the inherited authority has been deleted; he is "graceful" rather than tough, and his fury is transformed into a more flaccid demeanor that, the narrator explains, "he expected us to sympathize with" (155), a kind of passive entitlement. These revisions create a powerlessness in Genaro that make him more of a victim to the sociopolitical systems in H-2, but the greatest victimization that he incurs comes from the combined efforts of Julia and Lolita and adds a disturbing dimension to Porter's bitter attitude in H-2.

Lolita, with the almost stereotypical seducer name, is an actor from the Jewel Theatre who arrives to be part of the film. Genaro, because of his position as *hacendado*, was "expected" to make love to her. He makes the error, however, of bringing her into the hacienda. Julia reveals through the narrator that trysts are acceptable in the "modern" society of the highborn Spaniards, but ensconcing a mistress in the wife's home is not allowed. Julia rebels, revenges herself with other lovers, then takes    **173** Lolita as lover. Her actions both thwart and outrage Genaro, inflicting on him the most devastating of cuckoldings in a machismo society.

Not only does the love triangle underscore the powerlessness of the Spaniard landowner Genaro, but it deepens the sense of corruption as Porter sees it. While Porter seemed to have no qualms about extramarital affairs (in light of her nearly disabling obsession for Matthew Josephson), her biographer Joan Givner notes that Porter "had always felt indignant about homosexuality, and she thought the political group a vast network of gentlemen who gave lads good jobs in return for their favors."[14] In her mind, H-2's "perverted" additional element of homosexuality would shout corruption. Homosexuality may have been a personally absorbing issue for Porter at this time. The story's genesis corresponds with the time frame of personal problems she was having with Hart Crane, which allegedly interrupted her work and precipitated her ill health.[15] Perhaps the issue also served as an important device contributing to her creation of tone because she uses it again when she transforms Justino's story from that of a possibly accidental murder in H-1 to that of a love triangle in H-2.

In both versions of "Hacienda," Justino, a Mexican Indian whose name signifies "the just one," is talking to his sister and tossing a pistol in the air when the gun goes off. Justino's sister is killed, his friend

Vicente pursues and catches him rather violently, and Justino is jailed. In H-1 we must consider whether Justino shot her with malice. We must take into account that the other Indians say that he did not kill her on purpose. Even his name absolves him. The reader's sympathy, therefore, can easily lie with Justino. The characters support him, as does the narrator/author by her frequent descriptions, in H-1 only, of the Indian as wrongfully oppressed. In H-2, however, Porter has redirected the event so that it becomes another of the spokes pointing inward to corruption of every facet of life in Mexico. Andreyev explains that Vicente went after his lover, Justino, for jealous revenge because Justino had betrayed Vicente with his own sister. Carlos Montaña, a character entirely absent from H-1 and who represents the artist as a corrupted failure, also indicates this betrayal in an impromptu song he creates. No longer merely a question of accidental murder, Justino's story in H-2 becomes another faction of what Porter considers hopeless corruption—homosexuality and incest. Justino now risks losing the reader's sympathy. The accusation of murder becomes more concrete because of Porter's manipulation of modern phobias surrounding "suspicious" sexual elements.

**174**

The Russian director of the film being produced in "Hacienda" is called "the famous director" in H-1 and "Uspensky" in H-2. Uspensky represents another sexually perverted character in his transformation from H-1 into the second "Hacienda." Described disparagingly by Porter in H-2 as having the characteristics of a monkey (his clothes, his face, his beard, his philosophy on life), Uspensky has become a kind of satyr. Among his many indiscretions, he stages country plays to amuse and showcase himself, while "prodding the rear of a patient burro, accustomed to grief and indignation, with a phallus-shaped gourd"—using bestiality as another, barely concealed symbolic perversion. He "flatters the Mexicans by declaring they really were the most obscene he had found in the whole world" (153), a double play on Porter's part that shows degradation in both Uspensky's tastes and the Mexicans' values. Uspensky cannot desist from associating, audibly, any Southern women he meets with their frequency of rape by "those dreadful negroes" (154). When Uspensky catches cold, he sneezes disgustingly into his hands, becomes practically an invalid, and initiates the summoning of Doctor Volk to cure him. Neither Volk nor Uspensky's author-endowed illnesses—physical or psychological—are included in H-1. And Porter seems to have no thematic purpose for Volk, other than to accent Uspensky's unattractive character by way of sickness. She describes him in very complimentary terms that do not hint of irony, unless a parallel could be loosely drawn between his competency as a doctor and his failures as a billiards player. He never becomes part of the eccentric, central hacienda family.

Another large section that Porter added to the final version of "Hacienda" is the description of Velarde. Velarde is the epitome of the Mexican big-time gangster, and yet he operates in H-2 under the guise of a good revolutionary (156). Velarde is the man to whom Genaro states he will appeal on Justino's behalf. The appeal is fruitless. In a *que será* summation added near the end of H-2, Porter makes it clear that no good results will be garnered in any such situation with a government official, at least not without a payoff. She writes, inclusively of all time, "don Genaro and his fellow-*hacendados* would fret and curse, the Agrarians would raid, and the ambitious politicians in the capital would be stealing right and left enough to buy such haciendas for themselves" (168). Porter would give no leeway to any faction.

As in the story's attitude addendum toward politicians, a transformation also takes place between the two "Haciendas" regarding the soldier as fighter and defender. H-1 includes a primarily objective paragraph that describes the guards as sent by the government to defend the hacienda against the Agrarians, those revolutionaries who want to have the land divided among the people. Porter explains in "The Mexican Trinity" that this partitioning of land "menaces the Church and foreign investors."[16] For this reason, the soldiers were sent to the haciendas to protect both land and produce such as pulque.

The Mexican soldiers in H-1 are fairly invisible. One soldier is chased by one of the elegant dogs of the hacienda in an amusing but slightly denigrating scene. Porter explains in the story that these soldiers defend against the Agrarians who make the *hacendados'* life "a hell on earth" (564) and that the presence of the soldiers is a sign of government approval. Don J— has been known to wield a machine gun himself in times of great need, she writes, which also places the don in the role of soldier-protector.

In the second version of the story, three elements further illuminate Porter's revised attitude toward the soldier-protector, an attitude that has become plainly disdainful. First, the dog-chasing-soldier scene is drawn out to highlight the absurdity of the disgraced and powerless "fat-bottomed soldier." Second, Porter has added a sentence condemning the laziness of all the soldiers who ate their beans at Genaro's expense. Finally, the paragraph detailing the soldiers' actual battle-readiness has been deleted. Between H-1 and H-2, Genaro, the soldiers, and their purpose as fighting men who defend the hacienda (and in the larger sense, Mexico) have been made small and ridiculous. What remains in the story's mood is frustration, tension, and the author's vision that Mexico functions awry without possibility of being righted.

Porter's revisioning of the Mexican Indians' plight is a final major change between H-1 and H-2 that underlines her resignation to the decay and corruption throughout Mexico. The Indian in H-1 is portrayed as simple, primitive, and oppressed by the hated Spanish.[17] In a two-page effusion, Porter describes the cycle of oppression, the alcoholic drink called pulque, and the dependency on alcohol, which is not chosen by, but rather forced upon, the Indian. Pulque is a wine made from the fermented juice of the maguey plant, which was initially used in religious ceremonies to appease or communicate with the gods. It later became a popular drink and lost its religious meaning, representing a further corruption of the Mexican people. In "Hacienda," Porter states that pulque is distributed to control the Indians, who subsequently are unable or unwilling to contribute to their "own" revolution. The corruption of the Mexican Indian, and the Indian's perceived complicity in this hierarchy, becomes a final degradation that Porter could not forgive.

In H-1, Porter considers the Indian to be "stabled worse than his own burro, but he eats his corn and cannot be persuaded away from it. For who would give him corn but the master?" (566). Tied to the feudal sys-

**176**

tem by custom, love of birthplace, and fear of the risks of change, the Indians in H-1 are not held completely responsible by the author for a world they did not create. They are described as suffering tragically; their "dark faces carry a common memory, as the eyes of cruelly treated animals all look alike: they know that they suffer, they do not know why, and they cannot imagine a remedy" (558). The Indians in H-1 move as in a funeral procession "with no symbol of grief omitted" (558). Porter still believed, at this point in H-1, that given their freedom, the Indians would advance themselves to become relieved of the misery caused by enslavement to the *hacendados*. H-2's images of the Indians show that their corruption may match that of Mexico's other communities.

The Indians in H-2 are not the same issue with Porter as the tragic figures in the first version. What she previously condoned as primitivism is now scorned as ennui. Although she uses some of the same phrases as **177** in H-1 to describe the Indians in H-2, she has recreated them as "beautiful and hollow" (142), bored and artistically stylized figures rather than the bearers of societal crosses borne along through their own oppression. H-1's tired Indians, who are described as lashing themselves when they lash their burros (566), become apathetic in H-2, lashing the burros without despair or interest, working their way through another day's boredom (163). The "forced feeding" of pulque has transformed the Indians' joie de vivre, as the narrator tells us, into singing "in weariness and excitement" as they work in the pulqueria. These Indians are listless and bored except when confronted with vicarious thrills such as Justino's murdering his sister or public speculations on the sexual lives of the *hacendados*, the making of pulque, and anything to do with death. In H-2 Porter elaborates on the Mexican "love of death," the *fatalismo* that has become a spiritual habit. She calls it an "almost ecstatic death-expectancy" (143) and showcases this attitude in the heightened interest and comments surrounding the death of Justino's sister. Kennerly, as well as the Mexicans, becomes excited over the dead body, analyzing the lost possibilities of using it in the film. Granted, some of these morbidities would be intriguing to many people today as well, considering what in contemporary media seems most marketable to society. But Porter did not accent them while reshaping H-2 until *after* her disillusionment. They play a vital role in the story's transformation into a work that, as Jane Krause DeMouy explains it, finds "all human beings to be eminently corruptible."[18]

Other instances of corruption and apathy that were written into the second version of "Hacienda" also help contribute to the tone. The fleshed-out description of the young pugilist's braggart arrogance, which can be attributed only to his appearing in the film, complements Porter's H-2 view of machismo as predictable and pathetic. The Spanish overseer, who plays the film's villain, wears tight leather pants to the set, prepared to sit all day in habitual boredom. Porter crafts her anger through the cruelty of Betancourt to Carlos Montaña when he encourages Montaña's failure, through the emphasis on Lolita's masculine features, and through the longer descriptions of the decaying smell of the pulque, which seeps into every corner of the hacienda, just as moral decay blankets Mexico. All these devices contribute to H-2's weighty sense of deterioration of the revolutionary ideals Porter had once imagined existed in Mexico.

In *Understanding Katherine Anne Porter*, Darlene Unrue sees H-2 as a "more analytical representation of the events which inspired the first version," and she adds in *Truth and Vision in Katherine Anne Porter's Fiction* that Porter's "deeply bitter and futile attitude" pervades H-2.[19] Of the period in Porter's life just before she left Mexico forever, Givner states that Porter looked back on it with "the utmost horror."[20] Three years later, H-2 would still potently capture the sense of disappointment and the desperation of the author (and the author as narrator) to leave the hacienda and to leave Mexico to its stasis and greed.

Porter contrived not only to round out the characters of H-2 in her revisions but to emphasize heavily what was left undeveloped in the background of the first version: that the revolution in Mexico was a farce at that time and that corruption was the embraced lifestyle for all who lived there. The Mexican "true genius for individual expression without hypocrisy"[21] that Porter once proclaimed has been refashioned as sad and ridiculous in light of her disillusioned rewriting of "Hacienda."

178

# Notes

1. Katherine Anne Porter, *The Days Before* (New York: Harcourt, 1952), 240. Subsequent references to this collection of essays are noted parenthetically in the text.

2. Joan Givner, ed., *Katherine Anne Porter: Conversations* (Jackson: University Press of Mississippi, 1987), 78–98.

3. Janis P. Stout, *Katherine Anne Porter: A Sense of the Times* (Charlottesville: University Press of Virginia, 1995), 68.

4. Joan Givner, *Katherine Anne Porter: A Life* (New York: Simon & Schuster, 1982), 241. Subsequent references to this book are noted parenthetically in the text.

5. Givner, ed., *Conversations*, 124.

6. Darlene Harbour Unrue, *Truth and Vision in Katherine Anne Porter's Fiction* (Athens: University of Georgia Press, 1985), 39.

7. Porter, *The Days Before*, 254.

8. Unrue, *Truth and Vision*, 130.

9. Givner, *Katherine Anne Porter*, 242.

10. Givner, ed., *Conversations*, 120–34.

11. Unrue, *Truth and Vision*, 85.

12. *Virginia Quarterly Review* 8 (1932): 558. Subsequent references to H-1 are to this version and are noted parenthetically in the text.

13. *Collected Stories of Katherine Anne Porter* (New York: Harcourt, 1965). Subsequent references to H-2 are to this version and are noted parenthetically in the text.

14. Givner, *Katherine Anne Porter*, 239.

15. Ibid., 234–38.

16. Porter, *The Days Before*, 254.

17. Ibid., 251.

18. Jane Krause DeMouy, *Katherine Anne Porter's Women* (Austin: University of Texas Press, 1983), 95.

19. Darlene Unrue, *Understanding Katherine Anne Porter* (Columbia: University of South Carolina Press, 1988), 39; Unrue, *Truth and Vision*, 27–28.

20. Givner, *Katherine Anne Porter*, 242.

21. Porter, *The Days Before*, 241.

**179**

# Poems of the Civil War, Past and Present

hose who disparage Civil War novels by claiming that they have yet to include an American version of *War and Peace* will have an even easier time putting down Civil War poetry, which, despite Whitman's claim in *Memoranda During the War* (1875) that the events of 1861 to 1865 furnished material "far more grand, in my opinion, to the hands capable of it, than Homer's siege of Troy, or the French wars to Shakspere," can boast of nothing that rivals the *Iliad* or *Henry the Fifth*.¹ In *Patriotic Gore* (1962), Edmund Wilson puts the matter bluntly, dismissing thousands of lines of wartime verse as "barren reading" and claiming that the "period of the Civil War was not at all a favorable one for poetry."² I happen to think this judgment spectacularly wrong because the period of the Civil War gave us the greatest poems of Emily Dickinson, and those poems are more than enough to redeem any period. But Wilson does not share my opinion of Dickinson, whom he thinks "a little overrated" (489). Fair enough, but respect for his opinion would come more easily, at least to me, if Wilson did not also confess the unreliability of his reading with the statement that Dickinson "never, so far as I know, refers to the war in her poetry" (488):

> When I was small, a Woman died—
> Today—her Only Boy

Went up from the Potomac—
His face all Victory (1–4)[3]

Numbered 596 by editor Thomas H. Johnson in *The Poems of Emily Dickinson* (1955) and dated by him to around 1862, this poem refers to the death of Francis H. Dickinson of Amherst, Massachusetts, who was killed at Ball's Bluff, Virginia, on October 21, 1861. To appreciate the achievement of Dickinson's small elegy, we have only to compare it with a contemporary piece by Caroline Augusta Ball, whose elegy "The Jacket of Grey" gave its title to a volume published in 1866:

Fold it up carefully, lay it aside;
Tenderly touch it, look on it with pride;
For dear must it be to our hearts evermore,
The jacket of grey our loved soldier boy wore. (1–4)[4]

**181**

To the ears of the 1860s, Ball's endstopped rhyming couplets, which waltz along in the same one-two-three meter as "The Star-Spangled Banner," would have sounded much more like what poetry should be than Dickinson's imperfectly rhymed version of ballad or hymn meter. And to the sensibilities of most poetry readers in the 1860s, Ball's archaic diction, which, for example, refers to combat as "the fray" (7)—conveniently rhyming with "grey"—would have sounded appropriately elevated rather than hackneyed and stale. But beyond historical differences in taste between then and now lie more important differences that involve the representation of death in combat and the presence or absence of partisanship.

In Ball's vision, combat is a matter of unsheathed swords and lighted brands with no actual image of killing with lead or iron projectiles. Instead, she gives us a theatrical tableau of the aftermath of battle: "But our treasured one on the red battle field lay, / While the life-blood oozed out on the jacket of grey" (23–24). By contrast, Dickinson's vision is unsentimental and matter-of-fact in its compressed blending of geometry with the modern technology of bullets:

> How slowly
> The Seasons must have turned
> Till Bullets clipt an Angle
> And He passed quickly round— (5–8)

Ball elegizes with effusive lamentation ("Ah! vain, all, all vain were our prayers and our tears" [21]), Dickinson with terse understatement that reflects the increasingly impersonal and mechanical nature of combat. Not all readers will necessarily agree that the latter strategy is more effective than the former, but they should agree that whereas Ball's elegy limits itself to the boundaries of partisanship ("Can we ever forget when he joined the brave band, / Who rose in defence of our dear Southern land" [5–6]), Dickinson's enlarges its scope by moving beyond the specific death of one man from a small town in a small battle toward a generalized contemplation of perpetual death everywhere:

> I'm confident that Bravoes—
> Perpetual break, abroad
> For Braveries, remote as this
> In Scarlet Maryland— (17–20)

Those who agree with Wilson in thinking Dickinson overrated might also assume that she shows herself a little fuzzy on geography in the final line, since Ball's Bluff lies on the Virginia side of the Potomac, but my guess is that she wrote this poem about a year after Francis Dickinson's death, when the fighting at Sharpsburg-Antietam had turned Maryland "Scarlet" (a definite improvement over "Yonder Maryland" in another version of the poem), and no Northerner who read the newspapers as avidly as Dickinson could have been unaware of the exhibit of Alexander Gardner's photographs from the battlefield there. If I am right, Dickinson uses the death of someone known to her to approach the vast enormity of so many thousands unknown to her.

Except for our differences over Dickinson, however, I have to agree with Wilson that the period of the Civil War was not a golden age for

American poetry. Whitman published *Drum-Taps* in 1865 and Herman Melville followed with *Battle-Pieces* in 1866, but for all their memorable moments neither of these books is an unqualified success. Aside from poems by these two poets, the only two war poems from the 1860s, other than the lyrics of the minstrel song "Dixie," that general readers in the United States might still be able to recognize today are Julia Ward Howe's "The Battle Hymn of the Republic," composed, according to a plaque on the building, on November 21, 1861, at Willard's Hotel in Washington, and John Greenleaf Whittier's "Barbara Frietchie," originally collected in the volume *In War Time* (1864). Meanwhile, there is plenty of barren reading.

In the case of the Wilderness, for example, a modern reader coming from "The Battle Hymn of the Republic" has to struggle hard to read, or hear, James D. Gay's broadside "The Battle of the Wilderness," which I **183** happened across one day in the University of Virginia Special Collections, the catalog of which dates the poem between 1864 and 1869. Gay, who resided at 300 North 20th Street, above Vine Street, Philadelphia, advertised himself as "the celebrated Army song publisher and dealer," who sold his songs "beautifully illustrated with Battle scenes" in "large or small quantities" at his residence. The words for "The Battle of the Wilderness," unaccompanied by any music, appear on a single sheet that measures not quite five and a half by not quite nine and a half inches. At the top of the page appears one of Gay's battle scenes, which shows Federal soldiers, led by a sword-wielding officer on horseback, advancing in perfect order across an open space toward a distant line of Confederates, identified by the Stars and Bars rather than the more familiar battle flag. Between the opposing lines lie two apparently dead bodies and one wounded man. Behind the Confederates stands a single row of leafless trees through which one can see a range of high hills or low mountains resembling nothing visible from anywhere in the actual Wilderness. At the bottom of the page one sees that "J. D. Gay also publishes the different Army Hospitals Views which are beautifully colored" and which "will be sent by Mail." The song itself consists of ten four-line stanzas, not necessarily the worst of which is the sixth:

> They met them in the Wilderness, just at the break of day sirs,
> And fought them on the right and left, till Lee he ran away
>    sirs,
> And left some thousands on the field, he could not get away
>    sirs;
> But our Union boys they dressed their wounds, their dead
>    they put away sirs.
>
> CHORUS.—And that's just so—Ri, fal, de ral de laddy and
>    that's just so.

But perhaps it's not fair to pick on song lyrics unaccompanied by music, especially the song lyrics of someone self-employed and self-promoting. Perhaps we should look instead to a poem in the "Journal of Civilization," *Harper's Weekly*. In the issue of May 28, 1864, appears the unsigned poem "The Battle of the Wilderness," which opens with the biblical epigraph "The wilderness shall bloom" (Isa. 32:15).[5] Unfortunately, however, the shift from unaccompanied song to self-contained poem does not significantly improve the quality. "The Battle of the Wilderness," which celebrates with no doubts or second thoughts a Union victory on May 5 and 6, begins and ends with the same stanza:

> Victory! shout for victory
> On the battle-field again;
> For the bloom of the Wilderness
> Glory to God! Amen! (Stanzas 1 and 7)

Between the initial and final appearances of this stanza fall five others, each of which begins with the same line that opens the poem. Of the remaining fifteen lines, none manages to get beyond either convention or a partisanship that spills over into overt propaganda. The second stanza offers to those who mourn one of Ulysses S. Grant's 17,666 casualties the consolation, "Only by Death's dark roses / The lilies of peace shall grow"; the third urges, "Let a nation's heart rejoice"; the fourth finally descends from abstraction to mention the actual men who bade victory grow "From the bloom of the Wilderness / To the fruitage of the Po"; the fifth identifies freedom as what can blossom from the bloody "flowers / That have so purpled the Wilderness"; and the sixth caps the celebration with an unequivocating image of the victory "That flashes a morning light / From the bloom of Wilderness / Far into the years of right."

But again perhaps it is not fair to pick on an unsigned poem that appeared in a journal catering to a general readership. What about a poem from a real poet? Born in Richmond in 1823, John Reuben Thompson purchased the *Southern Literary Messenger* and became its editor in 1847. Before the launching of both *Harper's Magazine* and the *Atlantic Monthly*, the *Southern Literary Messenger*, which Edgar Allan Poe edited from December 1835 until January 1837, emerged as a leading literary journal. In addition to editing the *Messenger* longer than anyone else **185** (1847–60), Thompson also flourished as a poet, and his poems were collected, edited, and published by John S. Patton in 1920.[6] One of his poems, published in the New Orleans journal the *Crescent Monthly* in May 1865, when Thompson was living in London and editing the Confederate newspaper the *Index*, focuses on the most famous moment, at least from a Confederate perspective, in the Battle of the Wilderness:

> Dawn of a pleasant morning in May
> Broke through the wilderness cool and grey,
> While, perched in the tallest tree-tops, the birds
> Were carolling Mendelssohn's "Songs Without Words." (1)

Although some might wince at the unlikely final line of this opening stanza, Thompson's eighty-line poem "Lee to the Rear" still had admirers in the early twentieth century. According to Allan Nevins's *The Evening Post* (1922), almost seventy years after its publication nearly every Southern schoolboy still knew the poem.[7]

Thompson's grasp of actual conditions in the Wilderness is not strong. He locates the famous incident "Down on the left of the rebel lines" (1), when in fact General Robert E. Lee was on the right at the

Widow Tapp's farm, and his quaint evocation of "the tide of battle" rolling "Over the Wilderness, wood and wold" (3) obscures the reality that there was precious little wold, or unforested land, on the battlefield, especially along the Orange Plank Road near the Brock Road. Thompson also erases James Longstreet from his representation altogether, so that his version of the incident has none of the actual drama of Lee learning the identity of the Texas brigade and realizing that the anxiously awaited First Corps had finally arrived just in time to prevent the total collapse of the Confederate right. Finally, Thompson's image of "Calm and resolute Robert Lee" (2) bears no resemblance to the man whom many later described as having temporarily lost his sense of balance and perspective.

Despite these historical quibbles, however, and despite too many lines that recall Caroline Augusta Ball, both in their conventional language and their metrical predictability, "Lee to the Rear" marks an advance beyond the achievement of James Gay or the anonymous poet in *Harper's Weekly*. Although he stages the incident from a Confederate perspective, at least Thompson discards the egregious partisanship of Ball's "dear Southern land" (6), and he avoids the distasteful self-righteousness of the *Harper's Weekly* poet, a remarkable feat of restraint for someone also editing a newspaper devoted to Confederate propaganda. Furthermore, at least twice in his twenty stanzas Thompson manages to break through the crust of clichés like "banners rent," "columns riven," and "foemen slain." The couplet describing the roar of Federal artillery ("For still with their loud, deep, bull-dog bay, / The Yankee batteries blazed away" [2]) freshly transforms the mechanical into the animal, anticipating Stephen Crane's extensive use of the same technique in *Red Badge of Courage*—never mind that Federal artillery saw limited action in the Wilderness—and the quatrain in which Lee's soldiers tell him to go to the rear attempts a tonal pungency that Patton makes even more noticeable with genteel censorship in the 1920 *Poems:*

"We'll go forward, but you must go back"—
And they moved not an inch in the perilous track:

"Go to the rear, and we'll send them to h—!"
And the sound of the battle was lost in their yell. (3)

Whatever its other failings, Thompson's "Lee to the Rear" helps fulfill the prophecy of its own final stanza, "But the fame of the Wilderness
fight abides" (3) in part by mythologizing history but also in part by focusing on a specific moment and personalizing it in a way that differs
completely from the faceless anonymity of Gay's song or the *Harper's
Weekly* poem. Some might argue that to praise and value a nineteenth-
century poem for the kind of personalized specificity and focus that
characterizes so much twentieth-century poetry is to judge the former
retrospectively according to a standard that is historically inappropriate.
But such an argument would work only if the twentieth century had a
monopoly on valuing personalized specificity and focus, and it does not. **187**
With the development and spread of photography during the war, poets
who wanted to write about the fighting found themselves confronted by
two different modes of representation, one involving the familiar rhetorical formulas of conventional battle poetry, the other involving the minimal framing and description of arresting visual images.

That the photographic mode of representation held powerful attractions for at least one poet confronting the war is clear from the achievement of Whitman's shorter poems in *Drum-Taps*. Such superbly realized
pieces as "Cavalry Crossing a Ford," "Bivouac on a Mountain Side," "An
Army Corps on the March," and "By the Bivouac's Fitful Flame" com-
pensate for many of the poems, especially early in the volume, that suc-
cumb to the rhetorical excesses of *Harper's Weekly*ism. (Significantly, the
awful poem "Beat! Beat! Drums!" first appeared in *Harper's Weekly*.) As
the ordering of poems in *Drum-Taps* makes clear, Whitman himself perceived all too clearly the discrepancy between his loud belligerence and
his quieter watching. In the often anthologized poem "The Wound-
Dresser," he admits parenthetically that "Arous'd and angry, I'd thought
to beat the alarum, and urge relentless war, / But soon my fingers fail'd
me, my face droop'd and I resign'd myself, / To sit by the wounded and
soothe them, or silently watch the dead" (4–6).[8] But even in "The

Wound-Dresser," despite this apparent insight into his own motives and transformation, Whitman awkwardly pairs conventional battle rhetoric ("Soldier alert I arrive after a long march cover'd with sweat and dust, / In the nick of time I come, plunge in the fight, loudly shout in the rush of successful charge" [15–16]) with some of the greatest and most terrible lines to come out of the war:

> From the stump of the arm, the amputated hand,
> I undo the clotted lint, remove the slough, wash off the matter
> and blood,
> Back on his pillow the soldier bends with curv'd neck and
> side-falling head,
> His eyes are closed, his face is pale, he dares not look on the
> bloody stump,
> And has not yet look'd on it.
>
> . . . . . . . . . . . . . . . . . . . . . .
>
> I dress the perforated shoulder, the foot with the
> bullet-wound,
> Cleanse the one with a gnawing and putrid gangrene, so
> sickening, so offensive,
> While the attendant stands behind aside me holding the tray
> and the pail. (45–55)

It is hard to believe that only a slight shift in the stressing of "amputated," placing emphasis on the second syllable rather than on the first and third, would render the first line a metrical match for any in "The Jacket of Grey," and Whitman's artistry shows in many other touches as well, such as in the auditory fusion of prominent sounds from "perforated" and "wound" into "putrid." But the proof of these lines lies in their power to stun with a visual clarity wholly distinct from familiar rhetorical conventions about lifeblood oozing, a clarity that momentarily blinds us to their artistry.

Although flawed, *Drum-Taps* is hardly barren reading, and the same can be said for Melville's *Battle-Pieces,* published a year later.[9] When managing the competing tendencies toward, on the one hand, familiar

188

rhetorical formulas and, on the other, specifically focused clarity, Melville had many of the same problems as Whitman, but because Melville was not as good a poet as Whitman, his successes are fewer and more qualified. "The Portent," which closes with the image of John Brown as "The meteor of the war" (14), and "Shiloh" are both short enough to avoid major catastrophes and justify their inclusion in anthologies. But unlike Whitman, Melville constructed his book by writing poems to follow the chronology of the war. As a result, many of his poems, especially the longer ones, feel as though they were written merely in obedience to that chronology rather than to deep observation and feeling. A good example of Melville at both his best and worst is the two-part poem "The Armies of the Wilderness":

> Like snows the camps on Southern hills      **189**
> Lay all the winter long,
> Our levies there in patience stood—
> They stood in patience strong.
> On fronting slopes gleamed other camps
> Where faith as firmly clung:
> Ah, froward kin! so brave amiss—
> The zealots of the Wrong. (1–8)

As Dickinson makes abundantly clear to any skeptic, American poetry in any century can put the common meter of hymnody to good use, but although one can sing these opening lines to the tune of "O God, Our Help in Ages Past," Melville stumbles badly in this first stanza. If the only problem were his ignorance of the terrain and troop dispositions on both sides of the Rapidan (Lee's tent stood on the southern slope of Jerdone Mountain, north of the Plank Road and just west of where the Orange County Airport lies today, but the Union army wintered on relatively flat ground), the lapse would not exceed any of those in Thompson's "Lee to the Rear." But the much bigger problem that haunts not only "The Armies of the Wilderness" but all of *Battle-Pieces* is the bad fit between Melville's Union partisanship and his antiwar sentiments. The former gives us numerous clanky occurrences of the capitalized abstractions Right and Wrong, while the latter generates some of the more convincing lines in the volume, such as "All wars are boyish, and are fought by boys" ("The March into Virginia" [6]) and "What like a bullet can undeceive!" ("Shiloh" [16]).

The first part of "Armies of the Wilderness" has little to recommend it, other than an image of Federal soldiers, through "the pointed glass," watching Confederates play baseball ("They could have joined them in their sport / But for the vale's deep rent" [13–16]) and one of the few images in Civil War poetry of the massive deforestation caused by encamped armies: "And stumps of forests for dreary leagues / Like a massacre show" (91–92). But in the second part, when May arrives and Melville introduces Grant, the poem moves toward some of the best lines in *Battle-Pieces,* lines that Ken Burns admired enough to have George Plimpton read them during Burns's eight-minute recounting of the battle in his documentary:

**190**

> In glades they meet skull after skull
> Where pine-cones lay—the rusted gun,
> Green shoes full of bones, the mouldering coat
> And cuddled-up skeleton;
> And scores of such. Some start as in dreams,
> And comrades lost bemoan:
> By the edge of those wilds Stonewall had charged—
> But the Year and the Man were gone. (171–78)

Sung to the tune of "O God, Our Help," only two of these lines, the first and the sixth, would fit the pattern, and with the welcome shift into metrical variation, Melville momentarily discards his Unionist boosterism, although unfortunately it returns soon after Longstreet arrives on the scene ("But Heaven lent strength, the Right strove well, / And emerged from the Wilderness" [213–14]). As in the case of the excerpt from Whitman's "Wound-Dresser," what makes these lines so great, especially the first four, is the photographic focus on specific visual details that the men of Winfield Scott Hancock's Second Corps would have seen during their passage through the Chancellorsville battlefield toward the Brock Road. Furthermore, like Whitman, Melville delivers the visual force of the lines in conjunction with dense auditory patterning, as, for example, he binds the first four lines together by redistributing the prominent sounds of "skull" among the words "cuddled-up skeleton."

Two memorable passages from Whitman and Melville may not be sufficient to dissuade anyone from accepting Wilson's judgment that the Civil War was a bad time for poetry. But anyone who does accept that judgment needs to understand that American poets during and after the war not only failed to produce memorable war poetry. Most of them failed to produce memorable poetry, period. I understand that some will want to make a case for Stephen Crane or Edward Arlington Robinson or Trumbull Stickney or Adelaide Crapsey, but the fact is that between the time Whitman and Dickinson reached the heights of their powers and the time Robert Frost, Wallace Stevens, William Carlos Williams, Ezra Pound, T. S. Eliot, and Marianne Moore reached the heights of theirs, the pickings were slim. In frankly acknowledging this sag in American poetry, however, we need to guard against drawing easy conclusions about either cause and effect in literary history or cause and effect in the relation of war to poetry. Saying that the Civil War produced realism and realism does not foster lyric poetry, particularly the realism of war, gets us nowhere.

Despite the boundary-drawing in most recent anthologies of American literature, and despite the narratives endorsed by many teachers and scholars, the Civil War did not produce realism. I acknowledge that losing 2 percent of the population to disease and combat, as urban industrialism ground up rural agrarianism, led many among the maimed, the bereaved, and the dispossessed to discard certain romantic tendencies in favor of certain realistic ones. But it is too easy and naive to conclude that because the war was ugly and brutal, writers and readers suddenly awoke from the dreams of romance into the harsher light of realism. For one thing, all wars are ugly and brutal, but not all wars have been followed by greater realism in literature. If they were, then we would expect to see realism flourishing after the Revolution, the War of 1812, and the Mexican-

American War, but it didn't. In the twentieth century, we associate World War I with the disruptions of modernism and Vietnam with the dislocations of postmodernism, neither of which is the same as realism. And what about the influences on literary realism that have nothing to do with the Civil War? What about the invention of photography in 1837 and the development of the wet-plate negative in 1845? In numerous discussions of the new technology, we read that, unlike painting, photography captures reality. What about the discovery of gold in California in 1848, the massive westward migrations, and the development of a new kind of realistic observation in frontier literature? What about the influence of the French novelists—Balzac, who died the year of the Compromise of 1850; Flaubert, whose *Madame Bovary* appeared the year before the Dred Scott decision; and Zola, whose experiments in naturalism reflect nineteenth-century developments in science? Rather than claim that the Civil War engendered literary realism, it makes much more sense to say that some of the conditions that combined to produce war in North America during the nineteenth century also combined to produce realism there.

Nor do I buy the claim that something inherent in lyric poetry makes it incompatible with realism and, specifically, with the representation of war. If anything, a genre that intensifies brief bits of individual experience stands an excellent chance of producing memorable representations of events that far exceed the power of any one observer to comprehend the whole. Of course, the sweep of long novels and histories and memoirs can accomplish many things that a few lines of verse cannot. But as the undiminished power of Civil War photographs shows us, small, specific glimpses can also speak volumes. Why, then, aren't there more great Civil War poems?

One reason is that the first generation of major modern American poets did not focus on the Civil War, perhaps because the two world wars eclipsed it in their awareness, perhaps because they were busy looking abroad much of the time. Also, among Frost, Stevens, Williams, Pound, Moore, and Eliot, there is not a single Southerner, and although one does not have to be a Southerner to write about the war, I wonder, for example, what Williams's insistence on discovering the universal in the local might have meant if he had come from Virginia rather than New Jersey, or how our sense of Civil War poetry might differ if Faulkner's muse had caused him to keep developing his verse rather than devoting his energies to prose. Frost touched on the war in "The Black Cottage," a dramatic monologue included in *North of Boston* (1914), and in his polemical statements Pound often pointed to the Civil War as the beginning of American economic corruption and decadence. But otherwise the poets who now dominate anthologies of modern poetry mostly ignored the war.

This blank does not mean, however, that no poets born late in the nineteenth century ever turned their attention to the war. In Richard Marius's edition of *The Columbia Book of Civil War Poetry* (1994),[10] William Vaughn Moody, Edgar Lee Masters, Edward Arlington Robinson, Paul Laurence Dunbar, Carl Sandburg, Vachel Lindsay, John Gould Fletcher, Donald Davidson—Marius twice lists Davidson as having been **193** born in 1922, but he was actually born in 1893—and Stephen Vincent Benét are all represented. To be sure, we can't dismiss these poems as wholly without merit. The title poem of Davidson's volume *Lee in the Mountains* (1938), for example, shows Lee thinking to himself, "I heard the tangled / Cry of the Wilderness wounded, bloody with doom" (326), more compelling lines than anything in Gay, Thompson, or *Harper's Weekly*. But few of these poems appear in general anthologies.

Of these particular poets, the one who deserves a closer look here is Stephen Vincent Benét, whose epic poem *John Brown's Body* (1928) won the Pulitzer Prize in 1929. In his anthology, Marius represents the poem with two excerpts, "The Congressmen Came Out to See Bull Run" and "John Brown's Prayer" (27–31, 120–122), neither of which is especially likely to entice a contemporary reader into plowing through the entire poem. In his headnote to "The Congressmen Came Out to See Bull Run," Marius comments that Benét's "reputation has not endured" (27). Twenty years before Marius's postmortem, Daniel Aaron described the poem in *The Unwritten War* (1973) as "still widely (and I think mistakenly) regarded as the great Civil War epic."[11] The juxtaposition of these comments is a little confusing, since their chronology suggests that Benét's star, still shining brightly as late as Richard Nixon's presidency, suddenly fell during the subsequent twenty years. In fact, however,

Aaron's statement, which appears in a footnote, remains ambiguous. It does not say that *John Brown's Body* was still widely read in 1973—it wasn't—and it does not say whether Aaron thinks that someone else's mistake lies, on the one hand, in thinking Benét's epic great or, on the other, in thinking it the best of all the other Civil War epics that come to his mind. If he means the latter, it is hard to see why, since in 1973 it would have been difficult to name another serious contender.

Whatever others think of Benét's reputation, the United States Postal Service thought enough of him to honor the centennial of his birth with a commemorative stamp in 1998. It is not clear that anyone in the Postal Service actually read the poem, since the background for Benét's young (he only lived until 1943), bespectacled face is a few of the black soldiers from Saint-Gaudens's monument to Robert Gould Shaw and the Fifty-fourth Massachusetts. It's true that the cast of characters in *John Brown's Body* includes the unfortunately named Spade, a slave who runs away and ends up fighting at the Battle of the Crater in Petersburg. It's also true that despite the attention he pays to Southerners in his narrative, the title of Benét's poem, along with a prelude section called "The Slaver," makes it clear where his sympathies lie. But the message that the designers of the commemorative stamp seem to want to send has more to do with an idealized image of John Brown's legacy than with the poem that Benét actually wrote.

The poem Benét actually wrote contains much of value. Especially when one considers that it appeared not long after the first flush of modernist free verse, the broad spectrum of traditional poetic forms employed by Benét is impressive, from the opening sonnets of the "Invocation" to the common meter of "John Brown's Prayer" to the blank verse used throughout the poem. Inevitably, the technique of varying verse forms causes the epic to fragment into smaller poems, some of which do little more than advance the narrative, some of which dilate a particular moment, as in the case of the short lyric that accompanies Jack Ellyat's return to consciousness after he has been taken prisoner by the Confederates at Shiloh, escaped, and been given food and shelter by Melora Vilas:

194

> Cold comes back and pain comes back
> And the lizard, too,
> And the burden in the sack
> May be meant for you.
> Do not play the risen dunce
> With unrisen men.
> Lazarus was risen once
> But earth gaped again.[12]

Lyrics like the one from which this excerpt comes make a strong bid for memorability, and other remarkable moments and touches abound in *John Brown's Body*. In a prose section of Book Two, for instance, Benét introduces Whitman in a passage based on a section from the notes to *Memoranda During the War*, later incorporated into *Specimen Days* (1882), **195** about the return to Washington of exhausted Federal troops after the defeat at First Manassas–Bull Run; in Book Three, as Jack Ellyat thinks about escaping from the column of Federal prisoners, he confronts the ironic discrepancy between the reality of his situation and visual representations of the war in *Harper's Weekly:* "You had to escape like a drawing in *Harper's Weekly* / With stiff little men on horses like sickle-pears / Firing round frozen cream-puffs into your back" (130–31); and in Book Six Benét offers, in the midst of images of people for whom the war is not a daily reality, a wonderful portrait of Dickinson:

> A moth of a woman,
> Shut in a garden, lives on scraps of Eternity
> With a dog, a procession of sunsets and certain poems
> She scribbles on bits of paper. Such poems may be
> Ice-crystals, rubies cracked with refracted light,
> Or all vast death like a wide field in ten short lines.
> She writes to the tough, swart-minded Higginson
> Minding his negro troops in a lost bayou,
> "War feels to me like an oblique place." (263)

As for the Battle of the Wilderness in *John Brown's Body,* Benét's narrative pinches it in much the same way that Ken Burns's documentary film does. Book Eight contains an abridged version of "Lee to the Rear," but otherwise, in a poem that gives so many pages to First Manassas–Bull Run, the Wilderness is only one in a list of names:

> Follow the agony if you must and can
> By the brushwood names, by the bloody prints in the woods,
> Cold Harbor and Spottsylvania and Yellow Tavern
> And all the lost court-houses and country stores
> In the Wilderness, where the bitter fighting passed,
> (No fighting bitterer)—(321)

**196**     The criticism that Benét's ambitious poem is better in some places than in others should hardly disqualify it from the generous consideration of readers who have learned to live with the drastic ups and downs of Pound's *Cantos* (first collected, including Canto 120, in 1972), Hart Crane's *The Bridge* (1930), or Williams's *Paterson* (first collected in 1963). But even if the modernist competitors of *John Brown's Body* have crowded it out of most anthologies, one can see in those anthologies that with the next generation of American poets an important shift takes place in Civil War poetry. Instead of the major poets ignoring the war while only the minor ones write about it, the major poets begin to pay more attention. Beginning with Allen Tate, born the year after Benét, many important American poets wrote poems about the war, including (in order of birth) Langston Hughes, Robert Penn Warren, Charles Olson, Elizabeth Bishop, Randall Jarrell, John Berryman, and Robert Lowell. Of their poems, the two most familiar to anthology readers are Tate's dense, symbol-burdened "Ode to the Confederate Dead" (1928) and Lowell's sparer, more accessible response, "For the Union Dead" (1959), which meditates on Saint-Gaudens's monument to Colonel Shaw and the Massachusetts Fifty-fourth against the immediate backdrop of construction on Boston Common, as well as against the larger backdrop of desegregation:

Their monument sticks like a fishbone
in the city's throat.
Its Colonel is as lean
as a compass-needle.[13]

The second generation of modern poets found in the war many opportunities for good poetry, and subsequent generations have followed
with notable poems of their own so that we now have numerous poetic
representations of the war that successfully avoid sentimentality or partisanship or cliché. In the midst of this promising plenitude, the most
important development in recent Civil War poetry, and the one that
would be my nomination over *John Brown's Body* for the best Civil War
epic, assuming that a book-length narrative sequence of shorter poems
qualifies as an epic, is Andrew Hudgins's *After the Lost War* (1988).[14]     **197**
As Hudgins explains in a preface and headnote, this volume consists
of a sequence of forty-four poems "based on the life of the Georgia-born
poet and musician Sidney Lanier," who joined the Macon Volunteers;
was sent to Virginia; fought in the Battle of Chancellorsville and various
smaller engagements; was transferred to the Signals Corps and then, in
1864, to the blockade-runner *Lucy;* was captured and sent to Fort Look-
out, Maryland, where he spent three months; and returned to Macon in
broken health after the war. As Hudgins freely acknowledges, many of
the biographical details in the sequence derive from two biographies he
found especially useful, Edwin Mims's *Sidney Lanier* (1905) and Aubrey
Harrison Starke's *Sidney Lanier* (1933). Although he protects himself in
the preface with a disclaimer that "the voice of these poems will be unfamiliar to anyone who knows the writings of this historical figure" (ix),
in fact Hudgins's version of Lanier deserves credit for often preserving
many of the original tones. In his chapter "A Confederate Soldier," for
example, Mims quotes from a letter of June 11, 1866, Lanier's fond recollection of life at Fort Boykin on Burwell's Bay with his brother Clifford:
"Cliff and I never cease to talk of the beautiful women, the serenades, the
moonlight dashes on the beach of fair Burwell's Bay, and the spirited
brushes of our little force with the enemy."[15] Hudgins's version of this let-

ter, which opens the sixth section of "Serenades in Virginia: Summer 1863," sharpens the language into regular iambic meter while still tracing the contours of Lanier's voice:

> When Cliff and I discuss the war,
> we talk of lovely women, serenades,
> the moonlit dashes on the beach,
> the brushes of our force with theirs,
> with whom we clashed with more élan
> and consequence. (14)

Of the many fine poems in *After the Lost War*, several stand out for their ability to push a contemporary reader beyond naive idealization of the war toward keener awareness of the physical and psychological conditions behind the combat in Virginia, particularly "At Chancellorsville: The Battle of the Wilderness," "After the Wilderness: May 3, 1863," "Burial Detail," and "Reflections on Cold Harbor." Although the title of the first poem is puzzling—apparently Hudgins has confused the battles of 1863 and 1864—the poem itself transforms an instance of battlefield scavenging, as recounted by George Herbert Clarke in *Some Reminiscences and Early Letters of Sidney Lanier* (1907) and quoted in Starke's biography, into a scene of initiation for the young soldier.[16] His uniform "shabby with / continuous wear, worn down to threads," Lanier comes upon a dead Indiana corporal, shot in the thigh, whose shirt consists of "good / stout wool, unmarked by blood" (6). His brother Cliff advises him to take the shirt, but Lanier cannot bring himself to do so:

> Imagining
> the slack flesh shifting underneath
> my hands, the other-person stink
> of that man's shirt, so newly his,
> I cursed Clifford from his eyeballs to
> his feet. I'd never talked that way before
> and didn't know I could. (6)

Just as it initiates him into angry swearing, Chancellorsville initiates Lanier into something larger that cannot afford the luxury of squeamishness. Although another Confederate has taken the dead man's shirt by the time the brothers return to the corpse, the poem snaps closed with two cool lines that serve as shorthand notation for the profound changes that war effects in a man's sensibility:

> By autumn, we wore so much blue
> we could have passed for New York infantry. (6)

Hudgins excels at this kind of closure in which all the superfluous flesh of talking—all the embarrassing flourishes of Caroline Augusta Ball or James D. Gay or the *Harper's Weekly* poet or even Melville and Whitman at their respective worst—has long been worked off, leaving ample room for what Wallace Stevens, in a prose statement on the poetry of war published in *The Palm at the End of the Mind* (1971), calls "a consciousness of fact" to do its imaginative work.[17] Writing in 1942 in the shadow of World War II, Stevens realized that "consciousness of an immense war is a consciousness of fact" and that in "the presence of the violent reality of war, consciousness takes the place of imagination" (206). Stevens himself felt threatened by the encroachment of consciousness upon imagination and continually exhorted poets to resist the overwhelming reality of facts. And certainly when the brutal weight of brutal facts threatens to deaden the imagination altogether, such resistance is a matter of survival. But in *After the Lost War*, Hudgins shows us again and again that in the context of an immense war, the simple consciousness of simple fact can also startle the imagination into places it could never reach on its own.

The close of "After the Wilderness" furnishes my last example. After Chancellorsville, Lanier looks frantically for his brother Clifford "among the fields of dead / before we lost him to a common grave" (7). When he finally finds him, Clifford is bent above a dying squirrel ("A battlefield is full of trash like that— / dead birds and squirrels, bits of uniform" [7]), and in his obsessive attention to burying all the dead squirrels he finds in

"a dozen, tiny, separate graves" (7), he shows all too clearly that his colli-
sion with the immense war has momentarily burned his mind. When the
two young men finish the last of the tiny graves, Clifford breaks, as
Grant supposedly did after the Wilderness, and "sobbed as though they'd
been his unborn sons" (8). And then Hudgins, in iambic pentameter lines
that refuse to flinch under the nearly unbearable weight of what they lead
us to imagine, gives mere fact the last and overwhelming word:

> I wiped his tears and stroked his matted hair,
> and as I hugged him to my chest I saw
> he'd wet his pants. We called it Yankee tea. (8)

As the large achievement of *After the Lost War* shows, American poets
may yet fulfill the spirit, if not quite the letter, of Whitman's hyperbolic
prophecy, finding in the Civil War "indeed the Verteber of Poetry and
Art, (of personal character too,) for all future America." As the twenty-
first century opens, they may discover, or rediscover, what Whitman
called "the inexhaustible mine" of "native passion, first-class pictures,
tempests of life and death."[18] And if they do, and, if they can make room
in themselves for a consciousness of the facts of an immense war, the
Wilderness may bloom and keep blooming.

## Notes

1. Walt Whitman, *Memoranda During the War* (Boston: Applewood Books, 1990), 4.

2. Edmund Wilson, *Patriotic Gore: Studies in the Literature of the American Civil War* (New York: Oxford University Press, 1962), 466; subsequent references are noted parenthetically in the text.

3. Thomas H. Johnson, ed., *The Poems of Emily Dickinson*, 3 vols. (Cambridge, Mass.: Belknap Press of Harvard University Press, 1955), 2: 457. Subsequent references to Dickinson's poetry are to this edition.

4. Caroline Augusta Ball, *The Jacket of Grey and Other Fugitive Poems* (Charleston, S.C.: J. Walker, 1866); subsequent references are noted parenthetically in the text.

5. *Harper's Weekly* (May 28, 1864), 343.

6. *The Poems of John R. Thompson* (New York: Charles Scribner's Sons, 1920); all references to Thompson's poetry are to this edition and are by page number.

7. Allan Nevins, *The Evening Post: A Century of Journalism* (New York: Boni and Liveright, 1922), 408.

8. All citations of Whitman's poetry are to *Leaves of Grass: A Textual Variorum of the Printed Poems*, 3 vols., ed. Sculley Bradley, Harold W. Blodgett, Arthur Golden, and William White (New York: New York University Press, 1980), and are noted parenthetically.

9. All citations of *Battle-Pieces* are to the edition by Hennig Cohen (New York: Thomas Yoseloff, 1963) and are noted parenthetically.

10. Richard Marius, ed., *The Columbia Book of Civil War Poetry* (New York: Columbia University Press, 1994); all subsequent references to Marius's edition are by page number and are noted parenthetically.

11. Daniel Aaron, *The Unwritten War: American Writers and the Civil War* (London: Oxford University Press, 1973), 302.

12. Stephen Vincent Benét, *John Brown's Body* (New York: Doubleday, Doran, 1929), 137. All subsequent references to the poem are by page number and are noted parenthetically.

13. Robert Lowell, *For The Union Dead* (New York: Farrar, Straus, & Giroux, 1956), 71.

14. Andrew Hudgins, *After the Lost War: A Narrative* (Boston: Houghton Mifflin, 1988); all references to this volume are by page number and are noted parenthetically.

15. Edwin Mims, *Sidney Lanier* (Boston: Houghton Mifflin, 1905), 54–55.

16. See Aubrey Harrison Starke, *Sidney Lanier: A Biographical and Critical Study* (Chapel Hill: University of North Carolina Press, 1933), 50.

17. *The Palm at the End of the Mind: Selected Poems and a Play by Wallace Stevens*, ed. Holly Stevens (New York: Knopf, 1971), 206. Subsequent references are noted parenthetically.

18. Whitman, *Memoranda*, 4.

# "My Young Man of Mars"

## *The Gay, World War II Love Poetry of Dunstan Thompson*

How shall I let you know these words have meaning
Beyond the fakery, tricks of the tongue you wonder
At . . . ?

—Dunstan Thompson, "The Everlasting Gunman"

n the mid-1940s, Dunstan Thompson (1918–75) published two volumes of, chiefly, war poetry—*Poems* and *Lament for the Sleep-walker*—which were widely and, for the most part, enthusiastically reviewed.[1] Aware that Thompson was young, only twenty-four, when *Poems* appeared, Louise Bogan admitted, "His poems, when compared to the flat quatrains written in youth by . . . T. S. Eliot or the plain but heartfelt romantic sonnets of . . . young Santayana, scamper away with all prizes for virtuosity," while Louis Untermeyer described the collection as "nimble and yet disciplined" and "brilliant." Comparing Thompson's *Poems* and *Lament for the Sleepwalker,* Abbott Martin noted, "Mr. Thompson's first book of poems . . . was recognized . . . by discerning readers and reviewers as the very fine achievement of one of our younger poets. *Lament for the Sleepwalker* . . . will confirm the judgment of . . . earlier admirers," while John Hay called the second volume "intense" and "individual," confident its poems revealed the poet's "brilliance" and "courage."[2] Despite such accolades, Dunstan Thompson and his work disappeared from the literary scene by the end of the decade, and his posthumous *Poems 1950–1974* did nothing to reestablish his place in U.S. literary history.

Now, over fifty years since *Poems* appeared, the only mention of Thompson's stellar if brief career to have appeared in print for many decades is a solitary sentence in a survey of gay literature, chiefly fiction but also poetry and drama, published between 1900 and 1960: "In two books of war lyrics, the now-forgotten Dunstan Thompson . . . made his homosexuality as manifest as he could given his intricate and dense style."[3] A glance at either of Thompson's collections reveals that his style is often "intricate and dense," but it is just as often crystal clear. Furthermore, it is misleading to suggest, as the sentence does, that Thompson was unable to divulge his sexuality because his poetry's style prohibited him from doing so. The opposite is the actual case. Thompson's "intricate and dense style," along with, for example, his use of elegy, allowed him to reveal his sexuality—to those willing to read the poems closely. Indeed, of the several American poets of World War II whom we now identify as homosexual, Thompson was by far more openly gay in his poetry than any of the others.

203

Even the most experienced reader of poetry will probably stumble over the concluding stanza of Thompson's "Tarquin," the title of which is the name of a gay character in Lawrence Durrell's novel *The Black Book*—

> This bellboy beauty, this flamingo groom,
> Who left his nickname soul too little room
> For blood on blades of grass, must now turn over,
> Feel for the fatal flower, the hothouse sterile
> Rose, raised in no god's praise, and, like death, never
> Again enjoyed, must make his madness moral:
> Washed by the inland waters of the womb,
> The salt sheet is his shroud, the bed his tomb. (*Poems* 8)

—or will be at least momentarily baffled by these lines from "The Prince, His Madness, He Raves at Mirrors":

I am chilled as though a star
Of mobs and children came by traitor's gate
And climbed the water stair to break his neck
On the axe king's, all in winter sunshine. (*Lament* 29–33)

Perhaps one of the best examples of Thompson's "intricate and dense" style is the first poem of *Poems,* "Water Music," which begins

Over the river, sleeping, sleep your nights
Of never my delights, of famous flights,
Not mine, outshining moonstone stars, displayed
Like summer sailors from black water drawn
To dance on malachite, to prance parade
Past queens last-quarter afternoons of dawn,
First sunset mornings, break-of-day midnights,
O as the snow swans end their Rhenish flights. (*Poems* 1)

204

The "music" in this stanza of "Water Music" is overwhelming. Its first two lines and last two lines are rhyming couplets that surround a rhyming quatrain in much of the same way as the reader becomes surrounded by the entire stanza while reading it, but Thompson has also used internal rhyme and assonance/consonance, thus underscoring the rhyme scheme. In the second line, *delights* and *flights* rhyme; and in the next line, the music created by Thompson's auditory devices begins to build: *mine* and *outshining* rhyme, and the "st" of *moonstone* and *stars* repeat. In the fourth, fifth, and sixth lines, Thompson achieves a crescendo of sound: *summer, sailors,* and *water* rhyme; *dance* rhymes with *prance;* each "a" of *malachite* and *parade* are identical; the "qu" of *queens* is repeated in *quarter; past* and *last* rhyme; and the "ns" of *queens* echoes in *afternoons.* In the last couplet, the stanza achieves a quiet dénouement: the combination of "t" and "s" in *first* repeats in *midnights,* although the letters are flip-flopped, and the "en" of *end* reappears buried in *Rhenish.* Thompson also cross-rhymes internally and uses assonance or consonance from one line to the next. For example, in the first two lines, *over* and *river* of the first line rhyme with *never* in the second, and the long "e" of *sleeping* and *sleep* in line one echoes in *delight* in the second line—to cite only two of many possible examples. By using an end-word rhyme scheme as well as an internal-word web of rhymes and assonance/consonance, Thompson creates a substantial layer of sound, which may be "dense" to some but simply lush to others. The effect of the stanza's sonics is simple yet brilliant: readers are so overwhelmed by the auditory devices that, if they are not careful, they will be distracted from what the poem is saying.

Thompson creates even more intricacy in the stanza by its construction. Not only is the fifty-four-word stanza one sentence, but much of the sentence's syntax has been skewed, and most of the sentence belongs to one of three series of modifiers—two that are adjectival and one that is adverbial. The sentence's main clause, which is the subject of the stanza, is embedded within the first line: nights sleep. The rest of the line modifies the two words of the main clause and may be thus paraphrased: your nights sleep beyond the river which is also asleep. What follows in the next two lines is a sequence of adjectival prepositional phrases modifying the *nights* of the poem's unidentified you. The nights are never the narrator's "delights" and are never the narrator's "famous flights." They are brighter than stars and are similar to sailors who were drowned in their prime. At this point in the stanza, the adjectives, which are prepositional phrases, begin modifying *sailors* instead of *nights*. The sailors are resurrected from death "To dance" across a copper-like mineral often used in ornaments or jewelry in a parade-like manner past "queens." At this point, Thompson again shifts the sentence's focus. For the next two lines, he offers three adverbial prepositional phrases which modify *to prance* (the preposition of each phrase, *during*, is understood, not given). The sailors prance during afternoons the narrator describes as dawn, during mornings the narrator describes as sunset, and during midnights the narrator also describes as dawn. At the same time that the sailors prance, swans have either found rest along the Rhine River or have stopped escaping from the area through which the Rhine flows.

The narrator recognizes that a gap exists between himself and the as-yet-unidentified you. The gap between them is both real and figurative. Not only do the nights the you experiences exist away from the narrator,

205

that is, beyond the river that physically separates them, they belong only to the you who has not shared their delights with the narrator, *delights* introducing an obvious sexual overtone to the poem. Similarly, the you has experienced "nights . . . / . . . of famous flights"— escapes from the humdrum of life, the escapades of which many know—and has not shared them with the narrator either. Because the narrator has mentioned twice that he has been excluded from the life of you, his jealousy is apparent. It is obvious to the reader that the relationship the narrator once shared with the you was either sexual or romantic, but Thompson keeps the specifics of the relationship a mystery for the time being.

The narrator continues to lament his fate. He describes the nights of the you as glowing brightly; they outshine the stars, which are only moonstones by comparison, a lovely bit of hyperbole. If that were not enough, the narrator pushes the comparison even further, likening the stars to sailors who at summer, that is, at the height of their physical potency and desirability, have drowned. By including the "summer sailors" in the litany of modifiers that compose the stanza, Thompson reveals that the relationship between the narrator and the you is homosexual. No heterosexual narrator would liken his female beloved to a man. In fact, Thompson's use of the sailors emphasizes in a very subtle way a gay relationship because the stereotypic sailor is one of several icons of gay culture and gay desire.[4] By adding the sailor icon to the hyperbole he is constructing, the narrator reveals that the you's nights outshine one of the most attractive, most sexually potent, and most arousing fantasies he can imagine. In fact, by comparison, the sailors are dead to the narrator and even become ridiculous caricatures of a gay ideal. Resurrected from death by the narrator, they dance as if they were a part of an ornament and, being ornamental, they are superficial. They also *prance,* a word that derides the sailor/fantasy man, in a parade-like fashion not past generals surveying troops but past "queens," a gay slang term for effeminate men.[5] Thompson stresses the effeminacy, a negative in the gay subculture, of the ideal/fantasy man in comparison to the you whom the narrator loves. In short, Thompson's narrator rejects the icon/fantasy in favor of the you, saying the you is far superior—more attractive, more sexually potent, more arousing—than the ideal is. His hyperbole has upset the usual course of events in the world. A real individual, the you, is more of an ideal, more of a fantasy, than the gay subculture usually accepts as the ideal. With the elevation of the you above perfection, the laws of the narrator's universe have been flipped topsy-turvy: afternoons are dawns, mornings are sunsets, and midnights are mornings. In the narrator's world, what we accept as real has become surreal, what society has called unnatural—homosexuality—has become the mainstay.

In the stanza's last line, the narrator returns to the river of the first line with subtle closure. He identifies it as the Rhine, suggests that the you may live in one of the countries through which the Rhine flows, and introduces the fact of World War II's existence into the poem. The narrator explains that, while lamenting his separation from the you, swans either stop trying to escape from the Teutonic region of the world or come to rest in that region. In either case, the swans—so closely associated in our culture with fairy tales, in which they often play important roles, and thus are linked to "happily-ever-after" endings—suggest that the narrator sees the possibility of happiness in his life existing only in that region "Over the river," where the you resides.

The "story" of the narrator and the you is no Hero and Leander tale. In the first line, the narrator describes the river as "sleeping," inferring that it is sluggish, its current virtually nil and, thus, that he could cross it to his beloved. If crossing the river were an option, however, he would. He doesn't. Even if the river were only a creek, the narrator could not wade across. Culturally sanctioned regulations against male-male romantic/sexual relationships are too strongly ingrained in his psyche. His only option in pre-Stonewall America is to stand on the bank on this side of the river and lament his loss.

Indeed, lament is the most important facet of Dunstan Thompson's poetry, an elegiac impulse driving most of the work in *Poems* and the appropriately titled *Lament for the Sleepwalker*. While we could easily rationalize Thompson's focus on death by citing his World War II service, more is involved in his elegies than memorializing fallen comrades. Since the Sumerian *Epic of Gilgamesh*, gay poets have employed the elegy to express deeply felt emotions for another man. For many centuries, it was the only socially acceptable vehicle for such utterance, although after the classical period, the poet usually identified the subject of his elegy as friend, never lover. Thus the elegy in which a same-sex friend is eulogized became in many instances a code by which a gay poet could identify himself to gay readers.[6] Thompson was obviously aware of that long tradition, and he used it not only to identify himself as gay but to raise gay-related issues in his poetry. One of Thompson's finest poems, "This Tall Horseman, My Young Man of Mars," is not only a strong example of the twentieth-century elegy in general, and specifically of the gay elegy, it also clearly reveals how openly Thompson dealt in his poetry with his own homosexuality and with issues confronting gay men.

An Italian sonnet, the succinct elegy's first line is its title:

> This tall horseman, my young man of Mars,
> Scatters the gold dust from his hair, and takes
> Me to pieces like a gun. The myth forsakes
> Him slowly. Almost mortal, he shows the scars
> Where medals of honor, cut-steel stars,
> Pin death above the heart. But bends, but breaks
> In his hand, my love, whose wrecked machinery makes
> Time, the inventor, weep through a world of wars.
> Guilt like a rust enamels me. I breed
> A poison not this murdering youth may dare
> In one drop of blood to battle. No delight
> Is possible. Only at parting do we need
> Each other; together, we are not there
> At all. Love, I farewell you out of sight. (*Lament* 5)

By repeating the first line as title, Thompson introduces the relationship between the narrator and the "young man" immediately and twice so that it cannot escape the reader's notice. The narrator calls the "tall horseman" "*my* young man" (emphasis added), echoing how women once referred to their beaux, then transforms the youth into an icon, a fantasy, a knight-in-shining-armor figure whose hair, full of "gold dust," suggests a halo, implying his divine status. The youth's masculinity and beauty overwhelm the narrator, who admits that the youth "takes / [Him] to pieces like a gun." The narrator feels as if the youth has disassembled his body into individual parts in the same way a soldier takes his rifle apart to clean it. The Freudian gun simile emphasizes the youth's masculinity and sexual potency. Conversely, it underscores the narrator's lack of masculinity, sexual prowess, and control in the relationship. Symbolically, the youth plays the sexually active, even aggressive, role to the narrator's sexual passivity. We might assume, too, that the narrator has been passive in most, if not all, aspects of his life.

Regardless of how well the narrator creates the fantasy of the "young man of Mars," metamorphosing the youth into an icon/fantasy of ultramasculinity, reality intrudes: "The myth forsakes / Him." The "scars" that "he shows" the narrator threaten his stance as fantasy or icon. What the narrator thought was perfect is blemished, making the youth "Almost mortal." Evidently, the blemish is not enough to destroy the narrator's fantasy, only enough to give him pause. More important, the narrator realizes that the youth's heart is covered by "medals of honor, cut-steel stars" in a row across his "heart"—as if by armor. Not only is the youth's emotional life protected from the narrator by the medals, the medals separate him from the narrator and "Pin death" over his "heart," suggesting that the youth's ability to love is overshadowed by death, thus symbolically, dead itself. The youth may engage in a sexual relationship with the narrator but not in an emotional one. The narrator's path to the youth's "heart," the symbolic seat of love, is blocked, and the obstacle to his attaining love and happiness with the youth is, ironically, those very emblems—a military man, a hero, a knight-in-shining-armor—that had so attracted him initially. In short, the fantasy simultaneously invites a relationship and repels it; the "young man of Mars" is a temptation and a taboo. The youth has learned that love between men is futile during war because too often, too easily, one's beloved is killed or transferred out of one's life. Such a realization, which the narrator had not yet come to, has made the youth cynical, even cruel. The narrator helplessly watches as the youth "breaks / In his hand, [the narrator's] love" and hears "Time . . . weep through a world of wars" over the failed fantasy/icon the narrator had created around the youth, the "wrecked machinery" with which he intended to achieve love but attained only illusion. The "world of

**209**

wars" suggests not only the two world wars but also the many conflicts male-male sexual/romantic relationships face during war or peace globally and day-to-day in a homophobic world, the conflicts gay men face attempting to find love in a world that denies them the opportunities that it permits their heterosexual counterparts, the conflicts gay men face in their search for fulfillment and happiness. Although the narrator cannot yet mourn the destruction of what he believed would be love, he hears "Time" lament as if on his behalf.

Finding himself face-to-face with the death of his fantasy, the narrator confesses, "Guilt like a rust enamels me." He feels guilty for at least two reasons: because he is attracted to another man, to the youth, and because he realizes he has allowed himself to be attracted to a fantasy, not to a flesh-and-blood human being. Fantasy itself is not a problem; substituting fantasy for reality is. Guilt surrounds him completely, separating him from others, as well as protecting him from them as the youth's "medals of honor" had separated and protected him from the narrator and the pain of love that would eventually be killed off by one force or another. Yet because the narrator likens the guilt to "rust," the separation and protection it offers is temporary, even dangerous. The guilt/rust will eat through into his being. In fact, the narrator admits that he creates—the narrator's word is *breed*, an emphatically ironic choice of words because, as a gay man, he won't have children and because his attempt at producing an icon/fantasy was, to continue the metaphor, stillborn—the guilt that will eventually "poison" him, that the youth, and consequently love between men in general, cannot "battle" it successfully no matter how diligently they try. In the last four lines, the narrator sketches his relationship with the youth in utterly realistic, even cynical, terms. Because their relationship has been based on illusion, and is thus superficial, they have had "No delight," the object of any relationship however brief or lengthy. His self-identity is also threatened. It is so tightly intertwined with the fantasy that, when he and the youth part, he realizes they are less than complete human beings, the one needing the other to be complete, which in turn obliterates the individuality of each.

The ambiguity of the poem's last sentence, "Love, I farewell you out of sight," makes it the most powerful line in the elegy. On one level, the sentence emphasizes the tragedy of the narrator and the youth's relationship, the most recurring of all themes in gay literature, to remind us that love between men is doomed from the beginning and always ends tragically.[7] War destroys the fantasy the narrator adored. It "scarred" the youth, forcing the narrator to look at reality. To make matters worse, the youth destroys the narrator's love for him: he "bends . . . breaks / In his hand" the narrator's "heart," also forcing the narrator to look at reality. Having no other recourse but to accept his failure at love, the narrator simply watches the youth, whom the narrator addresses as "Love," leave, perhaps off to pick up, then bed, another man whom he will also leave or off to another battlefield where he will win even more "medals of honor." Regardless of the youth's future, the narrator's passivity has reached its climactic, logical end. His last gesture in the elegy is simply to wave good-bye to the youth—to "Love" itself—as he disappears, leaving the narrator waiting for the next icon, a tragic, pathetic image of the narrator. In its second possible interpretation, however, the sentence suggests that the narrator rejects passivity and by extension discards the fantasy "Love" that the youth/icon represents. Having realized that nothing exists in their relationship but illusion, the narrator dismisses the youth, his waving good-bye becoming a gesture of control. He expels the "young man of Mars," as well as the superficial relationship that an icon could only offer, from his life. The narrator's shifting stances at the elegy's conclusion is underscored by the fact that, in all but the last seven words of the poem, the narrator speaks *about* the "young man of Mars," as if he were not actually there, speaking *to* him only at the end, when dismissing him. The fantasy obscures the youth's true self from the narrator who cannot see the "young man" at all but only a "myth." In many ways, the narrator thus ironically mirrors the attitude of society at large, which sees only a stereotype, a "myth," when it views the narrator.

Although Thompson's narrator never actually mourns but allows Time, his stand-in, to lament briefly, concisely, he ends the elegy with a resolution that serves as a consolation, an element required in traditional elegies yet one twentieth-century elegists rarely include. He dismisses the icon because he knows a fantasy "Love" is temporary and detrimental. His "Love" for an icon is, of course, the embodiment of his dependence on, even addiction to, illusion. To reject his dependence is to shift his role from passive to active and thus to change his self-image. For the first time in the poem, and perhaps for the first time in his life, the narrator achieves control. He dismisses the "young man of Mars" in order to reject a superficial way of life, suggesting to the reader that, if he is aware enough to see past the superficial attractions of the fantasy and to find little of value, he may be strong enough in the future to locate the attributes needed to build real "Love" in another man. His resolve becomes a subtle consolation. Happiness, fulfillment, and love are possible to gay men but only to those strong enough to face reality.

"This Tall Horseman, My Young Man of Mars" is not the only poem in Dunstan Thompson's *Poems* and *Lament for the Sleepwalker* that tackles gay issues head-on. For those willing or able to read the books carefully as poetry is meant to be read, all poems in both collections do, but in varying degrees of subtlety. Although he wrote in the 1940s, decades before the advent of so-called gay liberation, Thompson was "out" to his readers but not in the same way that, for example, Allen Ginsberg could be. Writing in a tradition stemming from the beginnings of literature, not rebelling against it in order to create a new tradition, Thompson would never have written, "who let themselves be fucked in the ass by saintly motorcyclists, and screamed with joy," as Ginsberg did in his first book published nearly a decade after *Lament for the Sleepwalker*.[8] Instead, he wrote poetry that was less raw than Ginsberg's but no less obviously gay.

In these lines from "Largo," for instance, Thompson addresses the fact that gay men of his time had to conceal their gay relationships, even by marrying women to give themselves a veneer of heterosexuality:

more than friends, we fell
Together on the other side of love; where clocks
And mirrors were reversed to show
Ourselves as only we could know;
Where all the doors had secret locks

With double keys; and where the sliding panel, well
Concealed, gave us our exit through the palace wall.
There we have come and gone: twin kings, who roam at will
    Behind the court, behind the backs
    Of consort queens, behind the racks
On which their favorites lie who told them what to do.
                                       (*Poems* 21–26)

In "Return of the Hero," Thompson intertwines the theme of survivor's guilt which many soldiers, heterosexuals and homosexuals alike, who returned home after the war faced—". . . cries from the gulls were as nothing to the shrill cry / Caught in his throat as he thought of himself, the undrowned boy"—with the narrator's attempt to find love and its importance to his self-identity and to life in general:    **213**

If friendship were fake—which the poet affirmed and denied,
While he went from one bed to another in search of himself,
Until for the last time, or was it the first, he woke up the dead
To tell them "I've fallen in love," and half-joking, half
    Serious, sang them to sleep again—if friendship were
      fake,
    The hero reflected, his hand on the rail, then love was
    the rock. (*Lament* 39–42)

Thompson's depiction of a hustler and the man who buys him in "The Point of No Return" calls into question the notion of innocence—

See him now, how unhurried he destroys
The tick-tock meaning of the nursery boy's
Nostalgia for love's never-never land,
And, fairy-story prince turned toad, spews out
Not pearls, but girls' garters, when wizard wand
Waves him unwanton, just a Times Square tout:
His smile mints money, but his laugh enjoys
The spoilt child buying back pawn-broken toys. (*Poems* 9–10)

—while in "The Lay of the Battle of Tombland," the narrator's guilt over being homosexual turns the sexual impulse into a surrealistic horror:

> What could I cry but "Bombs Away,"
>     When the Man who was Hunchback spoke.
> "O live through this, and be my boy,"
>     He laughed, and his true voice broke.
>     . . . . . . . . . . . . . . . . . . . . . . . . . . . . . . .
> The Harelip Man knelt down to drink
>     Blood from the sewers, swore
> "You'll kiss me yet, and you'll thank
>     Me later, later, after the war. (*Lament* 3–4)

**214**    Despite such moments, love between men when it is open can prevent both physical and spiritual deaths, as Thompson so clearly reveals in "In All the Argosy of Your Bright Hair":

> When that damask duke took my heart for hound,
> I dogged him with praises, with poems, a beggar's homage.
> His blue eyes, fencing like a dance of swords,
> Ringed me from foemen, were night lights. I found
> He turned my head from death's entrancing image,
> Gold in the desert sun, who sang: "What words
> You want, I have." He saved me from my own hand. . . .
>                                                   (*Lament* 10–11)

It is now virtually impossible to ascertain why Dunstan Thompson's work disappeared from the literary landscape. Perhaps we can blame the time in which he wrote, one of utter homophobia. Indeed, of his many reviewers, only two broach the topic of his books' open homosexuality. H. P. Lazarus mentions that "Ganymede is present [in *Poems*] as bellboy, page, groom, sailor, and acolyte," aware that Ganymede was the prototypical pretty boy for gay poets and became a code gay poets adopted from ancient Greek mythology to disclose their own homosexuality to gay readers. Warren Beck identifies Richard Hager, the man to whom

Thompson dedicated "Nor Mars His Sword" in *Lament for the Sleep-walker,* as the person whom the narrator addresses throughout the poem, the narrator's "'death-in-life long lover.'"[9] Otherwise, reviewers are silent on the topic. Perhaps they were protecting Thompson; perhaps they didn't notice the homosexuality; perhaps they didn't think the books' gay content mattered. Because there is no official biography of Thompson and readers are left to piece together the facts of his life from blurbs on his books, we can only assume that Thompson may also be to blame for his obscurity. Having expatriated to England not long after his hitch in the U.S. Army was over, he may have not only removed himself physically from the U.S. literary milieu in which he initially grew but he may have made himself invisible to those who had, only a few years earlier, championed his work. In fact, in the all-too-brief blurb on the back cover of the posthumous *Poems 1950–1974,* readers are informed that Thompson died in 1975, only fifty-seven years of age, after "many years of illness." It is not only likely but probable that his illness kept him from the energy-sapping chore of submitting work for publication and he simply abandoned that task. Or perhaps, ultimately, Thompson's love for writing in traditional forms made him seem too rococo, too traditional, for the hip 1950s and 1960s, decades that were so obsessed with getting rid of fuddy-duddy ways and hand-me-down points of view that Thompson may simply have fallen victim to their cleaning house. Regardless of the possible reasons for his disappearance from literary history, it is obvious that, although either Robert Duncan or Allen Ginsberg are usually cited as the progenitors of gay poetry in this country, neither are strong candidates for the honor. Robert Duncan's first book, *Heavenly City, Earthly City,* was issued in the same year Thompson's second collection appeared,[10] and Allen Ginsberg's *Howl and Other Poems,* his first volume, was published nine years after Thompson's second. It is obvious, then, that not only does Dunstan Thompson not deserve the obscurity that has veiled his work from readers for many, many decades, his place as the first U.S. poet of European descent to tackle openly gay issues in his work should finally be recognized.

215

# Notes

1. I am concerned only with the poetry that appeared in the two volumes Thompson published during his life, *Poems* (New York: Scribner's, 1943) and *Lament for the Sleepwalker* (New York: Dodd, Mead, 1947). Hereafter, I will document quotations from those books within the essay by using *Poems* or *Lament* followed by the page number(s) on which the poem may be found. Thompson also published *The Phoenix in the Desert* (London: J. Lehmann, 1951), a travelogue; the novel *The Dove with the Bough of Olive* (New York: Simon and Schuster, 1954); and a seven-page chapbook, *The Song of Time: An English Poem Adapted from the French of Marguerite de Navarre* (Cambridge, Mass.: Cosmos Press, 1941), which appeared while he was an undergraduate at Harvard and may have been self-published. Philip Tower edited a posthumous collection of Thompson's work, *Poems 1950–1974* (Bungay, Suffolk, England: Paradigm Press, 1984).

2. Louise Bogan, "Verse," *New Yorker,* February 26, 1944, 84; Louis Untermeyer, "Among the Poets," *Yale Review* n.s., 34 (Winter 1945): 343; Abbott Martin, "Poets in Review," *New York Times Book Review,* October 12, 1947, 30; and John Hay, *Commonweal,* May 2, 1947, 75. Other reviewers were as laudatory of both collections. For example, Oscar Williams called *Poems* "the event of a poetic season rich in first books" ("Sincerity Is a Talent," *New Republic,* April 24, 1944, 581), and in their monumental survey of U.S. poetry, Horace Gregory and Marya Zaturenska labeled the volume "a brilliant first book of poems" (*A History of American Poetry, 1900–1940* [New York: Harcourt, Brace, 1946], 501), while based on his reading of *Lament,* Warren Beck pronounced Thompson "one of his generation's leading poets" (*Poetry,* July 1947, 222).

3. Joseph Cady, "American Literature: Gay Male, 1900–1969," in *Gay and Lesbian Literary Heritage,* ed. Claude J. Summers (New York: Holt, 1995), 34.

4. Several gay male icons—i.e., sexual fantasies—besides the "sailor" exist. All share attributes: they exhibit ultra-masculinity through such traits as a sharply defined musculature, insatiable sexual appetite, large penis; they often wear a specific "uniform," as policemen, for example, do; and they are typically active, even aggressively active, never passive, in sexual encounters. Each is, in a word, ultra-masculine and is also the opposite of the gay stereotype held by homophobic societies. Each member of the Village People, a singing group from the disco era, played the part of a different gay male icon.

5. *Queen* has been used as a term for effeminate, homosexual men since at least 1924, according to the *OED*.

6. An excellent introduction to the role of elegy in gay poetry is Stephen Guy Bray, "Elegy," in *Gay and Lesbian Literary Heritage,* ed. Summers, 217–19.

7. See the opening paragraphs of my "The Fifty-Seventh Second" (*American Book Review,* September–October 1995, 17, 30) for a brief discussion of gay literature's re-

liance on, even fostering of, tragedy as the outcome of male-male unions, which culminates in the AIDS literature of our day.

8. Allen Ginsberg, *Howl and Other Poems* (San Francisco: City Lights, 1956), 9–20.

9. H. P. Lazarus, "Poetry in Review," *Nation,* April 29, 1944, 519; and Warren Beck, "From the Most Mandrake Forest," *Poetry,* July 1947, 220.

10. Robert Duncan, *Heavenly City, Earthly City,* (Berkeley: Bern Porter, 1947).

# Warren's Ventriloquist

## *J. J. Audubon*

ames Weldon Johnson is said to have written his autobiography in five separate versions, a comic idea that, upon reflection, will startle few writers. *Who are you?* life asks the writing man. Robert Penn Warren's poetry, as intensely as that of any major contemporary poet, grapples with this question. His answers are shifting, multiple, contingent on circumstance. He said in *Fugitives' Reunion* that the greatness of an art lies in its ability to create and hold the single image of a man.[1] He knew a life is a history, a narrative, a journey for which the final redemption of meaning seldom, if ever, comes convincingly to the traveler. Yet he believed in poetry's redemptive life-telling that confronts fate, and he celebrated that in his strangely blended and iconic poem *Audubon: A Vision*, a poem of lyric voice performing narrative tasks.[2]

*Audubon: A Vision* seems a curious, aberrational poem however one approaches it. In her review of the book, Helen Vendler, a most reluctant admirer of Warren's, called it an elegy and a parable.[3] Others have called it a narrative and a history in verse. *Audubon* purports to chronicle the life of the American naturalist, artist, and entrepreneur John James Audubon, who lived from 1785 to 1851. The poem is spoken by an omniscient but hardly indifferent narrator. Its final moment, however, is given undeniably to, and is abruptly spoken by, the poet Robert Penn Warren who, almost defiantly, assumes an autobiographical post. If *Audubon's* pedigree seems an odd intercourse of the pastoral elegy and the frontier tall tale, the book is perhaps circumscribed only by recognizing that it is an autobiography disguised as a biography disguised as a narrative legend disguised as a narrative poem, all serving to forge the image of a man and a language in which he can exist.

What drew Warren to such an infolded, layered work? His early verse was indebted to the authorial effacement of modernists T. S. Eliot and Thomas Hardy who, in 1928, published his last book, *Winter Words.* Then a Rhodes Scholar at Oxford, Warren had been writing poems with John Crowe Ransom since 1921, and, as Allen Tate's roommate at Vanderbilt, he gleefully illustrated "The Waste Land" on their dormitory wall. Modernist that he was, he did not easily accept himself as subject or speaker of his poems. There is no overt autobiography that might have offered us, as James Olney says in *Metaphors of Self,* "the symptomatic key to all that he did and, naturally, to all that he was."[4] He refused the self-explaining statements such as poets are apt to make about the writing of poems—Poe's "Philosophy of Composition," for example, or fastidious Tate's "Narcissus as Narcissus." Yet Warren's first book, published in 1929, was a life study, *John Brown: The Making of a Martyr,*[5] and life study would be Warren's interest, whatever the genre he favored, over a remarkable seventy years of writing.

Unlike Hardy, who wrote his own biography and published it in his second wife's name, Warren often stated vigorous opposition to seeing his life rendered into biography. Yet he cooperated with Joseph Blotner, whose *Robert Penn Warren* appeared in 1996.[6] This "life" has, regrettably, too little of Warren's life in it. I am tempted to say that all we have, truly, of an indisputable Warren life is the collected interviews, *Robert Penn Warren Talking;*[7] but any Warren poem, a "talking," is an autobiography of a speculative, alert, self-measuring consciousness in an enigmatic world. His lives are never merely well-recorded historical events. Each poem is a visitation of a life engaged in a struggle between an interior self

**219**

and an exterior determinism; the struggle is always to observe a self who possesses and employs knowledge. It would be pretty to say this life was Warren's own—pretty but perhaps not wholly accurate. The life he offers is neither autobiographical nor biographical but dialectical and hypothetical, a living in, and of, words that compose a man. *Audubon: A Vision* is Warren's starkest rendering of that story.

James H. Justus tells us, in *The Achievement of Robert Penn Warren*, that the problem in Warren is always "an adequate selfhood, a breaking out of the debilitating sense of incompleteness and fragmentation. The price, he says, "for that integration of self is not the loss of certain spiritual certitudes, but their hopeful and sometimes desperate testing."⁸ Such testing is, of course, directed at self-repair and self-creation, and a full individuation requires living into consciousness. The Audubon of Warren's poetic biography passes precious little life, and what appears is far more cerebral than physical. No historian or student of Audubon has claimed the man owned the introspection Warren attributes to him in this poem, yet Warren requires, and gives him, a life of both significant deed and knowledge in order to demonstrate the value of humane ideas. Audubon's life, embodying the competing attractions to art's individualistic pursuit and community's self-compromises, and moreover displaying the embryonic struggles at the frontiers of country and imagination, seems in retrospect an ideal vessel for Warren's vitalizing.

It apparently looked otherwise to Warren. Published in 1969, the year I entered the United States Air Force and dead in the middle of the Vietnam War, *Audubon: A Vision* had proved difficult for Warren to write. He had started it in the 1940s, worked desultorily on it, but could not come to the "frame for it, the narrative line" despite the completed, sealed, and available life shape of the long dead Audubon. Rumors have indebted Warren to both Eudora Welty and Katherine Ann Porter, who had themselves employed Audubon. Finally, as Warren said, he determined to write the work in "snapshots of Audubon," and he claimed that *Audubon*'s form came to him in a sudden rush while he made up the bed.⁹ It is an amusing suggestion of a craft-driven modernist's negotiations with romantic inspiration.

Warren's narrative preparation and skills were established facts—a "long foreground" as Emerson said of Whitman's first work—well before *Audubon* became a gleam in his fancy.[10] His seventh book, *All the King's Men*, had won the Pulitzer Prize in 1946.[11] His eleventh, *Brother to Dragons*, published in 1955,[12] was a verse tale, much admired for its historical, philosophical, and moral probing of Thomas Jefferson's murdering nephews and juxtaposed to our national conviction of American righteousness. If Warren's form trouble seemed mitigatable by his abilities, Audubon's factual life was openly, indisputably available. The young explorer Jean Jacques Audubon, bastard son of a French sea captain and his Haitian mistress, had been treated by at least nine full biographies before Warren's work. Several were published in the 1960s when Warren's creation simmered and it seems at least likely that Warren would have read them. Audubon's *Ornithological Journals*, long in print and reissued in 1967,[13] would have given Warren as much self-perceived character and as many dramatic life events, boldly embroidered if not invented, as a novelist might desire. If Warren had ten Audubons to choose from, why was there a form problem? In fact, searching for a narrative line may have deflected Warren from recognizing that was not his difficulty at all. The trouble was a voice appropriately modulated.

Predictably terse, Warren's comments on the making of the poem imply that he lacked not so much a formed knowledge of Audubon as a feel for the inner man. The poem moved rapidly forward when, as Warren said, he began to see Audubon as "a man who has finally learned to accept his fate. The poem is about a man and his fate."[14] Warren, at the time of publication, was sixty-four, with two children roughly the age of those America had watched the Chicago police bludgeon the year before at the Democratic National Convention. Many of us recall how those years produced moments of decision, suddenly made, upon which entire lives seemed later to have followed. Warren's form problem apparently diminished as he came to feel drawn closer to Audubon's inner life.

Warren's attraction to Audubon's life story reaches deep into the sources of identity, beginning with a sense of a Kentucky connection in both lives. Beyond that, Warren's passion to live and work by the imagination and his feeling for the artist as both exile and frontiersman made Audubon a powerfully attractive ancestral model only two generations behind him. Audubon must have looked to Warren like the exemplary American success story as it ought to be rather than as it so often became—a tale of consumptive and exploitative greed that makes heroes of Gatsbys.

The point of Warren's original interest in Audubon will probably never be known, but we can be sure of an awareness by the mid-1930s. Always compelled by history's actors, Warren, during his tenure at Louisiana State University in the late 1930s, could hardly have been ignorant of Audubon. Lewis P. Simpson, in an essay that describes Warren's residences in Baton Rouge, observes that Warren so enjoyed driving his car, even over primitive roads, that he did not hesitate to purchase property twenty miles out from the university, commuting to his academic duties.[15] Only slightly farther to the northwest was the river village of St. Francisville, where Audubon had lived and painted the portrait of Miss Elizabeth Pirrie in the fall of 1821. Long synonymous with America's nature world, in Louisiana Audubon is virtually the emblem of an ancestry that is itself identified with raw vitality of creature and place. Bird prints, elaborately framed survivors of his great portfolios, grace living rooms, law offices, and dental parlors. Zoos, schools, and roads bear Audubon's name. Audubon, the old man, must have seemed to Warren, in 1936, as immediate as did that new man, Huey "the Kingfish" Long, and Audubon's effort to live as an artist must have been especially telling to Depression-era eyes.

When Warren left Louisiana for Minnesota in the fall of 1941, he remarked that no place would ever look the same—both indicting the rank frontierism of poverty politics and the relatively unchanged beauty Audubon had known. It might be hard for a man to make a life of art anywhere, but Audubon had done it in swamps and in circumstances that were lived daily in Louisiana. Warren knew Audubon was far from ordinary. He was, nevertheless, a come-here immigrant who landed in the East, lit out for the West, and who, though no genius, developed a talent for representational art. He also had the ability to organize people and resources to realize his talent's potential. Who was ever more American than Audubon, the entrepreneur marrying art and business? He spent desperate years, but in the end, as Hollywood would script it, Audubon triumphed. He wanted and got it all: his girl, Lucy, children, money, fame. He proved wrong the ubiquitous doubters and naysayers, the privileged and the established, becoming even before Poe our favorite icon, the rebel whose cause was a driving passion for an art turned to a vocation. This vocation amounted to a virtual autobiography of the New World man wrestling out an appropriate relation with determinist Nature. Before Audubon's portfolios, paintings of birds seemed cataloged, lifeless abstracts. Audubon put birds into life scenes, made them realistic, dramatic, and with background contexts gave them a life story. Discovering species theretofore unknown, he expanded the New World's American language with art and made it one whose consciousness remains and lives.

**223**

In *Robert Penn Warren and the American Imagination,* one of Warren's best readers, Hugh Ruppersberg, admires "the dialectic of idealism and pragmatism" that *Audubon* pursues.[16] But, fuzzily to my mind, he says Audubon "seeks to lose himself" in frontier wilds:

> He desires merger with nature, the loss of self, transcendence to an identity larger than his own—nature's. He learns in the forest that such a merger is unattainable: he inhabits the real world, of which the wilderness is a part. His thwarted desire for merger transmutes into a desire to preserve the wilderness of his vision in artistic form. Art becomes his means of merger, of transcendence (79–80).

I am inclined to think Ruppersberg is merely trapped in hyperbole until he remarks, "It is the ideal which matters" (80). Not the life aspiring to a gritty balance of ideal and actual? Where in Warren is the ideal so privileged, the same ideal that, like the zealot of good cause, becomes so often our worst enemy? Audubon doesn't want to be lost, to transcend anything, or to merge with anything—unless of course his passion for painting represents that merger. If so, it is odd that the poem unequivocally minimalizes practice of the art. Audubon's painting is mentioned only twice in the poem. This Audubon does not draw or paint; he watches, and we watch him *watching*. Or he scouts, hunts, conducts business, and is said to learn to define himself against the world. "The world declares itself" (95), Warren writes.[17] Audubon can declare nothing until he has a language of integrated being, a real self. The evidence of that self may be the painting, but we see little of it. Or it may be the growth of consciousness, and there is a deal of talk about that. How else is Warren to give this Ulysses an uncounterfeitable signature? How retrieve from the deadness of time and his own actual life story an Audubon whose speech lives to redeem us?—a form problem indeed.

Warren's solution was, at any rate, under his nose and it was imagistic, if not cinematic. He recognized in Audubon's bird portraits the artist's manipulation of foreground and background, the paradox of time and distance, bountiful wildness and rapacious civilization. He saw how Audubon contrived the illusion of life's movement to survive and even to flourish in the most natural contingency and circumstance. Audubon had painted birds from corpses he killed, putting them in realistic contrast to symbolic landscapes, a procedure that served as an opportunity to reveal Audubon's growth of consciousness. Warren knew, as Joseph Conrad had written, that art's intention must be to render the highest justice to the visible universe.[18] And, snapshot to snapshot, each idiosyncratic in length and subject, Warren caused a figure of Audubon to stand still, to watch, then leaped him years ahead by exposition, image bridges, even quoted passages from Audubon's journals, always emphasizing the helplessness of phenomena before determinist fate. But Warren had also learned from Conrad that for the greatest artist "justice to the visible universe" is not enough. That artist is "one for whom the documentation of the world is constantly striving to rise to the level of generalization about values, for whom the image strives to rise to symbol, for whom images always fall into a dialectical configuration."[19]

Because Warren's problem was the tale of the inner man, he needed a strategy to draw out the dialectical configuration he knew Audubon's life story carried. Typically, poems of the life story begin and end somewhere, survey events, and occupy a large stage of time, providing context that manifests struggle sufficient for a life's redemption of historical anonymity. *The Divine Comedy, The Prelude, Song of Myself,* Ted Hughes's *Crow,* and Elizabeth Bishop's *Geography III,* however diverse in strategical imperatives, remain life-story dramas. Warren once chastised John Greenleaf Whittier for failing to submit his poems to life tests, for an "unconditional surrender" to pure emotion, which meant Whittier and his poems did not know life fully enough.[20] What Audubon knew, and it was adequate, had been described in a scene in the *Ornithological Journals* called "The Prairie." Maria Audubon's edition of the journals notes that the incident occurred in the spring of 1812, in the upper midwest plains, when Audubon was thirty-seven years old.[21]

Warren transposes this scene to "The Dream He Never Knew the End of," section 2 of the book's seven parts. At 197 lines, the section represents nearly half of *Audubon.* Its domination of the whole is such that no other event in Audubon's life is given in anything more than shorthand exposition. Although Audubon said his journals were "food for the idle," they reveal him to have been a man of discipline, one greatly busied by a career to which he was utterly devoted, roving over the American frontier as few did, or could, obviously delighting in abundant experiences of every sort. Why, then, did Warren choose to represent his life in a single anecdote portraying Audubon as, at the least, accessory to murder?

The answer may lie in recognition of the responsibility that a man assumes for the life he walks in. To Warren, the quest for language is always a self-definition. Warren's poem begins in rhetoric with definitions of Audubon. Part 1 locates young Audubon mythically, historically, and chronologically by lies attached to his name and origin, by describing his passion for the woods and its mysteries, by his lack of language. Audubon remains a stiff and standoffish character, however; definitions, distancing and controlled as they are, revealing as they do Audubon's recognition of "How thin is the membrane between himself and the world" (86), fail to make an Audubon "self" knowable. Part 2, therefore, cuts to Audubon in action, seeking a night's shelter at a cabin he has come upon in the woods. Admitted by its resident hag, he feels himself

**225**

direly threatened by her and her two crude sons. Guilty of uncivil, in-
hospitable, and ugly behavior but not of actual assault, mother and sons
are hung to death, and left hanging, by Audubon and three conveniently
arrived quasi-regulators:

> The affair was not tidy: bough low, no drop, with the clients
> Simply hung up, feet not much clear of the ground, but not
> Quite close enough to permit any dancing.
> The affair was not quick: both sons long jerking and farting,
>     but she,
> From the first, without motion, frozen
> In a rage of will, an ecstacy of iron, as though
> This was the dream that, lifelong, she had dreamed toward.
> (92)

Watching her about to die, the narrator (in a droll pun by Warren)
"becomes aware that he is in the manly state" (92). A brilliant anecdote
of loneliness, fear, lust, murder, and complicity becomes, because of
Warren's gift of consciousness to Audubon, an allegorical window
through which a great life story springs. But whose story is it, Audubon's
or Warren's?

This narrative of evil and slippery justice telescopes a man's life to a
single event about which all else, before or after, must orbit like lesser
stars. It prepares for multiple readings, some of which Warren simply
does not follow—Audubon's responsibility for three deaths, for example, and the American Adam's hypocrisy. Some are faint soundings—
the fairy tale victim of the woods, a creation myth, a Narcissus myth,
the artist's individuation legend. What is given conflates the gift of
Audubon's biography and impressionistic portraits of the woods world.
Except for "The Dream He Never Knew the End Of," Warren abandons
narrative structure nearly presumptive for a life story and makes his
*Audubon* out of forms of rhetoric and lyric essentially in the manner of a
pastoral elegy. He does so to emphasize the dialectic of a man who passes
through crisis to control. Warren's problem all along has been to estab-

lish and sustain a voice that must carry a life tale without the abjured narrative chronology.

The unusually static structure of *Audubon* chains images to initiate rhythmic movement for that life voice. Warren's snapshots frame, isolate, and project continuity of image and event relationships; they support interpretability. Like panels in a morality play, these variably constructed moments arrange a stage furniture to contextualize an action that is only suggested, not actual. With Audubon we watch a marvelous bear, a bee-glade, a perfect blue of skies and ponds; we hear a thrilling tusked boar and the oceanic roar of buffalo. To that extent, we experience a life Audubon measured in his journals as "in all conscience *perhaps* as good as worlds unknown."[22] So genuinely sweet seems this life, as a "walk in the world" (93), that Audubon risks forgetting the rude lesson of the hanging tree. He may imagine life is ever bountiful even as he dreams of Lucy's lips that "gleam in the bright wind," but it is exactly then that he "cannot hear the sound of that wind" (99).

The reader can hear it well enough, however, for the voice of Warren's narrator strategically moves from liquid evocation of beauty to an intense and gravelly register that is naturalism's countervoice. This dual sounding directs us as clearly as Little Red Riding Hood's path. Braiding a pastoral celebration of nature with an abrupt, chopped, sometimes choked lingo of brutal, muscular consonants, of broken syntax, and of phrases sawed off to hover in white space, Warren carves a style that seems as documentary as his snapshots. Refusing the authority of an autobiographical "I," his panel poems yoke objectivity to a management of time and space by line signals and gestures readers of poetry are never quite prepared for, especially readers who expect the silky traditional voices. Warren baits us with a life story we already know, and may envy, only to overwhelm us with the drumming death-wind news all flesh is heir to.

The narrative of a life story assumes a unified pattern, even a metonymic shape that extends empirically backward and forward as it mimics chronology and implies paraphrasable meaning available only in comprehension of the whole. Thus the narrative shape subordinates lyric, image, and what Warren, after Conrad, called "dialectical configuration." Lyric, conversely, emphasizes the immediate image, here and now, as a carrier of transcendent opportunity. Subordinating narrative to lyric pressurizes art visually. It also invests discrete moments with density and may impart hypertropic significance to a single experience. Warren's life of *Audubon* does precisely that.

Most of what a man lives, like much of what passes for poetry, is surface, convention, the rounding off and filling in, the fitting into expected form that is interstitial between moments which are everything. Art being long and life short may encourage aberrant symmetry in poetry but, in life's beginning, middle, and end we feel the truest pattern exists. We may not trust the song of happy experience, but we cling to its hope because we have had moments of joy that validate the hope for more. Audubon's boyhood, his lonelinesses, his feelings about paintings, travel, a favorite landscape, even his dreams—arrive at a paltry sum, as Warren says: "He died, and was mourned, who had loved the world" (98). What he left behind were the paintings that collectively express "the dream / Of a season past all seasons" (98). According to Warren the maker/ watcher, this was enough. Or it ought to have been enough, for anyone's life story known through the detached perspective of time and space comes to little more. And yet that little more matters.

Readers of poetry, like readers of life stories, regard all pattern-breaking suspiciously. Had Dante abandoned his terza rima at any point, he would have evoked a no-confidence gasp from his audience. The establishment of the voice telling the life story carries the essential authenticity of life. Warren wanted that voice to register lyric response to Audubon's fate, but he chose to violate reader expectations of the life story form which legitimately might have emphasized greater balladic, metric, grammatic, and aesthetic regularity. The points of violation, or imbalance, are so extensive that they constitute a kind of antipoem, as the poem is itself a melange of genre strains. If we expect Audubon's long life spread visibly and symmetrically, Warren gives us several days. If we expect unity of time and place, Warren introduces a Northwest Orient airliner passing over the head of a narrator standing in no defined place. If we take Audubon to represent nature's exquisite beauty and permanent

228

succor, Warren's imagery is blunt in denial with a portrait of a sky like "the inflamed distance" where the dawn is "redder than meat" (85). Nowhere is Warren more undermining of expectations than in the most elemental unit of poetry, the line, whose rebellious and confident note is evident from the opening section of the poem (line function tends to be mirrored in Warren's stanzaic improprieties).

Beginning in medias res, his voice catechistical, surging against the left margin, rebounding, noisy with its alliteration, boisterous and yet controlled, if barely so, Warren flares the stagelights upon Audubon:

I

WAS NOT THE LOST DAUPHIN

Was not the lost dauphin, though handsome was only      **229**
Base-born and not even able
To make a decent living, was only
Himself, Jean Jacques, and his passion—what
Is man but his passion?

Saw,
Eastward and over the cypress swamp, the dawn,
Redder than meat, break:
And the large bird,
Long neck outthrust, wings crooked to scull air, moved
In a slow calligraphy, crank, flat, and black against
The color of God's blood spilt, as though
Pulled by a single string.

Saw,
It proceed across the inflamed distance.

Moccasins set in hoar frost, eyes fixed on the bird,
Thought: "On that sky it is black."
Thought: "In my mind it is white."

Thinking: "*Ardea occidentalis,* heron, the great one."
Dawn: his heart shook in the tension of the world.
Dawn: and what is your passion? (85)

Each of the first four stanzas consists of a single sentence broken across lines as jagged as rocky ground. Pronouns have been pruned away; sense momentum has been decapitated for felt instability at line's end, sometimes a dizzying interrogation. The sentences three times bark "Saw" and are then immediately tamped by details ensconced by commas, forcing the reader to pull forward against line inertia. By the time he has juxtaposed watching Audubon to the great heron, lyric tension winds so tight what Warren calls "the tension of the world" throbs. The sonic character of an opening in hymn meter so radically differs from Warren's that you can hear the life whoof from the words. Consider this revision:

I was not the lost dauphin though
        handsome was only Base-
born and not even able,
        to make a decent living, was

Only myself, Jean Jacques, and my
        passion—what is man but
his passion? Saw, eastward, over
        the cypress swamp, the dawn. . . .

A stanza of colloquial iambics goes no better, I think:

I wasn't any lost daupin, handsome,
just badly born, not able to make a
decent living, only myself, Jean Jacques
my passion—what is man but passion? I. . . .

The slackness in both decasyllabics and hymn meter points up the force with which Warren's improvised sound conveys rhythmically the drama of consciousness that is to come. Imagistically, sonically, literally, the first scene stands Audubon outside of nature's kingdom and gives him Adam's task of naming the creatures. The voice is not Audubon's; it is not Warren's. It is the voice of the biographer, hieratic and indisputable, correct for the prologue that sonorously marks this triadic moment with man, creature, and God.

This voice is the composition of an unusual line signature, one Warren evolved almost entirely after *Promises* (1957),[23] what might, arguably, be called the first of his major collections of poetry. It is especially unusual in establishing an identity in the free-verse idiom, which typically sacrifices line signature for content effect. Any two or three lines by Warren are readily known as his, but is it so for such poets as Milosz, Rich, or Walcott? Line employment and composition in *Audubon* is not radically different from Warren's late work, but it is pared to a functional **231** minimum that assaults unexpecting readers and in that assault carries the death-wind news of all flesh.

The common reader expects narrative verse presented in a conventional metric of more or less insistent regularity that concludes typically in patterned sound identity, or rhymes. Modern poets first abandoned rhymes and next put aside lines of recurring numbered elements, whether syllables or stress or both. This has produced dismay among the uninitiated who mostly do not write such lines. But it has led equally to a weakened conception of what a line is and what its functions may be. The line, generally stated, advances external action, describes scene or circumstance, and in various ways embodies the mind's consciousness. Lines are thus declarative, imagistic, or rhetorical.

The declarative states, informs, accumulates information. It is built ordinarily in standard English word order (subject, verb, complement) and seeks completion in thought or action, tending to make a statement sufficient unto itself which may be a full or a partial sentence. This line minimizes connotative suggestion while enhancing narrative or discursive movement and thus may be known as either a dramatic or a rhetorical line.

Where the declarative line tends to completion, the imagistic line tends toward continuity or spillage, hence it displays the resonance of enjambment. Indeed, the "poise" of a line in the grid of a poem's actions reflects the juxtaposition of two imperatives: movement toward depletion and movement toward renewal. An enjambed line is an opportunity for multiple, even contradictory meanings in the hovering instant of line's end. Here expression arises from the reader's expectation either sustained or altered by the intrusive white space. Line manipulation affects syntax, momentum, spatial experience, connotation, and even cognitive resolution while it establishes controlling cadence. Once established as a normative length, the line is usually sustained in order to avoid violations offensive to either the ear or the eye that seeks symmetry, the imperative foremost to poetry.

This resistance to pattern-breaking is so firm that any alteration of the expected order is regarded suspiciously. Readers balk at multiple caesurae, at arbitrary line breaks, at suspended or spatially dispersed parts of a single line, at breakage of words into syllables, and so on. Such violations are common to free verse and may suggest a particular kind of voice selection, one different from the stable voice of metric form.

Perhaps the resistance to pattern-breaking explains why some readers feel put off by an interrogatory line which Warren has made a staple of his introspective lyric. He will ask questions in the full or partial line, usually in a tone indicative of emotional intensity, one that clearly risks control of the poem's moment as the line admits uncertainty, pauses, or turns the poem's motion. Successfully handled, the line gains the power of surprise, of aggression and rebalancing, of emphasis, and often enough shifts transmission of external information to internal information.

Many more specialized line forms occur in Warren's composition of his idiosyncratic rocking back and forth that is the systolic action of the mind and the diastolic action of the body. Among them might be mentioned the fulcrum line, for pivoting; a paratactic line used to build a visual, rhythmic, or physical moment of balance; the paradox line which declares contradiction as truth-seeming; the tautological line which makes an ourabouros image, or circles; the staccato line that impedes the reader; the command line that intimidates; the ironic line emphasizing

232

the narrator's distance or expressing a strong attitude of difference from what he appears to say; the symbolic line which subordinates declaration to connotation; and the metaphor line carrying its figure of speech boldly.

Warren is a proven master of line-scoring and variety, but certainly his lines are perceived by some ears as inflexible and clumsy. Few poems, if any, achieve quality and complexity if they do not integrate every sort of line. But types of lines may dominate a poem to the extent that the poem seeks to tell a story of event and consequence, appreciate a scene, record information, or express the vital nature of an emotion. The individual and communal nature of lines establishes tone, by which we know what the writer thinks, and voice, the collective idiom through which the writer speaks.

Functions ordinarily define what a poetic line is. If lines historically **233** manifest a metric measure, in modern poetry lines may represent a metric, sonic, or visual strategy. I think it would be hard for a line to hold less than the word or part of a word that occupies a vertical unit of space on a page of composition. A line typically possesses two or more syllables because two syllables are required to make the smallest metric unit. A nonmetrical line could exist with any number of syllables.

Obviously, the function of such minimal lines would also be minimal, a matter of account where the line's act is to carry information and to choreograph the rhythmic movement. The old argument over what constitutes a lyric and what a narrative poem seems, of late, reheated by theoretical criticism which holds all tales suspect and language itself, being plastic, manipulable, and historically calloused, deceptive in referentiality. Writing requires referentiality to link reader and writer. The poetic line transmits that referential information but, as I have said, carries as well a rhythmic guide-voice especially significant to lyric poems.

With a Warren lyric the staple line is not the conventional declarative but more insistently a violated, isolated, and roughly staccato line. It will resist a symmetric syllable count, tend toward a clustered or "jammed" preponderance of stressed words, will extend a sinuous sentence over a number of lines and abruptly butt against it an equally rude short or half line, often enough interrupting with query, expostulation, or what I have heard called a wisdom statement, one that typically feels like a commentary unearned by and apart from the poem. The effect Warren seeks is that of a poetry so vital and surgent in energy it cannot be contained by conventions; it creates a boisterous colloquy. The effect of such language is power acquisition; we are meant to feel what is said can never be false, deceptive, or solipsistic. Nothing said is trivial. The will of this poetry defiantly emphasizes the cerebral and speculative action of the watching poet but so identifies it as a part of the manly action of his doing that even the static part of his nature becomes significant to the whole of living. The lines create immediacy, movement, for a form that is dominantly inactive, one that risks boring the reader without the illusion of character alteration and engagement.

**234**    But what can that mean? Warren has done nothing. The watcher is invented, a string of words only. And Aududon, evidence suggests, may well have fabricated all or part of his tale. If so, is this only much ado about nothing? I think it is more than that. *Audubon: A Vision* is an entertainment first, but an entertainment in the testing of moral response. Audubon does not actually kill the woman or her sons, any more than he sleeps with them. He does not abuse their hospitality. He does not, as Ruppersberg seems to think, betray the nature he exists with. He does not flee in fear. But the woodspeople are dead; the regulators have gone; he is left with the burden of what he has and has not done, what he has and has not seen, what he knows and does not know, what the world is. He has a view of things and a language is composed to express, indeed to embody that view. Once again we might imagine what we would have if Warren had done the poem in tidy couplets. And what if it were in elegiac quintets? Or in any form perfectly symmetrical and confidently continuous. One doesn't feel it could work any other way. But that is, perhaps, only because we have the poem as Warren made it, and this way is the brooding, male, violence-dreamed shape of the life that must have purpose or it is nightmare only. Warren has, that is, gambled, as all artists must, with a form that might create a living character.

Perhaps the most dazzling gamble in *Audubon: A Vision* is Warren's choice of an ending. Audubon dies in his bed, and time, which contains him, flows on; meaning continues and contains the beautiful birds who "cry / In a tongue multitudinous, often like music" (99). We seek to be equal to that. The ending is natural and follows the normal life story, even allowing for a certain flare of ripening gold light and drumroll of chill wind. Both the pastoral and the funeral elegy is served by Warren's celebration of the hero who goes before and redeems our best under-standing. To know him, we see, is to know ourselves, a gesture of linkage that increases our sense of purpose in a world so visibly whirlpool-like. But Warren is too much the man here on this ground to leave his gaze on the outer world, however mythically reverberant, for the immediacy might be lost. Audubon's story is a man's life, and an event of crushing consequence in that life, and a life lived in the teeth of that event and all others. Isn't it possible that any moment in any of our lives could have the same weight, hence the same grand beauty? Warren, in the closing poem, "Tell Me a Story," pleads for his own life story and for that singular life-defining moment, that fulcrum on which meaning tilts.

**235**

Unlike the broken, grinding edges and wheezy, corrosive hinges of the lines in the first six sections, lines in this final unit are self-contained, syntactically complete, barely and slowly spilling one to the next, like a soothing fountain. The shortness and the spare jab of unmodified infor-mation create a sense of the essential, the final, and the dignified. This voice, one conceives, is capable of *knowing* what it asks for—Time and distance and delight, all of which are aspects of *direction*, that which the great geese in naturalistic process already know. So we arrive at what Audubon came first to, his kinship—not a merger—with the geese in a world whose laws, knowledge or none, are inflexible and written before we have the first question to ask. But if we are like Audubon, and like the migrating geese, we are not them, are never to be them; nor are they us. Their fate is to go; our fate is to know, or try to know. And where we can-not truly know, we can and must seek the story, the shape of a life that might be lived, and in knowledge. James Olney writes, "In speaking of autobiography, one always feels that there is a great and present danger that the subject will slip away altogether, that it will vanish into thinnest air, leaving behind the perception that there is no such creature as auto-biography and that there never has been."[24] But where there is no story of self, there is no self and no other. Worse, perhaps, there is no hope, no possibility of future life. If we are to exist, Warren's *Audubon* shows us, it must be in some manner like Audubon's life, but with consciousness alert, aware of the membrane between us and the rest, but testing its ten-sile strength. In telling our life stories, whether as confession or dramatic enactment, we are like James Weldon Johnson trying to get life right. The older a writer grows, the less concerned is he to make distinctions between his life and another's and that, finally, may be the illuminating value of *Audubon*.

**236**

## Notes

1. Rob Roy Purdy, comp., *Fugitives' Reunion* (Nashville: Vanderbilt University Press, 1959), 143.

2. Robert Penn Warren, *Audubon: A Vision* (New York: Random House, 1969).

3. Helen Vendler, *Part of Nature, Part of Us* (Cambridge, Mass.: Harvard University Press, 1980), 88.

4. James Olney, *Metaphors of Self* (Princeton: Princeton University Press, 1972), 4.

5. Robert Penn Warren, *John Brown: The Making of a Martyr* (New York: Payson and Clarke, 1929).

6. Joseph Blotner, *Robert Penn Warren: A Biography* (New York: Random House, 1996).

7. Floyd C. Watkins and John T. Hiers Jr., *Robert Penn Warren Talking: Interviews, 1950–1978* (New York: Random House, 1980).

8. James H. Justus, *The Achievement of Robert Penn Warren* (Baton Rouge: Louisiana State University Press, 1981), 3.

9. Watkins and Hiers, *Robert Penn Warren Talking*, 235.

10. This well-known quotation appears in a letter from Emerson to Whitman dated July 21, 1855. The letter is reprinted in *Leaves of Grass*, ed. Jerome Loving (Oxford: Oxford University Press, 1990), 462.

11. Robert Penn Warren, *All the King's Men* (New York: Harcourt, Brace, 1946).

12. Robert Penn Warren, *Brother to Dragons* (New York: Random House, 1955); rev. 1979; rpt. (Baton Rouge: Louisiana State University Press, 1996).

13. Maria Audubon, *Audubon and His Journals*, 2 vols. (New York: Charles Scrib-ner's Sons, 1897), vol. 2.

14. Watkins and Hiers, *Robert Penn Warren Talking*, 235.

15. Lewis P. Simpson, "Robert Penn Warren and the South," *Southern Review* 26 (Winter 1990): 7–12.

16. Hugh Ruppersberg, *Robert Penn Warren and the American Imagination* (Athens: University of Georgia Press, 1990); references are noted parenthetically in the text.

17. All citations of *Audubon: A Vision* are to *Robert Penn Warren: Selected Poems, 1923–1975* (New York: Random House, 1972) and are by page number.

18. For Warren's remarks on Conrad, see "'The Great Mirage': Conrad and *Nostromo*" in Robert Penn Warren, *New and Selected Essays* (New York: Random House, 1989), 137–61.

19. Robert Penn Warren, *Selected Essays* (New York: Random House, 1951), 58.

20. Warren's extensive remarks on Whittier appear in "John Greenleaf Whittier: Poetry as Experience" in Warren's *New and Selected Essays*, 235–83.

21. *Audubon*, 230.

22. Ibid.

23. Robert Penn Warren, *Promises: Poems, 1954–1956* (New York: Random House, 1957).

24. Olney, "Autobiography and the Cultural Moment: A Thematic, Historical, and Bibliographical Introduction," in *Autobiography: Essays Theoretical and Critical*, ed. James Olney, p. 4.

**237**

# Stephen Dedalus and the New Formalism

"If 'isms' are allowed to survive at all, they should at least
be made to feel their loneliness."
—Theodor Adorno, *Aesthetic Theory*

**had** best begin by declaring my intentions because they will
occasionally be waylaid along the crooked path that I have
chosen to pursue them. I want to have a look at a few of the mission statements of the New Formalist poetic movement, which
means that some of these essays are now over a decade old. They
caused something of a stir when they were originally published,
at least among those who are stirred by matters of poetic form,
and I would like to reexamine them now because their polemic,
with the passage of time, is not nearly so polemical as it once
was—hindsight is not only accurate, it is even-tempered as well.
I am primarily interested in the critical procedures of the New
Formalists, but I will pay little attention to their opinions of specific writers; I will concentrate instead on the declarations and
various *artes poeticae* that characterize what Dick Allen, a confessed adherent, has labeled with missionary enthusiasm the
"movement's theory, practice, and outreach."[1] To clarify my
intentions even further, I will do a bit of name-dropping. For
example, W. H. Auden's adroit recognition of poetry's inability to make things happen—the year was 1939—was partner to
his underlying assumption that criticism, responsibly practiced,
could in fact make several things happen, and so I am concerned
with the nearly oafish notion of critical integrity, a concern that

as Auden knew ultimately involved the rigors of introspection: "All the judgments," he wrote, "aesthetic or moral, that we pass, however objective we try to make them, are in part a rationalization and in part a corrective discipline of our subjective wishes."[2] I hope, in short, to uncover a few of the subjective wishes that seem to me typical of much New Formalist speculation.

The New Formalists—I use the title indiscriminately, as do their advocates and critics—depend both on their poetry and their criticism to enshrine their literary values, and in this respect their program accords with most self-proclaimed literary movements. Not all of the poets aligned with the group write criticism, but then those poets who do are sometimes said not to write poetry very well. And some of the poets who are associated with the group—often those the group would most want to enlist—express little interest in enlistment. An ability to write poetry, an ability to write criticism, and an ability to organize a program dedicated to the promulgation of certain kinds of poetry and certain kinds of criticism—these are talents seldom found thriving in a single writer, but the ambitious author remains happily unaware of the rarity of such a sidereal conjunction. Yet I will not press the matter of consistency—literary history teaches that no one should expect poets to practice uniformly in their poetry what they preach vehemently in their prose. The literary theory or criticism of any era rarely reflects the diverse strengths of the poetry that distinguishes it.

**239**

I am concerned with what I might call for lack of a better phrase the New Formalist literary history, and I am most specifically concerned with the quietist nostalgia for past literary accomplishment that often accompanied their proliferating diagnoses of our own poetry's current ills. But I am not using the term "nostalgia" as Ira Sadoff, for example, used it in his "Neo-Formalism: A Dangerous Nostalgia," and I ought to be clear about our differences. Sadoff has apparently discovered that the New Formalists have a "social as well as a linguistic agenda" and that "when they link pseudo-populism (the 'general reader') to regular meter, they disguise their nostalgia for moral and linguistic certainty, for a universal ('everyone agrees') and univocal way of conserving culture."[3] But there is no more harm, it seems to me, in proposing a "univocal" or conservative model of culture through poetry or criticism than there is in assuming that a liberal eclecticism remains unblemished by its own notion of "moral and linguistic certainty." Both approaches to reading poetry and writing about it avoid what Auden saw as one of the essential, corrective functions of criticism—its capacity to temper our most subjective wishes.

Sadoff's objections to the New Formalist program, while indicting one form of nostalgia, heartily embrace another: "American poets, partially because they have become more and more marginalized, have forgotten the scope of the project of poetry, have perhaps lost faith in recovering access to those ambitions" (9). Those who have recently taken a census know that the margins are teeming with writers—even Shakespeare is there, according to some—and most of our poets, the New Formalists included, will ultimately be received by the elite, huddled masses gathered in the margins. Sadoff worries about the diminished presence of poetry in American culture, and his diagnosis reveals the numbingly familiar symptoms: "the desperate loneliness of the American poet" (10); "a culture that considers art a commodity" (10); "the executives at Gulf and Western" (10); "[James] Merrill's privileged personal history" (9) and of course—what indictment of poetry is credible nowadays without her?—"Helen Vendler" (7). Ironically, though, Sadoff's nostalgia is essentially the New Formalist nostalgia because they both cast winsome glances over their shoulders to a time, unlike our present era of deprivation, when poets were valued by their cultures.

There are other similarities. Both Sadoff and Bruce Bawer, another adherent, have spotted Vendler in the enemy's trenches. Bawer's hesitations about Vendler's work originally appeared in the *Hudson Review*, and like Sadoff, Bawer is indignant, probably even saddened, that "the audience for poetry has dwindled down to a precious few."[4] But three pages later, Bawer's scant readership recovers its numbers quickly when Vendler appears as "poetry critic to the multitudes" (615). The nostalgia that engenders these central confusions about the poet's place in American culture reflects an admirable concern for the state of contemporary poetry; Bawer and Sadoff are both neatly trimmed in the forms and visages of duty, but their services are offered to the same lordly nostalgia.

I must confess, at least in this essay, to care nothing at all about the health of contemporary poetry, and this alone will go a long way toward distinguishing my interest in nostalgia from Sadoff's interest. I am far more concerned with the health of our literary past, especially as it is viewed through the nostalgic spectacles that I have found seated squarely on several New Formalist noses. If anything I have to say about reading literature from the past pertains to the creation of it in the present, then my purpose has been doubly served, but again, unlike Bawer or Sadoff, The Care and Maintenance of Contemporary Verse is not the manual I have come to compose. I want next to look at a few passages from an essay titled "Metrical Illiteracy," by Brad Leithauser, a lucid poet, critic, and novelist, who became for a while, perhaps against his will, one of the **241** New Formalist's most prominent members. I have chosen this piece not because it expresses ideas that are uniquely Leithauser's but because it deploys so effectively a rhetoric of nostalgia to explain the mediocrities that have mobilized much New Formalist critical procedure. This rhetoric, as I will indicate, masks a concept of literary history that is largely insupportable. "Hesitantly then," Leithauser writes, "I would suggest that a second generalization might safely be tendered: there is a widespread perception that we are not living in a golden age of poetry, and that mediocrity prevails in the periodicals and on the bookstore shelves."[5] Most readers of contemporary poetry and criticism have become familiar with this charge, and Leithauser's observation, whether one agrees with it or not, is accurate. We *do* hear a lot about mediocrity. The proposed origin of this mediocrity, as the title of the essay indicates, is found in the current and widespread illiteracy among our young poets concerning traditional poetic form. English poetry, it is implied, has not always been so possessed by such mediocrity: "There was a time," Leithauser continues later in the essay, "when poets might naturally, as a part of their culture, be steeped in verse, a time when anonymous ballads could flourish and perhaps even help a society find and define itself" (43). *There was a time when*—I want to examine this winsome claim because it has traditionally surfaced whenever a culture's literary accomplishments have been disparaged.

To do so, I will make good on my promise to pursue a crooked path. I am most comfortable discussing issues of this sort when confined to a text, and for my confinement I have chosen James Joyce's *A Portrait of the Artist as a Young Man*. When worrying about literary history's relation to contemporary writing, I have always found it sensible to listen to what Joyce has to say because he made a career of worrying about it, and he worries a good deal more eloquently than I do. In this case I find it even more sensible to listen with special care to a work of fiction that delivers its aesthetic theory robed in characterization, not only fleshing out the theory but also couching the implicit question of artistic form within the originating framework of a young artist's development. In the face of the New Formalist's concern for our own young poets, nothing would seem more to the point.

Stephen Dedalus, to use Auden's terminology, often seems no more than a bundle of "subjective wishes" continually corrected by his growing knowledge of aesthetics and poetic form. These corrections gradually give Stephen his earliest inklings of what constitutes the coherent literary sensibility, while they force him to recognize that the various authors he had plundered to gain this sensibility share an overriding concern: they have all argued plangently for their own individuation, so much so that they would see their works as successful only to the degree that they have resisted assimilation into Stephen's or into any other organizing tradition. This resistance to assimilation is fundamental to Joyce's notion of literary history and aesthetics, and it pervades much twentieth-century writing on culture and politics. The New Formalist notion of literary history, as I will show later, has quietly removed this resistive strain from the literature and, in doing so, has been able to coax a familiar and domesticated complicity from any author it pleases, while simultaneously lobotomizing the long and diversified tradition of English letters.

Joyce is very clear about the wrongheadedness of reading this way, and one of the early and definitive aesthetic experiences that Stephen undergoes speaks directly to this problem. In the latter half of the second chapter of *A Portrait of the Artist as a Young Man,* Stephen takes a walk after the annual Whitsuntide play at Belvedere College. This was not the first time that a crisis in Stephen's life had given birth to a grim constitutional, nor would it be the last, and in its narrative significance, this short jaunt down Marlborough Street pales in comparison to the impassioned foray that landed him in the middle of the red-light district. But Stephen always walks with purpose, and Joyce always drops his purposeful clues. The Whitsuntide play had revealed to the young man one of the fundamental lessons of artistic creation—"It surprised him," Joyce says of his young hero, "to see that the play which he had known at rehearsals for a disjointed lifeless thing had suddenly assumed a life of its own."[6] Aesthetics 101, perhaps, but Stephen is still, remember, an apprentice.

Invigoration, as Victor Frankenstein learned, encourages independence, and Mary Shelley's representation of the imaginative dialectic that adheres between creator and creature has survived fully intact in the twentieth century—the most intimate energies of the individual artist will ultimately be sacrificed to the larger, formal integrity of the resulting creation. Language, Joyce implies, whether plied in conversation or drama or poetry or fiction, is inherently a formal medium. To say, then, from the theorist's perspective, that it is impossible to write a formless poem is pedantry; but to say it from the writer's perspective is to recognize not only that every poem, upon completion, exhibits a formal integrity—this is why mediocre poems are so bothersome, so dogged— but also to discover that many kinds of formal integrity are available to the resourceful artist. Joyce places this experience early in Stephen's life because its lesson, a simple one, is for the artist an essential one.

Upon first confronting it, young writers are likely to find this integrity unreasonable, ominous, and frightening because it would seem to require what T. S. Eliot famously referred to in "Tradition and the Individual Talent" as the continual dissolution of personality. And young writers, who often have little but their personality, will be loath to see it go. When Stephen realized, with fear and loathing, that the play had "assumed a life of its own," he acknowledged the play's formal existence, its essential independence from the actors and the playwright. This represents an essential step in Stephen's maturation as an artist because it

243

forces him to confront the inalienable autonomy of the play's aesthetic order; from here, it is only a short step—a step, as we shall see, that occurs in *Ulysses*—to viewing the literary tradition in terms, not of its easy availability but of its inherent resistance, its definitive strangeness when confronted with readers indiscriminately appropriating the literature for their own schemes and interpretations. Epiphany, vision, inspiration—all of these terms have been evoked as their inadequacy to describe the experience has been confessed, but the knowledge gained from the sudden discovery of art's essential *otherness* humbles and renovates, and it has been an important subject matter in the epiphanic tradition at least since the eighteenth century. Stephen's dominant notion of complexity in literature depends to a large degree on his ability to recognize this particular independent formality of the work at hand; his fevered dash down Marlborough Street marks him, in the literal sense of the phrase, as a young or, perhaps, a new formalist.

Discussions about poetic form often pertain solely to prosody, and the New Formalists understandably have worried about the obliteration of the metrical line by the "self-absorbed, often narcissistic poems characteristic since the 1960's."[7] Those who share their worries agree with their treatises, and those who do not share them find their arguments unconvincing. Because it would clumsily apply a quantitative measurement (the classical scheme) to a language that is loudly accentual in its phonic system, metrical analysis in English is a haphazard business at best, and the results of any prolonged scansion will rarely change a reader's mind about a poem's overall worth. But the Whitsuntide passage from *A Portrait* is valuable because it makes a larger point: as soon as a work of art assumes "a life of its own," to use Joyce's words, its existence—its life— is identified through its assumed form, and the terms of the prosodist's trade describe the most prominent aspects of that form. But even the most inspired scansion fails to elucidate the central mystery of aesthetic form—its ability to sustain, as Joyce puts it, this "life of its own," and this failure has traditionally fostered a misrepresentation of the quickening and restless spirit of English poetics. For the most part, this insight is of little use to much contemporary critical theory because it doggedly reestablishes boundary lines between so-called critical and creative work.

But this same insight just as doggedly appears in the "creative" work of those authors who identify poetic form with the kind of thorny diversity necessary for authentic development in technique.

Historically, when critics have undertaken the task of comparing the literary accomplishments of their own to those of the past, the ancestors have often taken the laurels. Part of the reason for this concerns our persistent blindness when surveying the field of contemporary poetry—the purest innovations are often hidden from the most perceptive eye by their own purity. Pope, to cite an ancestor who has won some of these laurels and would seem unreceptive to Joyce's formal adventurism, was well aware of the *je ne sais quoi* of form when he spoke early on in *An Essay on Criticism* of the *"nameless Graces* which no Methods teach." Poetic form, when examined at this lofty level, is allowed to acknowledge its volatility and paradoxically to encourage the skepticism that the **245** strongest innovators of our literary tradition have embedded in their own sense of form. When Wordsworth, to take another example, announced at the end of the first book of *The Prelude* that he intended to tell "the story of [his] life," and then proceeded to do so over the next forty years, amassing over seven thousand lines of blank verse, part of the human dimension of his account lies in the deep uncertainty that often informs his speculations about the nature of his project, particularly as it might suffer by comparison to a tradition of poetry that he sincerely, it seems to me, labels "of ampler and more varied argument."

This has important implications for the New Formalists or anyone who would initiate a historical comparison of various literatures. Critics who recognize the mediocre work of contemporary literature are often seduced into dredging up a well-known paragon of virtue from the past and setting it against the current mediocrity, as if the one might somehow transform the other. Inasmuch as these recommendations of excellence are historically supported, however, they often do not reflect the various and essential skepticisms that are central to an underlying concept of form because to acknowledge these skepticisms would indicate that their chosen models of accomplishment were as uncertain about their achievements as we are about our own. The assessing voice, then, loses its credibility.

Leithauser correctly realizes that mediocrity has not been the special gift to letters of the late twentieth century: "Mediocre poems have always preponderated in the periodicals and on the bookstore shelves, and always will" (41). Its current preponderance, as we saw earlier, is owing to our poets' metrical illiteracy, and as an example of how the formal tradition in English poetry provides ample accommodation for the "fertile ferment of quiet revolution," Leithauser discusses the checkered history of the sonnet (42). The form, we are instructed, displayed an "overtaking brilliance" under Shakespeare, Donne, Milton, and Herbert, disappeared and was "born again" with Wordsworth, and after many changes, found itself in the hands of Cummings and Pound "successfully sporting *thee's* and *hath's* and other locutions that Wordsworth himself on a good day probably would have eschewed as old-fashioned" (42).

**246**     But what is the value of recognizing mediocrity in contemporary letters if its antidote lies in critical pronouncements informing us that Shakespeare, Donne, Milton, and Wordsworth were accomplished sonneteers? Leithauser emphasizes that "the search for new methods and the impatience with tired ones . . . have generated much of the brilliance and excitement of English literature," and when speaking of the substantial changes, the various repudiations that distinguish the history of the sonnet, he reminds us that "this process of repudiation . . . is all taking place within the larger domain of English formal poetry" (42). But the phrase "English formal poetry," when used in this context, domesticates the often radical language of individuality, the strenuous resistance to assimilation, that informs the poetry collected under the phrase. Romantic models of the imagination insisted on the innate recalcitrance of poetic genius—Wordsworth's "solitude," for example—and this version still determines much of our thinking about the poetic enterprise. Whether we recognize a distinctive modernist program or not, we can acknowledge, at least, the survival over the past two centuries of a sensibility suspicious of historical assessments that would assemble several centuries of poetry as seamless evidence for *any* prosecution.

The intentions of the New Formalist criticism often seem more blatantly self-serving than even the most interested criticism practiced by the most interested poets. The unspoken, subjective wish—to recall

Auden—that informs Leithauser's argument would run something like this: "And remember, it is within this domain, among these giants of 'English formal poetry,' that I hang my hat." But to speak of "English formal poetry" in Leithauser's sense is to speak of practically everything written before 1900 and a good deal of it written afterward; the phrase represents a savvy but indiscriminate means of enlisting an entire literature in service of the program, and such a broad conscription is unconvincing. Again, how useful, when attempting to cure the ills of our poetry, is a phrase that would insist on corraling the extensive differences between Herbert and Cummings, for example, within the unworkably vague boundaries of "formal poetry"? It is a matter of emphasis and, finally, a matter of critical acuity. Both poets have written poems that end at the fourteenth line, manipulate generic conventions, and make use of a similar metrical scheme, loosely scanned; but at the far extremes represented by Herbert and Cummings, their cultural differences alone, their overriding schemes of language, their unique, often antithetical historical situations, are far more numerous than their similarities. When viewed in this light, literary history becomes less available as an all-purpose panacea for mediocrity and reveals to the contemporary poet the vigorous individuality that might encourage the formal excellence that Leithauser justifiably praises.

Joyce was skeptical, even fearful, of this broadly appropriating vision of the literary tradition, and Stephen confronts it later in the novel, providing an example of how this struggle against such monolithic appropriation represents an essential component in the formation of the young artist. In the last chapter of the novel, Stephen is walking again, and this time, having had three cups of tea, he is prepared for animated conversation. Later in the afternoon, he meets Lynch, his friendly foil, and their talk turns to the philosophical subjects that lately have engaged Stephen. As they approach Merrion Square, Stephen continues his disquisition on "universal beauty," and the writings of Aquinas provide him with his *classicus locus* for an applied aesthetics. Wholeness, harmony, and radiance: these are the Aquinian qualities evident in the beautiful, and it is the translation of the third member of the triad—Stephen read Aquinas in

Latin—that has most troubled him. His attempts to articulate his understanding of the term "radiance" seem continually to deploy the narrow,
particularized jargon of "literary talk," and he will accept only those versions that would broaden the term's field of reference. When he finally
arrives at an assessment of the word, his method depends on analogy, an
inherently selective scheme and one that signals the founding of the distinctive Dedalan literary sensibility:

> The radiance of which he [Aquinas] speaks is the scholastic
> *quidditas,* the *whatness* of a thing. This supreme quality is felt
> by the artist when the esthetic image is first conceived in his
> imagination. The mind in that mysterious instant Shelley
> likened beautifully to a fading coal.[8]

**248**

From the *Summa Theologica* to "A Defence of Poetry"—a sizable leap but
one that reveals in Stephen the earliest flutterings of the critical curiosity, the first acquisition of a particularized historical sense that revels in
its ability to select and reject, paying the necessary homage to the clashing particularity that writers, if they are to find room for their own pro-
ductions, must hear in voices from the past.

As we have seen, to speak of the woe that is in contemporary writing
is often to envision a past of confident and assured accomplishment, but
the evidence indicates that literary wrist-slapping has become a staple of
English literary history. Sidney (*Astrophel and Stella,* I, II), Jonson ("Ode
to Himself"), Pope (*Essay on Criticism*), Johnson (the *Rambler* essays on
pastoral poetry), Wordsworth ("Preface" to *Lyrical Ballads*), Arnold
("The Function of Criticism at the Present Time"), and Pound (*A B C of
Reading*) all at one time or another inveighed against the mediocrity of
their age, but like Stephen, their vision of literary history was discriminating, even separatist. Eliot's review of Grierson's anthology of the
Metaphysical poets assaulted the "quaint and pleasant taste" that had
previously greeted these poets, and his essay represents in one sense a
deep dissatisfaction with his generation's assessment of seventeenth-
century poetry. When Eliot begins in the same essay to speculate on the
creative process in general, he bases his ideas not on an indiscriminate re-

spect for his literary past but again, much like Stephen, on the recognition of the irreconcilable discordances that distinguished the seventeenth century no less than our own.

In 1920, a few years after Joyce had published Stephen's story, Eliot claimed in "Tradition and the Individual Talent" that poets who hoped to continue beyond their twenty-fifth year must acquire the historical sense, and although this essay appeared a year before the essay on the Metaphysical poets, the latter provides the example, methodologically at least, of how such a historical sense is acquired. Eliot's hesitations about Milton's accomplishment, in fact, particularly his enlightened and perverse comparison of *Paradise Lost* to Joyce's *Work in Progress*, as *Finnegan's Wake* was then called, are similar in their inspired impishness to Stephen's own confrontational tastes—when pressed by Heron to name the greatest poet, Stephen ceremoniously dissented from Tennyson, the respectable choice, and nominated Byron, the immoral Presbyterian. **249** Stephen suffered for his heresy as Nash and Boland gave him a thumping, punctuated by the command to admit that Byron was "no good." Stephen resisted the inquisition until he was able to escape "half blinded with tears, clenching his fists madly and sobbing."[9] Whether deprecating with Eliot or sobbing with Stephen, the writer who would look to the past in hopes of acquiring the historical sense must be able to recognize there the same amount of discord, cacophony, and disagreement that is regularly said to characterize contemporary writing, and it is just this sort of evaluative temperament—finicky, insistent—that structures the most influential historical criticism written by poets. "The past," as Eliot wrote in "Tradition and the Individual Talent," "should be altered by the present as much as the present is directed by the past."

Criticism, when written in this vein, implicitly recognizes the protean aspect of taste while it makes a virtue of discrimination—the lineage that Stephen draws between Aquinas and Shelley represents one of his earliest discriminations, and having already recognized the essential formal integrity of the Whitsuntide play, he has begun to realize that in the long procession of literary history aesthetic integrity takes many forms, often of irreconcilable differences. These irreconcilable differences, which

might serve as the foundation for forging new styles or finding new re-
suscitating lines of development, are obscured by the normative phrase
"English formal tradition." The multiplicity of these aesthetic forms will
generate a multiplicity of advocates, particularly when advocacy is the
game at hand, and I want to pursue several of the implications that arise
from this notion of multiplicity since it too pertains to the critical
methodology deployed now and again by the New Formalists.

Taste, which is nowadays seen to be very old-fashioned, has historically provided both critics and artists one of several criteria with which
to judge literary accomplishment, and as the various schools of criticism
or poetry advocate their programs, conceptions of taste, mostly unde-
fined, lead them to assert the superiority of one work over another. Even
those methodologies—Marxism, for example—that claim to avoid the
agenda-heavy linearity that structures the old canon insist on the privi-
lege of their own perspective. Embedded in the Marxist position, as in
any other angle of observation, is the imperial idea of rectitude, the conviction that the information uncovered by the one method is somehow
more significant and valuable than the information made available by the
other method. New Formalism, because it is not nearly so well defined as
Marxism, bears its agenda, however constituted, quietly and often without examination, and such unexamined confidence often leads to pre-
sumptuously authoritarian criticism.

250

But any form of literary scrutiny arises from a set of special interests,
and a disagreement about the ultimate worth of a specific work of literature is often nothing more than a disagreement about the propriety of
those special interests. Although fashion and consensus inevitably exact
their toll from the renegade—until it became fashionable to be the renegade—those critics who most vehemently attack another's particular
perspective reveal, whether they will or not, the perspectivist quality of all
forms of critical discourse, including their own. I veer toward the position of the extreme relativist, always open to the logical embarrassment
that hounds them: "All values are relative," argue such critics, "except," re-
join their opponents, "your statement that all values are relative." To the degree that the argument addresses both the literary work itself and the system of values by which the work is being appraised, the criticism honestly

recognizes the volatility of its origins, and it is this kind of criticism, self-effacing but self-aware, that changes or, at least, sharpens our opinions.

Toleration, even when it is polemically motivated, is the sine qua non of convincing criticism because belief, over and above the invigorating truths of scholarship, accounts for the fundamental motivation of the critic. No proof exists that will demonstrate the exclusive validity of the Marxist approach to literature, but the Marxist critic, or the New Critic, or the deconstructionist, certainly *believes* in the effectiveness of the chosen method. And belief, for it to remain a belief, avoiding the brittle constrictions of dogma, must cultivate toleration. Poetry, on the other hand, particularly poetry of the highest accomplishment, often seems a grand system of elaborately enunciated intolerances, and the most effective assessments of the past will recognize this. The influences that shape a poet's work, especially when they involve the works of other poets, reveal themselves to the reader in the spirit of antagonism or sympathy, but once they are present in either manifestation, they argue vociferously against the admission of other diverting voices. If the word "tradition," as used in the phrase "English formal tradition," is meant to indicate a formal continuity, then the word applies most aptly to the mediocre verse that makes up the lion's share of an era's literary output because it is there that we find *real,* though numbing, regularity. What is traditional, however, about a sonnet by Cummings or Herbert is its willingness to alter the most fundamental sensibilities that have informed the tradition, and this irrepressible adventurousness ought to be emphasized over and above its obvious allegiance to "English formal poetry." A poet's work achieves a singular, individual articulation when it implicitly declares, "This voice and no other." The work must first exist in its uniqueness, and initially this uniqueness will seem divisive or, at least, confrontational. From Aquinas to Shelley (and not to Wordsworth or to Coleridge—this is Stephen's point): Stephen is forging exclusive connections from the past—he is making his literary history—and those connections will unabashedly bear the imprint of his critical intelligence.

If one goal of the New Formalists is to resuscitate contemporary poetry by reestablishing various traditions of poetic form—the "traditions of meter and rhyme," as Allen tagged them[10]—then the adherents of the movement must also recognize that many of these metered and rhymed works of literature, the very ones that they might enlist during their indictment, reveal a native discomfort with making traditions. Eliot was clearly aware of this endemic restlessness, and his best criticism reflects this awareness; the last paragraph of his essay on the Metaphysicals, for example, is rife with an understanding of how multifaceted, even contradictory, is the "main current of English poetry," and how often the strength of a single personality, in this case that of Dr. Johnson, "a dangerous person to disagree with," forms the canons of taste. Clearly, Eliot focuses on the particularities of each writer, on those traits that render each one utterly unlike the other one:

> It would be a fruitful work, and one requiring a substantial book, to break up the classification of Johnson (for there has been none since) and exhibit these poets in all their difference of kind and degree, from the massive music of Donne to the faint pleasing tinkle of Aurelian Townshend.[11]

An authentic and revisionary literary identity is often accompanied by a kind of timorousness, an uncertainty on behalf of the author at his having attempted such a bold revision. One source of complexity in the most ambitious literature originates in the self-conscious diffidence heard when an author attempts to modify, ever so slightly, the conventions of a genre—Milton's revisions, for example, of the pastoral elegy in "Lycidas"—and those critics and writers who would appropriate any strain of English and American verse must hear this note of diffidence and realize that authors from the seventeenth century were often as unsure of their own accomplishment as we are of ours. And this uncertainty, this radical disagreement concerning the nature of poetic accomplishment, ought to be reflected by our own avoidance of these broadly appropriating interpretations of literary history. Their work was not originally conceived to serve the stuffy didacticism of the late twentieth century, and to press it into such service is to mangle it beyond recognition.

The best examples of a discriminating critical practice often occur in essays written by poets examining the work of another poet, particularly that of a poet from an historical era: Johnson, Coleridge, Pope, and Hecht on Shakespeare; Arnold and Yeats on Shelley; Heaney on Wordsworth; Pinsky on Freneau; and Auden on Byron. These are but a few. Yet here principles of exclusion and discrimination, rather than undifferentiated approbation, allow the reader to observe the ongoing formation of a highly individualized poetic tradition—the poet's reading list—and this critical reading, for many poets, is one of the important activities of the poetic imagination. Eliot, among others, warned against the criticism practiced by a poet because the poet's critical activities are often rallying cries for the poet's own work. But I would have it no other way; the fashioning of a literary identity depends on just this sort of interested selection and exclusion—just this sort of engaged reading. Had Stephen become the writer he had envisioned, Shelley and Aquinas would likely have been among the members of his own selected canon. And although Stephen issues no literary manifestos, he is probably dissatisfied, as are all writers, with a good deal of the literature that is currently being produced. But for Stephen, the past does not exist, to use Eliot's phrase from "Tradition and the Individual Talent," as a "lump" or "indiscriminate bolus" of accomplishment. A radically varied congregation of voices, the past exhibits precisely those qualities required of those who would attempt to understand it: discrimination, bias, and judgment. In his essay "Exceptions and Rules," Howard Nemerov ponders the poet's reading of the proverb "The exception proves the rule," and his assessment accurately characterizes the poet's sanguinely divisive approach to literary history. For the poet, Nemerov writes, "the exception turns out to be, or proves to be, the rule."[12]

**253**

No major literary epoch, as I indicated earlier, has deprived itself of the titillating notion that the accomplishments of the present generation are undistinguished and that the current generation—excepting, of course, the prosecutors—are ill-equipped, beset as they are by the deprivations of contemporary life, to receive the lessons offered by the ennobled works that crowd the past. "It is certain," Jonson wrote nearly four centuries ago in the dedicatory "Epistle" to *Volpone*, "that too much license of Poetasters, in this time, hath much deformed their mistress."[13] The passage of time has done little to allay the fears of our literary survivalists. That so much of the critical prose appearing under the aegis of the New Formalism is bothered by the current state of contemporary poetry ought to indicate that a reformation is imminent. Reformations proceed at varying paces, but their necessity is most often justified in the context of an impending cataclysmic loss: Allen, in the aforementioned issue of *Crosscurrents,* confesses to an "anxiety for poetry's survival as a vital art."[14] I can envy no one who fancies himself living on the cusp of poetry's moribundity, but neither can I envy the fancy that placed him there.

Yet if poetry is to survive as a vital art, then poets presumably must begin to write vital poems, and much New Formalist doctrine has been designed to explain both how that might be done and where examples of such poetry might currently be found. The movement has not yet written its equivalent to Wordsworth's "Preface," but this is probably because Wordsworth and Coleridge did not think of themselves as Romantic poets, while the New Formalists do think of themselves as the New Formalists—critical statements issued by committees must submit to the generalities that will house the differing perspectives of its members, while those issued by one overbearing man enjoy the benefit of sharp, and in Wordsworth's case, intelligent eccentricity. But another, more central problem confronts all literary movements or "isms," as Theodor Adorno labeled them, and it concerns the peculiar logic that is often used to justify the need for such movements.

Because the writers who would participate in this revisionary movement indicate that American poetry is currently besieged by mediocrity, they often envision themselves as united against it. Nothing is immune to mediocrity, and no one, where poetry is concerned, values it. Definitions that emphasize unity, however, depend on a methodology designed to discover the common literary values that will both organize the group and respond to the ills currently seen to afflict the culture. This works well enough for testing allegiances and compiling membership lists. But typically this same practice has structured many of the discussions concerning American and English literary history—with their defining incompatibilities muzzled, a broad and specious array of writers from various centuries inexplicably appears as evidence for the prosecution.

But unanimity is no more characteristic of the past than it is of the present, and this is one of the final lessons that Joyce's young artist takes to heart. When we last see Stephen in episode 17 of *Ulysses,* he is sitting with Leopold Bloom in Bloom's kitchen. As they begin their discussion of the Egyptian hieroglyphs and the Greek and Roman alphabets, the narrator asks two questions—Joyce has adopted a catechetical structure for the episode—that succinctly portray the final development of Stephen's critical intelligence, a critical intelligence based on his fresh understanding of the past:

> What was Stephen's auditive sensation?
> He heard in a profound ancient male unfamiliar melody the accumulation of the past.
> What was Bloom's visual sensation?
> He saw in a quick young male familiar form the predestination of a future.[15]

**255**

The "sensations" of the two characters are briefly joined to represent a comprehensive historical scheme in which hope for the future depends on recognizing the "unfamiliar melody" of the past, the melody that, because of its strangeness, initially resists critical categorization.

A half-century later, Adorno was making similar claims in his *Aesthetic Theory,* and because his own philosophical observations are so strikingly similar to Joyce's fictive account, Adorno's thoughts on the subject almost seem a commentary on Stephen's and Leopold's conversation:

> When something becomes too familiar it stops making sense. What is immediately accessible is bound to be lifeless as well . . . . If one perceives art as anything other than strange, one does not perceive it at all.[16]

Various political imperatives conditioned Adorno's theories, of course, and an explanation of them would necessarily confront the long-standing tradition that places the sovereign, creating self in opposition to the assimilative forces that define the workings of a dominant culture. Here, it is enough to understand that Stephen realizes that any broad appropriation—in essence, a familiarization—of the varied gallery of voices that constitute Irish history risks losing the essential integrity of those voices. The past, to invoke Eliot once more, is not a "lump, an indiscriminate bolus"; it is crowded with dissenting, individual talents that often, as they rail against misinterpretation by their contemporaries, give voice to an abiding resentment at being resigned by a later generation to an accomplished "time when." There is no reason to assume that Cummings or Herbert would be flattered by an assessment of their abilities that landed them in the same category. And to recruit either of them as proto–New Formalists is simply perverse.

Both Leithauser and Allen are genuinely concerned about the current

**256**  state of contemporary poetry. But Leithauser, in the same essay, fears as much for the survival of our literary past as he does for what Allen termed the "vital art" of poetry. In "Metrical Illiteracy," Leithauser writes:

> Ours is a clangorous and increasingly violent age, and the art of poetry, in all its subtleties and near-fatal unsexiness, is easily lost in the din and jostle. It will take years for any young poet who has spent his share of time at the movies, where knifings and garrotings and eviscerations are served up with such ferociously unblinking exactitude, or at rock concerts where the very walls are set to shuddering, to appreciate the delicate but prodigious violence packed into a sonnet like Milton's "On the Late Massacre in Piedmont." (44)

What seems characteristic here of much New Formalist criticism is the argumentative tone, the note of wearied and musty authority that resonates from a gambit like "Ours is a clangorous and increasingly violent age." "So what," I wish Dickens were here to say, "ours was the marsh country," which he did say. Wordsworth too worried in his "Preface" about the "multitude of causes, unknown to former times . . . acting with a combined force to blunt the discriminating powers of the mind," and he even worried, like Leithauser, about the "invaluable works of our elder writers," which at the time were "being driven into neglect by frantic novels and stupid German tragedies and deluges of idle and extravagant stories in verse."[17] America no more invented the horrific sensationalism of the Texas chainsaw murders than England did those "clowns, conjurors, posture-masters, [and] harlequins" that Wordsworth saw at Sadler's Wells and recorded in the seventh book of *The Prelude*.[18] The New Formalist exasperation with contemporary letters loses a good deal of credibility when its donnish discriminations issue from such an indiscriminate reading of literary history.

Critics who praise a great deal of contemporary poetry, Randall Jarrell once argued, are bad critics; and poets, it could be further argued, who are blithely happy about the current state of letters are bad poets. Public dissatisfaction often blazes the straightest trail to recognition, and nostalgia for the past, as long as it encourages an accompanying recognition of the past's essential strangeness and unfamiliarity, offers the most effective sedative such dissatisfactions have engendered. But I am in danger here of not recognizing the real owner of my thought. In his own "Preface" to Shakespeare's plays Dr. Johnson wrote:

> Some seem to admire indiscriminately whatever has been long preserved, without considering that time has sometimes co-operated with chance; all perhaps are more willing to honor past than present excellence. . . . The great contention of criticism is to find the faults of the moderns, and the beauties of the ancients. While an author is yet living we estimate his powers by his worst performance, and when he is dead we rate them best.[19]

In this profession, there is a lot to be said for dying. Our clangorous age, in a century or so, will be the object of a wistful poet's daydreams, and it would not be an altogether bad thing to locate now the Golden Age that future generations will foist on us. Perhaps some of the New Formalists will reside there, but it is their poetry and not their criticism that will grant them their citizenship. Various writers—often in groups—will always be concerned to administer antidotes to the ailing literature of their time, and no one should begrudge them the opportunity to do so. In lieu of a Golden Age, however, a consensus of opinion on two matters will have to do: first, Ben Jonson listened to unamplified music and still, in "Ode to Himself," declared his intentions to "leave the loathed stage, / And the more loathsome age"; second, Joyce thought it important that Stephen recognize in Bloom an "unfamiliar" past, one that resists appropriation and assumption, because the exception, as Nemerov reminds the poet, turns out to be the rule.

**258**

## Notes

1. Dick Allen, "Transcending the Self," *Crosscurrents* 8 (January 1989): 6n.

2. W. H. Auden, *The Dyer's Hand* (New York: Vintage Books, 1968), 6.

3. Ira Sadoff, "Neo-Formalism: A Dangerous Nostalgia," *American Poetry Review* 19 (January, 1990): 7. Subsequent references are noted parenthetically in the text.

4. Bruce Bawer, "Helen Vendler, Poetry Critic," *Hudson Review* 41 (Winter 1989): 613. Subsequent references are noted parenthetically in the text.

5. Brad Leithauser, "Metrical Illiteracy," *New Criterion* 1 (January, 1983): 41. Subsequent references are noted parenthetically in the text.

6. James Joyce, *A Portrait of the Artist as a Young Man* (New York: Penguin, Centennial Edition, 1986), 85.

7. Allen, "Transcending the Self," 5.

8. Joyce, *A Portrait*, 213.

9. Ibid., 80–82.

10. Allen, "Transcending the Self," 5.

11. T. S. Eliot, *Selected Essays of T. S. Eliot* (New York: Harcourt, Brace & World, 1950), 250.

12. Howard Nemerov, *Figures of Thought* (Boston: David R. Godine, 1978), 42.

13. Ben Jonson, *Volpone,* ed. R. B. Parker (Manchester: Manchester University Press, 1983), 70.

14. Allen, "Transcending the Self," 6.

15. James Joyce, *Ulysses,* ed. Hans Gabler (New York: Vintage Books, 1986), 565.

16. Theodor Adorno, *Aesthetic Theory* (London: Routledge & Kegan Paul, 1986), 262–63.

17. William Wordsworth, *Selected Poems and Prefaces,* ed. Jack Stillinger (Boston: Houghton Mifflin, 1965), 449.

18. Ibid., 278.

19. Samuel Johnson, *Johnson on Shakespeare,* ed. Walter Raleigh (Oxford: Oxford University Press, 1965), 9.

# A Bibliography of the Writings
# of Ray Lewis White

## Books

1.  *The Achievement of Sherwood Anderson: Essays in Criticism.* Chapel Hill: University of North Carolina Press, 1966; Chapel Hill: Chapel Hill Books, [1966].

2.  *Sherwood Anderson, Return to Winesburg: Selections from Four Years of Writing for a Country Newspaper.* Chapel Hill: University of North Carolina Press, 1967.

3.  *Gore Vidal.* New York: Twayne Publishers, 1968; New Haven: College and University Press, [1968]. Partially reprinted in *Gore Vidal: Writer Against the Grain.* Edited by Jay Parini. New York: Columbia University Press, 1992, 120–36.

4.  *Sherwood Anderson's "A Story Teller's Story": A Critical Text.* Cleveland: Press of Case Western Reserve University, 1968.

5.  *Sherwood Anderson's Memoirs: A Critical Edition.* Chapel Hill: University of North Carolina Press, 1969.

6.  *Checklist of Sherwood Anderson.* Columbus: Charles E. Merrill, 1969.

7.  *Sherwood Anderson's "Tar: A Midwest Childhood"—A Critical Text.* Cleveland: Press of Case Western Reserve University, 1969.

8.  *Studies in "Winesburg, Ohio."* Columbus: Charles E. Merrill, 1971.

9.  *Sherwood Anderson's "Marching Men": A Critical Text.* Cleveland: Press of Case Western Reserve University, 1972.

10. *Sherwood Anderson/Gertrude Stein: Correspondence and Personal Essays.* Chapel Hill: University of North Carolina Press, 1972; *Sherwood Anderson/Gertrude Stein: Briefwechsel und Ausgewahlte Essays.* Translated by Jürgen Dierking. Frankfurt: Suhrkamp Verlag, 1985; *Sherwood Anderson/Gertrude Stein: Venticinque arance per venticinque cents–Lettere 1921–1941.* Translated by Marina Premoli. Milan: Rosellina Archinto, 1988.

11. *Sherwood Anderson: A Reference Guide.* Boston: G. K. Hall, 1977.

12. *Heinrich Böll in America, 1954–1970.* Hildesheim: Georg Olms Verlag, 1979.

13. *Pär Lagerkvist in America.* Stockholm: Almqvist & Wiksell, 1979.

14. *Günter Grass in America: The Early Years.* Hildesheim: Georg Olms Verlag, 1981.

15. *R. K. Narayan: The American Reception, 1953–1970.* Gulbarga, India: JIWE, 1983.

16. *Gertrude Stein and Alice B. Toklas: A Reference Guide.* Boston: G. K. Hall, 1984.

17. *Arnold Zweig in the USA.* Bern: Peter Lang Verlag, 1986.

18. *Index to Best American Short Stories and O. Henry Prize Stories.* Boston: G. K. Hall, 1988.

19. *Sherwood Anderson: Early Writings.* Kent, Ohio: Kent State University Press, 1989.

20. *"Winesburg, Ohio": An Exploration.* Boston: Twayne, 1990.

21. *Sherwood Anderson's Secret Love Letters: For Eleanor—A Letter a Day.* Baton Rouge: Louisiana State University Press, 1991; *Für Eleanor: Geheime Briefe an die Geliebte—Ein Nachlass von Sherwood Anderson.* Translated by Gerhard Kelling. Hamburg-Bremen: Achilla Presse Verlagsbuchhandlung, 1994.

22. *Winesburg, Ohio: A Norton Critical Edition.* New York: Norton, 1996. (with Charles E. Modlin)

23. *Sherwood Anderson's "Winesburg, Ohio": With Variant Readings and Annotations.* Athens: Ohio University Press, 1997.

## Articles

24. "The Original for Sherwood Anderson's *Kit Brandon*." *Newberry Library Bulletin* 6 (December 1965): 196–99.

25. "Hemingway's Private Explanation of *The Torrents of Spring*." *Modern Fiction Studies* 13 (Summer 1967): 261–63.

26. "Sherwood Anderson's First Published Story." *Readers & Writers* 1 (April 1968): 32–37.

27. "A Checklist of Sherwood Anderson Studies, 1959–1969." *Newberry Library Bulletin* 6 (July 1971): 288–302.

28. "Sherwood Anderson: Country Editor." *Milner Library Newsletter* 3 (Spring 1971): 4–6.

29. "Sherwood Anderson." In *The Politics of Twentieth-Century Novelists.* Edited by George A. Panichas. New York: Hawthorn Books, 1971, 251–62.

30. "Sherwood Anderson: A Collection of Critical Essays." *Old Northwest* 1 (September 1975): 327–30.

31. "A Sherwood Anderson Checklist, 1970–1971." *Winesburg Eagle: The Official Publication of the Sherwood Anderson Society* 1 (November 1975): 4–5.

32. "A Sherwood Anderson Checklist, 1972–1973." *Winesburg Eagle: The Official Publication of the Sherwood Anderson Society* 1 (April 1976): 7–8.

33. "*Winesburg* in Translation: Ohio in the World." *Ohioana Quarterly* 19 (Summer 1976): 58–60.

34. "'The Warmth of Desire': Sex in Anderson's Novels." In *Sherwood Anderson: The Dimensions of His Literary Art.* Edited by David D. Anderson. East Lansing: Michigan State University Press, 1976, 24–40.

35. "Sherwood Anderson and *The American Spectator* Conference: Dictators and Drunks." *American Notes and Queries* 15 (September 1976): 6–9.

36. "Query." *American Notes and Queries* 15 (September 1976): 13.

37. "A Sherwood Anderson Checklist, 1974–75." *Winesburg Eagle: The Official Publication of the Sherwood Anderson Society* 2 (November 1976): 4.

38. "Nathanael West: Additional Reviews of His Work, 1933–57." *Yale University Library Gazette* 11 (April 1977): 218–32.

39. "Sherwood Anderson, Ben Hecht, and *Erik Dorn.*" *American Literature* 49 (May 1977): 238–41.

40. "*Winesburg, Ohio*: A Lost Chicago Review." *Winesburg Eagle: The Official Publication of the Sherwood Anderson Society* 2 (April 1977): 2.

41. "Sherwood Anderson in Print." *Winesburg Eagle: The Official Publication of the Sherwood Anderson Society* 2 (April 1977): 3–4. (with Douglas Rogers)

42. "*Winesburg, Ohio*: First Impression Errors." *Papers of the Bibliographical Society of America* 71 (April–June 1977): 222–23.

43. "Sherwood Anderson: A Centennial Bibliography." *Ohioana Quarterly* 20 (Winter 1977): 172–73.

44. "Sherwood Anderson: Fugitive Pamphlets and Broadsides, 1918–1940." *Studies in Bibliography* 31 (1978): 257–63.

45. "Anderson in Chicago Newspapers: A Supplementary List." *Winesburg Eagle: The Official Publication of the Sherwood Anderson Society* 3 (November 1977): 3–5. (with Diana Haskell)

46. "Sherwood Anderson Meets John Steinbeck: 1939." *Steinbeck Quarterly* 11 (Winter 1978): 20–22.

47. "Whatever Happened to Willard Motley? A Documentary." *MidAmerica* 5 (1978): 111–37.

48. "Mencken's Lost Review of *Winesburg, Ohio.*" *Notes on Modern American Literature* 2 (Spring 1978): 1–3.

49. "*Winesburg* in 1919: The Publisher's Catalog Copy." *Winesburg Eagle: The Official Publication of the Sherwood Anderson Society* 3 (April 1978): 3–4.

50. "Hemingway's *Islands in the Stream*: A Collection of Additional Reviews." *Library Chronicle* (University of Pennsylvania) 43 (Spring 1978): 81–98.

51. "*Winesburg, Ohio*: The Earliest Non-English-Language Review." *Winesburg Eagle: The Official Publication of the Sherwood Anderson Society* 3 (April 1978): 2–3.

52. "Kawabata Yasunari in the United States, 1956–1970, Part I." *Hon No Shu Hen* (October 1978): 54–64.

53. "Ben Hecht on *The Vegetable*: A Lost Chicago Review." *Fitzgerald/Hemingway Annual* (1978): 97–98.

54. "*The Fifth Column and Four Stories of the Spanish Civil War*: 38 Additional Reviews." *Fitzgerald/Hemingway Annual* (1978): 273–82.

55. "Eldridge Cleaver's *Soul on Ice*: A Book Review Digest." *College Language Association Journal* 31 (June 1978): 556–66.

56. "Raja Rao's *The Cat and Shakespeare in the U.S.A.*" *Journal of Indian Writing in English* 7 (January 1979): 24–29.

57. "*Winesburg, Ohio*: A Unique 1919 Ohio Review." *Ohioana Quarterly* 22 (Spring 1979): 12–13.

58. "Steinbeck and de Maupassant: A Parallel Occurrence." *Steinbeck Quarterly* 12 (Winter–Spring 1979): 27–29.

59. "Evan S. Connell, Jr.'s *Mrs. Bridge* and *Mr. Bridge*: A Critical Documentary." *MidAmerica* 6 (1979): 141–59.

60. "Kawabata Yasunari in the United States, 1956–1970, Part II." *Hon No Shu Hen* (August 1979): 24–36.

61. "Zelda Fitzgerald's *Save Me the Waltz*: A Collection of Reviews from 1932–1933." *Fitzgerald/Hemingway Annual* (1979): 163–68.

62. "Of Time and *Winesburg, Ohio*: An Experiment in Chronology." *Modern Fiction Studies* 25 (Winter 1979–80): 658–66.

63. "*The Pat Hobby Stories*: A File of Reviews." *Fitzgerald/Hemingway Annual* (1979): 177–80.

64. "The Early Fiction of William H. Gass: A Critical Documentary." *MidAmerica* 8 (1980): 164–77.

65. Review of Roy A. Medvedev, *Problems in the Literary Biography of Mikhail Sholokhov*. *Journal of Modern Literature* 7 (Supplement 1979): 814.

66. "Anderson's Private Reaction to *The Torrents of Spring*." *Modern Fiction Studies* 26 (Winter 1980–81): 635–37.

67. "Wallace Stevens: A Collection of Reviews of His Works, 1931–1967." *Wallace Stevens Journal* 4 (Spring 1980): 5–23.

68. " 'Death in the Woods': Anderson's Earliest Version." *Winesburg Eagle: The Official Publication of the Sherwood Anderson Society* 7 (April 1982): 1–3.

69. "*Winesburg, Ohio*: The Unique Alternate Draft of 'Nobody Knows.'" *Winesburg Eagle: The Official Publication of the Sherwood Anderson Society* 8 (November 1982): 3–5.

70. "Raja Rao's *The Serpent and the Rope* in the U.S.A." *Journal of Indian Writing in English* 10 (January–July 1982): 41–51.

71. "The Chicago Renaissance Discovers Gertrude Stein." *American Notes and Queries* 20 (March–April 1982): 111–13.

72. "*The Chicago Literary Times*: A Description and a Book Review Index." *MidAmerica* 9 (1982): 139–47.

73. " 'Implications of Obscenity': The English Trial of *Many Marriages*." *Journal of Modern Literature* 10 (March 1983): 153–58.

74. "Anderson Country." *Iron Mountain Review* 1 (Spring 1983): 3–9.

75. "Soloxov in the United States: A Collection of the Periodical Columns, 1934–1967." *Russian Language Journal* 37 (Winter–Spring 1983): 147–76.

76. "H. L. Mencken Discovers Gertrude Stein." *Notes on Modern American Literature* 7 (Spring–Summer 1983): 1–2.

77. "*The Grapes of Wrath* and the Critics of 1939." *Resources for American Literary Study* 13 (Autumn 1983): 134–64.

78. "*Vom Winde Verweht: Gone With the Wind* in Nazi Germany." *Southern Studies* 22 (Winter 1983): 401–406.

79. "*Winesburg, Ohio*: The Story Titles." *Winesburg Eagle: The Official Publication of the Sherwood Anderson Society* 10 (November 1984): 6–7.

80. "The Revisions in *Windy McPherson's Son*, Sherwood Anderson's First Novel." *Midwestern Miscellany* 12 (1984): 23–52.

81. "*Winesburg, Ohio*: The Table of Contents." *Notes on Modern American Literature* 8 (Autumn 1984): 1–4.

82. *"Raintree County* and the Critics of '48." *MidAmerica* 11 (1984): 149–70.

83. Review of Jane L. Walker, *The Making of a Modernist: Gertrude Stein from "Three Lives" to "Tender Buttons." American Literature* 57 (March 1985): 165–66.

84. *"Winesburg, Ohio*: First Printings, Variants, and Errors." *Winesburg Eagle: The Official Publication of the Sherwood Anderson Society* 10 (April 1985): 1–3.

85. "The Manuscripts of *Winesburg, Ohio." Winesburg Eagle: The Official Publication of the Sherwood Anderson Society* 11 (November 1985): 4–10.

86. "The Two *Grapes of Wrath." Notes on Modern American Literature* 9 (Fall 1985): 1–3.

87. "The Novels of C. Hugh Holman." *Southern Literary Journal* 18 (Spring 1986): 83–95.

88. Review of Claire Bruyère, *Sherwood Anderson: L'impuissance créatrice. Winesburg Eagle: The Official Publication of the Sherwood Anderson Society* 12 (November 1986): 3.

89. "The Paris *Ex Libris*: A Description and an Index." *Bulletin of Bibliography* 44 (March 1987): 24–34.

90. "Sherwood Anderson and the Real Winesburg, Ohio." *Winesburg Eagle: The Official Publication of the Sherwood Anderson Society* 12 (April 1987): 1–4.

91. "Socrates in *Winesburg." Notes on Modern American Literature* 10 (Spring–Summer 1986): 3–6.

92. "Anderson's Eulogy for Laura Lou Copenhaver." *Winesburg Eagle: The Official Publication of the Sherwood Anderson Society* 13 (November 1987): 3.

93. "John Dos Passos and the Federal Bureau of Investigation." *Journal of Modern Literature* 14 (Summer 1987): 97–110.

94. "Re: Unpublished Literary Manuscripts." *Illinois English Bulletin* 76 (Fall 1988): 26–30.

95. "Anderson's Epitaph." *Winesburg Eagle: The Official Publication of the Sherwood Anderson Society* 14 (Winter 1989): 3–4.

96. "'As His Home Town Knew Him': Sherwood Anderson's Last Trip Home." *MidAmerica* 14 (1987): 74–88.

97. Review of *The Letters of Gertrude Stein and Carl Van Vechten, 1913–1946. Resources for American Literary Study* 16 (1986–87): 190–93.

98. "John Barth." *Twentieth-Century Romance and Historical Writers*, 2d ed. Chicago: St. James Press, 1990, 34–35.

99. "Ross Lockridge." *Twentieth-Century Romance and Historical Writers*, 2d ed. Chicago: St. James Press, 1990, 401–2.

100. "Anderson, Blakelock, and 'Blackfoot's Masterpiece. '" *Winesburg Eagle: The Official Publication of the Sherwood Anderson Society* 15 (Winter 1990): 8–10.

101. "A Walking Tour of Winesburg, Ohio." *Arts & Sciences Lectures: First 20 Years.* Edited by Richard H. Dammers. Normal: Illinois State University, 1990, 330–41.

102. "Sherwood Anderson, American Labor, and Danville, Virginia." *Winesburg Eagle: The Official Publication of the Sherwood Anderson Society* 15 (Summer 1990): 1–9.

103. Review of Charles E. Modlin, ed., *Sherwood Anderson's Love Letters to Eleanor Copenhaver Anderson*; and Linda Wagner-Martin, *The Modern American Novel, 1914–1945*. *Modern Fiction Studies* 36 (Winter 1990): 557–59.

104. "Anderson, Faulkner, and a Unique Al Jackson Tale." *Winesburg Eagle: The Official Publication of the Sherwood Anderson Society* 16 (Summer 1991): 5–8.

105. "Sherwood Anderson's 'The Newspaper and the Modern Age.'" *Old Northwest* 15 (Winter 1991–1992): 213–31.

106. "Anderson's Elegy for Gil Stephenson." *Winesburg Eagle: The Official Publication of the Sherwood Anderson Society* 17 (Summer 1992): 9–10.

107. "Sherwood Anderson." *Bibliography of American Fiction: 1866–1918*. Edited by James Nagel and Gwen L. Nagel. New York: Facts, 1993, 50–54.

108. Review of John E. Hallwas, ed. *Spoon River Anthology: An Annotated Edition*. *Illinois Historical Journal* 86 (Summer 1993): 136–37.

109. "Anderson and the Smith Family Scandal." *Winesburg Eagle: The Official Publication of the Sherwood Anderson Society* 18 (Summer 1993): 10–12.

110. "Introduction." *Windy McPherson's Son*. By Sherwood Anderson. Urbana: University of Illinois Press, 1993, ix–xxxii.

111. Review of Sidney P. Moss and Carolyn J. Moss, *Charles Dickens and His Chicago Relatives: A Documentary Narrative*. *Illinois Historical Journal* 88 (Summer 1995): 138–39.

112. "Anderson's Will and Estate." *Winesburg Eagle: The Official Publication of the Sherwood Anderson Society* 21 (Summer 1996): 3–5.

113. "Sherwood Anderson: Dissertations, Theses, Research Papers, 1924–1995." *Winesburg Eagle: The Official Publication of the Sherwood Anderson Society* 22 (Summer 1997): 7–12.

# Contributors

JACKSON J. BENSON is Emeritus Professor of American Literature at San Diego State University. He is the author of the authorized biography, *The True Adventures of John Steinbeck, Writer* (Heinemann, 1984), which won the PEN-WEST USA award for nonfiction. His latest book is *Wallace Stegner: His Life and Work* (Viking, 1996), which won the David Woolley and Beatrice Cannon Evans Biography Award.

SIDNEY BURRIS is Associate Professor of English and Director of the Honors Program in the William J. Fulbright College of Arts and Sciences at the University of Arkansas. He is the author of *The Poetry of Resistance: Seamus Heaney and the Pastoral Tradition* (Ohio, 1989) and *A Day at the Races* (Utah, 1989), a volume of poetry that won the Utah Press Poetry Competition.

ROBERT COCHRAN is Professor of English and Director of the Center for Arkansas and Regional Studies at the University of Arkansas. Among his books on literature and folklore are *Samuel Beckett: A Study of the Short Fiction* (Twayne, 1991) and *Vance Randolph: An Ozark Life* (Illinois, 1995). His most recent book is *Singing in Zion: Music and Song in the Life of an Arkansas Family* (Arkansas, 1999).

STEPHEN CUSHMAN is Professor of English at the University of Virginia. He is the author of *William Carlos Williams and the Meanings of Measure* (Yale, 1985), *Fictions of Form in American Poetry* (Princeton, 1993), and *Bloody Promenande: Reflections on a Civil War Battle* (Virginia, 1999), as well as a volume of poems, *Blue Pajamas* (Louisiana State, 1998).

JIM ELLEDGE is a poet/scholar who teaches in the Creative Writing Program at Illinois State University and the founder and director of Thorngate Road, a press. His most recent books are *Four Chapters of Coming Forth by Day*, a slim limited-edition collection of excerpts from his prose-poem novel; *The Circuit of Heaven,* his fifth collection of poetry; and *Real Things: An Anthology of Popular Culture in American Poetry* (Indiana, 1999), which he co-edited with Susan Swartwout.

ANN FISHER-WIRTH teaches American literature, creative writing, and nature writing at the University of Mississippi. The author of *William Carlos Williams and Autobiography: The Woods of His Own Nature* (Pennsylvania State, 1989), she has published numerous poems and essays, including several on Willa Cather. She is working on a book on Cather, and has recently completed a book manuscript of poems.

JOHN CALDWELL GUILDS holds the Distinguished Professorship in Humanities at the University of Arkansas. The biographer and editor of William Gilmore Simms, he is widely published in nineteenth-century American literature. His *Simms: A Literary Life* (Arkansas, 1992) was awarded the SCMLA Book Prize for 1993 as well as the Best Book prize by the South Carolina Historical Society (1993). The American novel is his particular interest.

DAVID B. KESTERSON is Professor of English and Interim Vice President for Academic Affairs at the University of North Texas. He co-founded the Nathaniel Hawthorne Society, served as its first president, and edited the *Hawthorne Society Newsletter* (now the *Nathaniel Hawthorne Review*) for its first eight years. He has published extensively on Hawthorne (including articles and an edited collection of essays on *The Marble Faun* [Merrill, 1971]) and on American humor. He is also president of the Society for the Study of Southern Literature and past president of the American Humor Association.

KENETH KINNAMON is Ethel Pumphrey Stephens Professor of English at the University of Arkansas. Among his books are *The Emergence of Richard Wright* (Illinois, 1972), *A Richard Wright Bibliography* (Greenwood, 1988), *New Essays on Native Son* (Cambridge, 1990), and, with Richard Barksdale, *Black Writers of America* (Macmillan, 1972).

NOEL POLK is Professor of English at the University of Southern Mississippi. He is the author of books and essays on William Faulkner and Eudora Welty, and is the editor of Faulkner's texts for the Library of America. Among his books are *Eudora Welty: A Bibliography of Her Work* (Mississippi,

1993) and *Children of the Dark House: Text and Context in Faulkner* (Mississippi, 1996).

MICHAEL REYNOLDS, Emeritus Professor of English at North Carolina State University, is the author of a five-volume biography of Ernest Hemingway, the most recent volume of which is *Hemingway: The 1930s* (Norton, 1997). He is also the author of *Hemingway's First War: The Making of "A Farewell to Arms"* (Princeton, 1976), and numerous articles on Hemingway and American literature.

DAVE SMITH is Boyd Professor of American Literature at Louisiana State University and co-editor of the *Southern Review*. Among his books of poetry are *Fate's Kite* (Louisiana State, 1996), *Floating on Solitude* (Illinois, 1997), *Night Pleasures* (Bloodaxe Books, 1993), and *The Roundhouse Voices* (Harper & Row, 1985). He is also the author of *The Essential Poe* (Ecco, 1992), *Cuba Night* (Morrow, 1990), and *Local Assays: On Contemporary American Poetry* (Illinois, 1985), editor of *The Pure Clear Word: Essays on the Poetry of James Wright* (Illinois, 1982), and co-editor of *The Morrow Anthology of Younger American Poets* (Morrow, 1985).

SUSAN SWARTWOUT teaches creative writing, contemporary American literature, and independent-press publishing at Southeast Missouri State University. She is the co-editor with Jim Elledge of *Real Things: An Anthology of Popular Culture in American Poetry* (Indiana, 1999) and the author of two poetry collections: *Freak* and *Uncommon Ground.*

LINDA WAGNER-MARTIN is Hanes Professor of English at the University of North Carolina, Chapel Hill. She writes on modern American authors and texts—Stein, Hemingway, Faulkner, Plath, Williams, Frost. Co-editor of *The Oxford Companion to Women's Writing in the United States* (Oxford, 1995) and its anthology *The Oxford Book of Women's Writing in the United States* (Oxford, 1995), she also edits the contemporary section of the Heath anthology. Her most recent book is *Sylvia Plath, A Literary Life* (St. Martin's, 1999).

BRIAN WILKIE, Professor of English at the University of Arkansas, is the author of *Romantic Poets and Epic Tradition* (Wisconsin, 1965), co-author of *Blake's "Four Zoas": The Design of a Dream* (Harvard, 1978), and most recently, co-editor of the two-volume *Literature of the Western World.*

# Index

275